Collins | English for Exams

IELTS
PREPARATION AND PRACTICE

Published by Collins
An imprint of HarperCollins Publishers
1 Robroyston Gate
Glasgow
G33 1JN

HarperCollins Publishers
Macken House, 39/40 Mayor Street Upper, Dublin 1,
D01 C9W8, Ireland

First edition 2021

10 9 8 7 6 5 4 3

This book contains FSC™ certified paper and other controlled
sources to ensure responsible forest management.

For more information visit: www.harpercollins.co.uk/green

If you would like to comment on any aspect of this book, please
contact us at the given address or online.

E-mail: dictionaries@harpercollins.co.uk

 facebook.com/collinselt

 @CollinsELT

Authors: Fiona Aish, Jo Tomlinson and Anneli Williams
Editor: Alison Macaulay
Research & Development: Celia Wigley
For the Publisher: Gillian Bowman and Kerry Ferguson
Typesetter: Jouve, India
Printer: Ashford Colour Ltd, UK
Audio recorded and produced by ID Audio, London

Acknowledgements
Photo credits: Page 98 © Roman Babakin / Shutterstock. All other
photos from Shutterstock.

Page 93: 'Distribution of deer' map redrawn from The Mammal
Society (www.mammal.org.uk).

The Publishers gratefully acknowledge the permission granted to
reproduce the copyright material in this book. Whilst every effort
has been made to trace the copyright holders, in cases where
this has been unsuccessful, or if any have inadvertently been
overlooked, the Publishers would gladly receive any information
enabling them to rectify any error or omission at the first
opportunity.

All exam-style questions and sample answers in this title were
written by the authors.

About the authors
Jo Tomlinson and Fiona Aish are co-owners of Target English,
a language consultancy specializing in materials development,
test production and teacher training. With MAs in Language
Testing and ELT & Applied Linguistics, they have over forty years'
teaching experience between them in areas such as general
English, test preparation and academic English. They now work
with a variety of organizations developing bespoke course and
test materials, as well as training teachers in test preparation
and production. Jo and Fiona would like to thank Andrea
Langton, Alison Macaulay, Celia Wigley and all the team at
HarperCollins for their advice and support.

Anneli Williams has taught English for Academic Purposes at the
University of Glasgow for over 25 years, developing extensive
experience preparing students for the IELTS examination as well
as for academic study within university settings. She would like
to thank her partner Steven, her daughter Ruby, and her editors
Alison Macaulay and Andrea Langton for their support.

Contents

Introduction

Who is this book for?

Collins IELTS Preparation and Practice will prepare you for the IELTS test, whether you are taking the test for the first time or re-sitting the test. It has been written for learners with band score 5–5.5 who are trying to achieve band score 6.5 or higher.

The structured approach, comprehensive answer key and model answers have been designed so that you can use the materials to study on your own. However, the book can also be used as a supplementary course for IELTS preparation classes.

Content

Collins IELTS Preparation and Practice is divided into four sections and 38 units. Each section focuses on one of the four parts of the IELTS test. The Reading and Listening sections cover all of the main task types that students encounter in the IELTS test, providing practice of the skills, techniques and language that are needed to improve your score in the test. The Writing and Speaking units cover all of the key language skills that you will need in order to improve your score in all sections of these parts of the test. The aims listed at the start of each unit specify the key skills, techniques and language covered in the unit. In this way, you can focus on particular parts of the test or even specific task types that you need to improve, or you can work through all of the sections.

Additionally, the book provides exam strategies telling you what to expect and how best to succeed in the test.

Exam information is presented in clear, easy-to-read boxes.

Exam tips in each unit highlight essential exam techniques and can be rapidly reviewed at a glance.

Unit structure

Each unit is divided into three parts.

Part 1 introduces the task type or skill that is covered in the unit. Exercises ensure that you understand what is required in a particular task and how the different parts of the test are assessed. In the Writing and Speaking sections, you will learn which aspects of language are assessed and how a band score of 5.0 differs from a band score of 6.5 or 7.0.

Part 2 provides step-by-step exercises and guidance on specific question types and skills that appear in the IELTS test.

Exam information and *Exam tips* show you how to approach each question type and help you develop successful test-taking strategies.

Part 3 provides typical exam practice questions for the same task or exam skill that you practised in Part 2, allowing you to put what you have learned into practice.

Answer key and audio scripts

At the end of the book you will find full audio scripts of all the tracks on the audio recording. You should refer to these where instructed in the text. You can also use them for further speaking practice, recording your work and comparing your pronunciation against the recordings.

A comprehensive answer key is provided for all sections of the book, including detailed notes on why certain answers are correct or incorrect and sample answers for writing and speaking tasks where appropriate.

Using the audio

This icon 🔊 indicates that there is an audio track to listen to. You can download the audio files at www.collins.co.uk/eltresources.

Using the book for self-study

If you are new to IELTS, we recommend that you work systematically through the 38 units in order to familiarize yourself with all the parts of the test. If you are a more experienced learner, you can use the aims listed at the start of each unit to select the most useful exercises.

Having access to someone who can provide informed feedback on the practice exercises is an advantage. However, you can still learn a lot working alone or with a study partner willing to give and receive peer feedback.

The exercises in this book will help you to identify which areas of language you need to improve in order to boost your IELTS score. You should then make use of other language learning materials (grammar and vocabulary practice books and online materials, learner dictionaries and authentic materials such as English-language television, films and newspapers) to help you improve your problem areas.

Part 1: Language development

Ideally, you should begin each unit by working through the exercises in *Part 1*. This will familiarize you with the task type or language skill and show you how the IELTS examiners assess answers. Try to answer the questions without looking at a dictionary in order to develop the skill of inferring the meaning of unfamiliar words from context.

Part 2: Development

Work through the *Part 2* exercises from beginning to end. It is important to study the *Exam information* and *Exam tips* about each of the question types, so that you become familiar with how to approach the different question types in the test. The strategies covered should be thoroughly mastered so that during the actual exam you are fully prepared for each section. All of the answers can be found in the Answer key at the back of the book. Many of the answers give detailed information about why particular answers are correct or incorrect, so it's important to refer to the key after each exercise. This will help you to understand how to improve your score.

Part 3: Practice

This section contains typical exam practice questions and tasks. Some of these are structured questions and others are typical exam-style tasks to be completed as in the IELTS test. After you have done the practice, it is a good idea to spend some time reviewing why certain answers are correct. For this reason we suggest you approach this part in the following way:

First do the practice. Here, you should focus on answering the questions correctly. You should try and complete Part 3 under test conditions if possible, where this is appropriate. For example, listen only once to listening exercises, and set yourself a time limit for reading and writing tasks. Do not look at the Audio script while doing the exam practice questions. After you have finished the practice questions, make sure the format and spelling of your answers are correct. You should do this within the time limit. Then, check your answers using the Answer key at the back of the book and the Audio script.

You can find additional exam practice in the *Collins Practice Tests for IELTS* range, which has three books with four tests in each.

Collins also offers a wide range of exam preparation books, including our Skills for IELTS series (*Reading for IELTS, Writing for IELTS, Listening for IELTS* and *Speaking for IELTS*) and our *IELTS Dictionary*. Please go to www.collins.co.uk/elt to find these and other resources.

The International English Language Testing System (IELTS) test

IELTS is jointly managed by the British Council, Cambridge ESOL Examinations and IDP Education, Australia. There are two versions of the test:

- Academic
- General Training

Academic is for students wishing to study at undergraduate or postgraduate levels in an English-medium environment.

General Training is for people who wish to migrate to an English-speaking country. This book is primarily for students taking the Academic version.

The test

There are four modules:

Listening	30 minutes, plus 10 minutes for transferring answers to the answer sheet
	NB: the audio is heard *only once*.
	Approx. ten questions per part
	Section 1: two speakers discuss a social situation
	Section 2: one speaker talks about a non-academic topic
	Section 3: up to four speakers discuss an educational project
	Section 4: one speaker gives a talk of general academic interest
Reading	60 minutes
	three texts, taken from authentic sources, on general academic topics. They may contain diagrams, charts, etc.
	40 questions: may include multiple choice, sentence completion, completing a diagram, graph or chart, choosing headings, yes/no, true/false questions, classification and matching exercises.
Writing	Task 1: 20 minutes: description of a table, chart, graph or diagram (150 words minimum)
	Task 2: 40 minutes: an essay in response to an argument or problem (250 words minimum)
Speaking	11–14 minutes
	A three-part face-to-face oral interview with an examiner. The interview is recorded.
	Part 1: introductions and general questions (4–5 mins)
	Part 2: individual long turn (3–4 mins): the candidate is given a task, has one minute to prepare, then talks for 1–2 minutes, with some questions from the examiner.
	Part 3: two-way discussion (4–5 mins): the examiner asks further questions on the topic from Part 2 and gives the candidate the opportunity to discuss more abstract issues or ideas.
Timetabling	Listening, Reading and Writing must be taken on the same day, and in the order listed above. Speaking can be taken up to seven days before or after the other modules.
Scoring	Each section is given a band score. The average of the four scores produces the Overall Band Score. You do not pass or fail IELTS; you receive a score.

IELTS and the Common European Framework of Reference

The CEFR shows the level of the learner and is used for many English as a Foreign Language examinations. The table below shows the approximate CEFR level and the equivalent IELTS Overall Band Score:

CEFR description	CEFR level	IELTS Band Score
Proficient user	C2	9
(Advanced)	C1	7–8
Independent user	B2	5–6.5
(Intermediate – Upper Intermediate)	B1	4–5

This table contains the general descriptors for the band scores 1–9:

IELTS Band Scores		
9	Expert user	Has fully operational command of the language: appropriate, accurate and fluent with complete understanding.
8	Very good user	Has fully operational command of the language, with only occasional unsystematic inaccuracies and inappropriacies. Misunderstandings may occur in unfamiliar situations. Handles complex detailed argumentation well.
7	Good user	Has operational command of the language, though with occasional inaccuracies, inappropriacies and misunderstandings in some situations. Generally handles complex language well and understands detailed reasoning.
6	Competent user	Has generally effective command of the language despite some inaccuracies, inappropriacies and misunderstandings. Can use and understand fairly complex language, particularly in familiar situations.
5	Modest user	Has partial command of the language, coping with overall meaning in most situations, though is likely to make many mistakes. Should be able to handle basic communication in own field.
4	Limited user	Basic competence is limited to familiar situations. Has frequent problems in understanding and expression. Is not able to use complex language.
3	Extremely limited user	Conveys and understands only general meaning in very familiar situations. Frequent breakdowns in communication occur.
2	Intermittent user	Has great difficulty understanding spoken and written English.
1	Non user	Essentially has no ability to use the language except a few isolated words.
0	Did not attempt the test	Did not answer the questions.

Marking

The Listening and Reading papers have 40 items, each worth one mark if correctly answered. Here are some examples of how marks are translated into band scores:

Listening: 16 out of 40 correct answers: band score 5
              23 out of 40 correct answers: band score 6
              30 out of 40 correct answers: band score 7

Reading: 15 out of 40 correct answers: band score 5
             23 out of 40 correct answers: band score 6
             30 out of 40 correct answers: band score 7

Writing and Speaking are marked according to performance descriptors.

Writing: examiners award a band score for each of four areas with equal weighting:

- Task achievement (Task 1), Task response (Task 2)
- Coherence and cohesion
- Lexical resource
- Grammatical range and accuracy

Speaking: examiners award a band score for each of four areas with equal weighting:

- Fluency and coherence
- Lexical resource
- Grammatical range and accuracy
- Pronunciation

For full details of how the examination is scored and marked, go to: www.ielts.org

1 General and academic listening

Aims | Understanding the Listening test format; Understanding general and academic English features; Identifying general and academic features

Part 1: Understanding the Listening test format

1 Read the exam information and Parts 1–4 and decide if statements 1–5 are TRUE or FALSE.

1 You can choose which part of the test you want to answer. TRUE / FALSE
2 There are two monologues and two dialogues. TRUE / FALSE
3 The parts go from academic language to more general language. TRUE / FALSE
4 Each recording will be repeated. TRUE / FALSE
5 You need to write your answers on an answer sheet. TRUE / FALSE

ℹ Exam information: Introducing the Listening test format

The IELTS Listening test lasts around 30 minutes, with an extra ten minutes to write your answers on the answer sheet. There are four parts to the test, each with ten questions. Answer the questions in order; they are all worth one point. You will only have ONE chance to listen, and you may hear speech in a range of different accents, like British, Canadian or Australian.

The Listening test

Part 1 a conversation between two speakers, which is usually transactional. This means a conversation where there is a transaction of some kind. This could be someone buying something or asking for information.

Part 2 a monologue (only one main speaker) about something which is general in nature. For example, a talk about a sports centre or tour information.

Part 3 a conversation that is based in an educational or training context, so for example you might hear students discussing a project, or you might hear a student discussing their work with a tutor.

Part 4 a monologue on an academic subject. This is usually in the style of a lecture. The lecture may use some difficult vocabulary, but the theme will be something generally accessible.

Generally, the parts get more difficult as the test proceeds. You can have any question type in any part of the exam.

2 Read the scenarios in 1–8. In which part of the IELTS test would you expect to see them?

1 A talk on how languages affect our emotional development.
2 A man buying some new clothes.
3 A man explaining facilities in a new shopping centre.
4 Two students talking about their environmental project work.
5 A woman explaining the holiday camp rules and timetable.
6 A woman asking for information about nearby restaurants.
7 A lecture about the development of driverless cars.
8 A tutor helping a student with their research project.

> **Exam tip**
> You will always hear the answers in the order that that you hear the audio.

Part 2: Understanding general and academic English features

> ### *i* Exam information: Understanding general and academic English features
>
> The language used in general and academic contexts is slightly different. In Parts 1 and 2 of the IELTS Listening test, you will hear English that is more general in style. Part 4 will use more academic language (Part 3 to a lesser extent will also use some academic features of language). There can be a mixture of these features, and you are likely to hear this in Part 3 of the test, where students and tutors are speaking in a conversation.

3 Read the information in the table and complete headings 1 and 2 with *General* or *Academic*, according to which column lists general English features and which lists academic features.

1 _____ English	2 _____ English
Uses phrasal verbs	Uses single word verbs
Most people can't get by without a regular income.	*Most people can't survive without a regular income.*
Uses a verb-based sentence structure	Uses more noun-phrases
Food prices have been rising since 2000 because of transport costs.	*The rise in food prices since 2000 is due to transport costs.*
Rhetorical contexts include – social, transactional, informational	Rhetorical functions include – evaluating, defining, describing, explaining
General vocabulary	Academic vocabulary
Generally uses more idiomatic-based expressions	Doesn't generally use idioms
Can be informal (e.g. between friends) and more formal (e.g. customer, sales assistant)	Is usually more formal in style

4 Read audio extracts 1 and 2 and decide which one is academic and which is general.

1 *"This cinema has been open since 1953 and has been at the heart of the local community all this time. That's why we've decided to give it a makeover and open up a coffee shop on the ground floor, as well as giving each of the screens an upgrade."*

2 *"The impact of cinema on modern society is vast. While films are a reflection of society, they also serve to shape opinions in general. This can be seen by many films that have a social or political element to their themes."*

5 Read the paragraphs again and mark the features of general and academic English. Which text has an informative purpose and which has an explanatory purpose?

🔆 Exam tip

You can improve your academic vocabulary by reading articles and listening to talks on research and world issues. An academic word list can also help you expand your academic vocabulary.

Part 3: Identifying general and academic features

6 Read and listen to the extracts of a listening test, A–D, and answer questions 1 and 2.

🔊 02

1 Which part of the test is each extract from?

2 What features of general or academic English can you identify?

A

"Welcome to the StayFit Gym! Here's your member card. I'll show you around so you know what you need to do. Firstly, you probably saw the café by the entrance. It's open the same hours as the gym, 8 a.m. till 10 p.m., so you can grab a bite to eat at any time. On the left here, you'll see the changing rooms. All you need to do to open it is to is put a dollar into the locker, which you'll get back at the end."

B

Professor Davis:	*You only have three more weeks before you need to submit this, but some sections need a lot more work.*
Adam:	*I did have problems finding resources for background reading. There aren't many books on the subject.*
Professor Davis:	*Maybe not, but there are plenty of primary studies that you can reference.*

C

"The rise of online learning has been due to two main factors – the socio-political context and the advancement of technology. While the convenience of learning at home means that many people can access education at a time that is convenient to them, technology also means they can do this via computer or mobile, and in a format they enjoy."

D

Tourist:	*Excuse me. I'm looking for information about the city. Can you help me?*
Assistant:	*Yes, we've got a city guide here. It's free, so you can just pick one up. Do you need any specific help?*
Tourist:	*Well, I'm looking for place I can take my kids to.*

2 Listening to English

Aims | Typical speakers in the Listening paper (speakers' accents); **Features of English pronunciation** (following connected speech, weak and strong forms, the schwa sound, intonation and emphasis); **Practising multiple-choice**

Part 1: Typical speakers in the Listening paper

Exam information: Speakers' accents

In the Listening test, you will hear people talking naturally at an average speed, not too fast or slow. You will hear a range of gentle accents from different parts of the UK, the USA and Australia. Familiarize yourself with different accents before you take the test.

1 Listen to four speakers and match them to accents A–D.

🔊 03

Speaker 1 ____
Speaker 2 ____
Speaker 3 ____
Speaker 4 ____

A American
B Australian
C English
D Scottish

 **Exam tip**

You can use the Internet, films and TV programmes to practise listening to different English accents.

Part 2: Features of English pronunciation

Exam information: Following connected speech

When people speak naturally, their words flow and connect together and they don't pause between each word. This is called connected speech and there are different ways speakers do this.

2 Read the information in the table and complete the types of connection with the words from the box. Number 1 is an example.

change   disappear   join   link

Type of connection	Explanation	Examples
1 Sounds <u>link</u> together	When one word ends in a consonant and the next word begins with a vowel, speakers usually **connect** these words together.	1 Take‿it‿all‿out. 2 I went‿out‿at‿eight‿o'clock.
2 Sounds _____ together	When a word ends with a consonant and the next word begins with the same consonant, speakers usually say them as **one sound**.	3 She's studying now. 4 I cannot tell you.
3 Sounds _____	When a word ends with a /t/ or /d/ sound and the next word begins with a consonant, speakers usually **don't say** the /t/ or /d/ sound	5 We must do it. 6 Pass me the salt and pepper.
4 Sounds _____	When two consonant sounds form a **new sound**	7 <u>Do you</u> want to go? (jou) 8 I'll <u>meet you</u> later. (meechou)

3 Listen to the examples from the table above and notice how the speaker connects the words.
 Practise saying the phrases.

4 Read the conversation and indicate where you think the words are connected and the type of connection.

Robert: Hi, Susanna. How are you? I'm making lunch for us.
Susanna: Oh, thanks. Would you like any help?
Robert: That would be great.
Susanna: OK. Tell me what to do.
Robert: Could you get a couple of glasses of water and cut up some bread.

5 Listen and check your answers to exercise 4.

ⓘ Exam information: Weak and strong forms

English speakers usually say the content words (nouns, verbs, adjectives) with more emphasis or stress than other words. These are called strong and weak forms. Weak forms include articles (*a, the*), prepositions (*in, for*), auxiliary verbs (*has, can, would*), contracted forms (*I'm, could've, won't*), and the negative form *not*. Understanding the weak forms is important because they add more information such as when something happened (past, present, future), the location of something or the frequency or quantity of something.

6 Listen to part of a conversation between a student and her professor and answer the questions.

1 Which of the statements A–C is correct?

   A The revision videos are on the university online learning system.

   B Professor Watkins is going to send Kate some online revision videos.

   C Kate needs to prepare more for her final exam.

2 Was Kate pleased with her last exam results? _____.

7 Look at page 160 and read and listen to the conversation again. Then answer the questions.

1 Are the underlined words or the bold words easier to hear? Why?

2 Do the underlined or the bold words help you to answer the questions in exercise 6 correctly?

ⓘ Exam information: The schwa sound

This is the most common sound in English. It is a short, weak sound, not a strong sound, and it appears in many words. Being able to recognize this sound will help you improve your listening skills. Listen to the schwa sound.

8 Read and listen to the first part of a school welcome talk. What do you notice about the pronunciation of the <u>underlined</u> sounds?

"Go<u>o</u>d morning everyone <u>a</u>nd welc<u>o</u>me t<u>o</u> th<u>e</u> information day at Hobart's English School. Now, I want you t<u>o</u> rememb<u>er</u> th<u>a</u>t we value all stud<u>e</u>nts here."

9 Read and listen to the next part of the talk and underline the schwa sounds.

"We are totally focused on helping you to get the best out of your time at the school. Now, you should've received a welcome pack when you came in. Inside you can see that there's a map of the campus and some general information."

ⓘ Exam information: Intonation and emphasis

Speakers communicate different meanings, feelings and emotions through the sound of their voice. For example, speakers use rising intonation to show surprise, and falling intonation to show that they are bored. Speakers stress specific words that are important or because they disagree with another speaker. In the Listening test, being able to identify the meaning behind changes in intonation and emphasis can lead to the correct answers.

10 Listen to Annie, Leon and Harry discussing a project and answer the questions. Circle the correct name.

1	Who is feeling **disappointed** with the **project**?	Annie	Leon	Harry
2	Which person is **worried** about the **situation**?	Annie	Leon	Harry
3	Which person is **relieved** with the **decision**?	Annie	Leon	Harry

Part 3: Practising multiple-choice

11 Listen and complete Part 1.

Part 1

🔊
11

Questions 1–8. Choose the correct letter, A, B or C.

1 What would Jessica like to do on Friday night?

A study

B take a walk

C go to the gym

2 What do Jessica and Ben decide to do on Friday night?

A go to the cinema

B watch a film at Ben's flat

C go to a restaurant

3 How does Ben feel about the decision at first?

A angry

B happy

C disappointed

4 What is Jessica interested in?

A the cinema café

B making cakes

C visiting her sister

5 What do Jessica and Ben disagree on?

A films

B food

C TV

6 How does Ben feel at the end of the conversation?

A upset

B excited

C relieved

7 What is Ben's accent?

A American

B Australian

C Scottish

8 What is Jessica's accent?

A Australian

B British

C American

3 Short-answer questions

Part 1: Understanding the question type

 Exam information: Short-answer questions

Short-answer questions test your ability to listen for specific information, such as places, reasons or times. You read a question, listen and then write a short answer. Some questions ask students to list two or three points.

You will see a word limit for these questions (e.g. NO MORE THAN THREE WORDS AND/OR A NUMBER). You will lose marks for writing more than the word limit. Hyphenated words (e.g. well-known) count as single words. These question types can be in ANY part of the Listening test.

1   Read the exam information. Then look at the example task and decide what is wrong with the first answer.

   Where are they going on holiday?

   ...*They are going to Australia...* ✗

   ....*Australia....* ✓

2   Look at tasks A and B and decide which part of the Listening test they are from. Refer to Unit 1, page 8 for information about the content of each part.

A What event happens on Saturdays?   ....*book club*......   How much is a library card?   ......*$3.50*......

B What TWO activities does Mark want to do?   • ......*sailing*......   • ....*tennis*.......

Part 2: Answering short-answer questions

 Exam information: Understanding the question

Look carefully at the question before you listen to predict the kind of information you are listening out for. Question words like *which, who, where, when, why* and *how* are very common but expect other types of question forms too.

 **Exam tip**

When writing answers, you must always use words that you hear in the audio and you cannot change these words. e.g. if you hear *to go*, you cannot write *going*.

 **Exam tip**

If you spell your answer incorrectly, you will not get the question right. Leave enough time to check your spelling carefully at the end of your exam.

3 Read the Exam information and look at the two tasks A and B. Then answer questions 1–4.

1 What is another way of saying 'At what time'? **which / who / where / when / why / how**
2 What is another way of saying 'In which two places'? **which / who / where / when / why / how**
3 Which of these answers are possible / not possible for question A? Explain why.

Monday morning   7.45 p.m.   half past eleven   12.30 a.m.   twelve thirty

4 Brainstorm possible answers for question B.

A **Write no more than TWO WORDS AND/OR a NUMBER for your answer.**
At what time is the plane leaving?

_____

B **Write no more than TWO WORDS AND/OR a NUMBER for your answer.**
In which two places were the birds sighted?

_____

ⓘ Exam information: Rephrasing the question

In the Listening test, the information you hear will not use the same words as the question. Try rephrasing the question by predicting synonyms you may hear.

4 Read the Exam information. Then answer questions 1 and 2 about question B in exercise 3.

1 The word *bird* doesn't have any exact synonyms, but which of these words are related to the word *bird* and so may be used in the audio? blackbird / squirrel / crow / herd / flock / chick / puppy
2 Brainstorm other words with a similar meaning to *sighted*.
There are many ways this question may be paraphrased in the text. You have to be ready to listen for this, so you know the answer is coming.

5 Look at the following sentences. Which three sentences might indicate that the answer to the question 'In which two places were the <u>birds sighted</u>?' is coming?

1 These blackbirds have been spotted in only a few locations throughout the continent …
2 The birds often nest in locations that are very …
3 There have only been a couple of sightings of these birds …
4 They've been observed in only a few locations …
5 Their habitats are often warm, dry and away from …

ⓘ Exam information: Avoiding wrong answers

In the Listening test, you will probably hear other options that may sound like possible answers. Listen carefully, as there are options to distract you into choosing the wrong answer.

6 Read the Exam information, question C and the audio script. Then answer questions 1–4.

1 What tense is the question in?
2 Find three possible location answers in the audio script.
3 Which of the possibilities is correct?
4 Why are the other possibilities wrong?

C Where is the event taking place?

_____

"The spring festival is normally held at the town hall but because of renovations it will be held for the first time in the main square … in front of the community centre."

7 Read the sample questions D–F and the audio scripts. Then answer questions 1 and 2.

1 What are the possible answers for each question?
2 Identify which answers are wrong and which are the correct ones.

D Write no more than ONE WORD AND/OR a NUMBER for your answer.
Name TWO language courses that are now available at the Wordz Academy:

_____

_____

"Here at the Wordz Academy we used to run a popular Russian course, but unfortunately the teacher left at the end of the year, so it's no longer available. We've got Polish running now and we're planning on running Japanese early next year. Ooh, we've also got a French class but it's evenings only."

E Write no more than THREE WORDS AND/OR a NUMBER for your answer.
What natural event are they going to study?

_____

What will Anna do?

_____

Peter: _Hmm … I'm not sure what we should research for our presentation … we've got to pick one of the natural events we've already studied …_
Anna: _So we've got the choice of earthquakes, droughts, wildfires or volcanic eruptions. Everyone is going to do eruptions so let's not pick that. Do you have a preference?_
Peter: _Yeah, I think I'd prefer droughts._
Anna: _Hmm … I was away for that week. What about wildfires?_
Peter: _OK. It will be more interesting that earthquakes! Do you want to do the speech or prepare the slides?_
Anna: _I think I'd prefer to leave the speech to you, if that's OK. I get nervous in front of a crowd._

F Write no more than TWO WORDS AND/OR a NUMBER for your answer.
With which TWO activities did stars help us in the past?

_____

_____

"We now know that stars tell us a great deal about the history of the solar system, but this was a relatively recent discovery. However, stars were used more than a thousand years ago too. In fact, they were of great assistance in many areas of life. While the sun and the moon were used to tell the time of day, star positioning informed people of seasonal changes, which was essential for planting crops. They were also used for navigating at sea as the stars worked as a map for sailors."

 **Exam tip**

When writing answers, you must use capitalization correctly. If you are unsure about which words need capitalization, write all your answers in capital letters, e.g. FRENCH, PREPARE THE SLIDES

Part 3: Practising short-answer questions

8 Listen and complete Parts 1 and 3.

Part 1

🔊 **12**

Listen to the conversation between a customer and a travel agent. Answer questions 1–5.

Write NO MORE THAN TWO WORDS AND/OR A NUMBER for each answer.

Where does the man choose to go on holiday?

1 _____

How much does the holiday cost?

2 _____

Name THREE things that are included in the cost.

3 _____

4 _____

5 _____

Part 3

🔊 **13**

Listen to the students discuss their research project. Answer questions 6–10.

Write NO MORE THAN THREE WORDS AND/OR A NUMBER for each answer.

In which TWO areas do national parks need to improve?

6 _____

7 _____

What are they going to work on now?

8 _____

What TWO things does their professor want?

9 _____

10 _____

4 Completion questions 1

Aims | Understanding the question types (sentence and summary questions); **Answering sentence and summary completions** (following instructions, what makes a sentence, making predictions, checking your answers); **Practising completion questions**

Part 1: Understanding the question types

i Exam information: Sentence and summary questions

In sentence and summary questions, you have to complete gaps with a word or words from the audio. There is a word limit for each gap; for example, NO MORE THAN TWO WORDS AND/OR A NUMBER. You may see these question types in any part of the Listening exam.

1 Complete the descriptions with the words in the box.

sentence completion   summary completion

1   In _____ questions, there are separate sentences, each with a single gap to complete.
2   In _____ questions, there are one or two paragraphs with spaces to complete.

☀ **Exam tip**
Learn how words are counted in the IELTS test. For example, hyphenated words (e.g. *long-term, fifty-five*) count as one word.

2 Look at tasks A and B and answer questions 1 and 2.

1   Which task A or B is a sentence completion task, and which is a summary completion task?
2   What part of the exam do you think they are from? See Unit 1 page 8 for a description of each part of the test.

A *Legends are normally* **1** _____ *over time to make them remain believable. They usually contain a* **2** _____ *meaning which may help people conform to certain beliefs. There is generally a basis for most legends in* **3** _____, *which means that although people may not be sure of their truth, they are never entirely doubted.*

B *The local history museum* **1** _____ *on the 5th of November.*

The top floor restaurant is only open **2** _____.

Admission is free for **3** _____.

There is a **4** _____ *for elderly people before midday.*

Part 2: Answering sentence and summary completions

 Exam information: Following instructions

It is important to follow the instructions carefully. For example, in completion tasks it may say NO MORE THAN TWO WORDS AND/OR A NUMBER. This means that each gap must have one or two words only.

3 Look at the question and audio script below. What do you think the answer could be?

1 radio-controlled
2 car
3 radio-controlled car
4 video games console
5 console

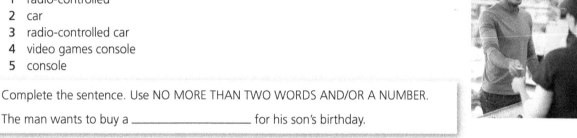

Complete the sentence. Use NO MORE THAN TWO WORDS AND/OR A NUMBER.

The man wants to buy a _____ for his son's birthday.

Man:	*I'm looking for something for my son … it's his birthday soon!*
Shop assistant:	*Hmmm … We've got the latest video games consoles. Would he like something like that?*
Man:	*No … I'm looking for a radio-controlled car. He's mad on racing!*

4 Look at the questions and audio script excerpt below. What words complete the gaps? Do you need to use all three words?

Complete the sentence. Use no more than THREE WORDS AND /OR A NUMBER.

The shopping centre was built behind the _____.

"So, here we are at the entrance to the shopping centre. This was actually a big open-air market many years ago, and this new centre was built just 15 years ago. Here, in front of us, you can see the clock tower, which is the oldest monument in the town."

 Exam information: What makes a sentence?

Understanding the parts of a sentence is essential for completion questions, as this can tell you what kind of information goes in the gaps. The most basic sentences have a subject, a verb and usually an object. However, other clauses can be added to this structure.

5 Read the sentences below and circle the sections containing the subject, verb and object. Underline the other clauses. The first one has been completed as an example.

1 (The _____ took off) <u>for the first time in 1852</u>.

2 The number of calories recommended for people depends on _____.

3 Students can _____ their tutors at 6 p.m. onwards.

4 For teenagers, texting apps are now the most common way to _____.

6 Read the sentences in exercise 5 again and decide what type of word is required for the answer.

1 a noun is required for the subject of the sentence

🔆 Exam tip

Learning about sentence structure and parts of speech can not only help you with Reading and Listening completion questions, it can help you understand more complicated sentences in texts and improve your writing.

ⓘ Exam information: Making predictions

Knowing what kind of word goes in the gap can help you predict answers, but there are also many other ways of predicting what might complete the gap. Thinking about possible answers before you listen will get you ready for listening. The words around the gaps can help you do this.

7 Read the sentence completions 1–4 and answer two questions about each one.

1 The _____ <u>took off</u> for the first time in <u>1852</u>.

What kind of things take off?

What kind of things might have taken off in 1852?

2 The <u>number of calories</u> recommended for people depends on _____.

What does the word *calories* tell us about the topic?

What does recommended calories usually depend on?

3 <u>Students</u> can _____ their <u>tutors</u> at <u>6 p.m. onwards</u>.

What does students and tutors tell you about the topic?

What kinds of things can students do with tutors?

4 For <u>teenagers</u>, <u>texting apps</u> are now the most common <u>way</u> to _____.

What kinds of things can you do on texting apps?

What might teenagers do with these apps?

🔆 Exam tip

You must write words from the recording in your answers. DO NOT write your own words. The words surrounding the gaps will often be paraphrased but the answers to complete the gaps are never paraphrased.

Part 2: Answering multiple-choice questions

 Exam information: Understanding the question in different parts of the test

Multiple-choice questions appear in all parts of the Listening test, but they may test quite different sub-skills. For example, there are questions that test your ability to hear specific details, general ideas, main points, similarities and differences.

2 Look at the Part 1 and Part 4 multiple-choice questions and read the audio extracts. Then answer the questions 1–5.

Part 1

Listen to someone asking about film times at a cinema.

1 What time does the film start?
   A 8.00 p.m.
   B 5.45 p.m.
   C 7.15 p.m.

"The film is going to be on earlier this week. It did start at 8.00, but because it's so popular with kids, the start time has been moved to quarter to six. It finishes at about quarter past seven."

Part 4

Listen to a lecture on Internet marketing.

1 The lecturer thinks that the biggest challenge for small businesses is
   A keeping up to date with the latest technology.
   B using their budget in the most efficient way.
   C choosing the right tone for their audience.

"Internet marketing has become the way that the majority of companies increase their customer base and visibility. Most people think that this is relatively easy but keeping pace with the latest technological trends is a full-time job from the smallest to the biggest companies in the world. Even the largest multinational corporations get their tone wrong once in a while. For companies just starting out, money spent on marketing online needs to be spent wisely, and this requires expertise. As a result, many small businesses fall at this first hurdle."

1 Does the question in Part 1 or Part 4 focus on simple, factual information?
2 Does the question in Part 1 or Part 4 avoid using much paraphrase?
3 Does Part 1 or Part 4 focus on ideas?
4 Which question uses a lot of paraphrase?
5 Are all the options mentioned in the audio extracts?

Exam tip

You always have some time before the recording to read the questions, so use it to think of possible paraphrases for the question and options.

 Exam information: Focusing on common synonyms

You will usually hear all the options mentioned in the audio. Some of the words will be exactly the same as in the question and others will be paraphrased. Remember that the answers will usually be paraphrased, so if you hear one of the options exactly, it may not be the correct answer.

3 Read Task B in exercise 1 again. Write some synonyms for the words below. The first one has been done as an example.

1 important *essential, necessary, vital*   4 amount _____

2 cost _____   5 life _____

3 design _____   6 time _____

4 Think of some synonyms for some of the words in Tasks A and C in exercise 1.

ℹ️ Exam information: Noticing small differences in options

In multiple-choice questions that focus on factual information, the options can be quite similar. It is important to focus on the small differences before listening.

5 How are the options A–C similar in 1 and 2? Why might it be difficult to choose the correct answer?

1 What kind of holiday does the customer
want to book?
A a beach holiday
B a sightseeing holiday
C a walking holiday

2 The town has a good selection of
A supermarkets
B restaurants
C cafés

6 Listen and answer questions 1 and 2 in exercise 5.
🔊
16

7 Look at the audio script for exercise 6 on page 163 and underline the answers to questions 1 and 2. What synonyms are used in the audio script?

ℹ️ Exam information: Understanding concepts in options

For questions that focus on concepts or ideas it is important to think of different ways you may hear the information mentioned in the question and options.

8 Think of some synonyms for the underlined words in the question and the options.

There are <u>fewer</u> <u>women</u> <u>working</u> in the <u>IT industry</u> <u>because</u>

A of a <u>lack</u> of female <u>role models</u>.   _____

B it is <u>difficult</u> to get <u>promoted</u>.   _____

C <u>companies</u> <u>prefer</u> to <u>hire</u> <u>men</u>.   _____

9 Listen and answer the question in exercise 8.
🔊
17

Part 3: Practising multiple choice

10 Listen and complete Parts 1 and 4.

Part 1

Questions 1–4. Choose the correct letter, A, B or C.

1   When will the man return the car?

    A   Sunday morning

    B   Monday morning

    C   Monday afternoon

2   What kind of vehicle does he choose?

    A   family car

    B   economy car

    C   luxury car

3   How is the man going to pay for the car?

    A   cash

    B   card

    C   cash and card

4   What time will the office close on Friday?

    A   4.30 p.m.

    B   8.00 p.m.

    C   7.00 p.m.

Part 4

Questions 5 and 6.

5   Listen to the lecture. Which TWO reasons does the lecturer give for the value of gold?

    A   its beauty

    B   its history

    C   its rarity

    D   its strength

    E   its flexibility

    F   its image

6   Choose the correct letter A, B or C. What lesser-known use of gold does the lecturer talk about?

    A   how it keeps aircraft cabins warm

    B   how it can improve visibility for pilots

    C   how it connects equipment in planes

6 Matching questions

Aims | Understanding the question types; Answering matching questions
(understanding the order of information, understanding distractors in matching questions,
paraphrasing in matching questions); **Practising matching questions**

Part 1: Understanding the question types

In matching questions, you have to match some information to a list of items, such as place names, reasons
for doing something or types of technology. The information on the recording comes in the same order as the
numbered statements, but the answer options (A, B, C, etc.) are random. You must write the letter on your
answer sheet. This question type tests your ability to understand details as well as the relationship between
different kinds of information.

1 Look at the sample matching questions 1 and 2 and answer questions 1–3.

> 1 What does the speaker say about the museums? Write the correct letter A, B or C.
> 1 It is good value for money.
> 2 The app is free for students.
> 3 The staff are knowledgeable.
> 4 It's an excellent choice for families.
>
> A The National Gallery of Landscapes
> B The Gallery of Textiles
> C The Ancient Arts Gallery
>
> 2 Match the students to the different projects that they are working on at the moment. Write the
> correct letter A, B or C.
> 1 Animal conservation
> 2 Animal behaviour
> 3 Species evolution
>
> A Jack
> B Lisa
> C Ana

1 What should you write on your answer sheet?
2 In which question do you need to choose an option more
   than once?
3 In which part of the test might you see the questions above?

 Exam tip

When you have to match a
statement to people's names, listen
carefully from the beginning and
take note when they refer to each
other by name.

Part 2: Answering matching questions

 Exam information: Understanding the order of information

You can use the numbered statements to predict what you might hear on the recording. These numbered statements also tell you the order you'll hear information.

2 Look at statements 1–4 in question 1 in exercise 1 and number the topics in the box in the order you think you will hear them.

employees _____   costs _____   technology _____   visitors _____

3 Read the first part of the audio script and underline two sentences connected to exercise 1, question 1, sentence 1 (*It is good value for money*).

"Good morning everyone. My name is Georgia and I'd like to go give you some details about the city's museums as this afternoon you have time to explore the city yourselves. There are lots of interesting places for families as well as adults. The National Gallery of Landscapes is free, but I don't think it's worth spending too much time there unless you want to learn about ancient geography. In my opinion there are better places. So, for example, even though you have to pay for the Ancient Arts Gallery, there is so much to see and there's something for everyone so in my view the price is completely justified."

 Exam tip

You may also hear words linked to the other statements, and these might confuse you, but remember that you will always hear the questions in number order.

 Exam information: Understanding distractors in matching questions

It is important to read both the statements and the items carefully, so you know what you are listening for. You may hear more than one item related to a statement, but only one will be correct.

4 Look at the audio script in exercise 3 again and answer questions 1–4. You will see that the speaker talks about more than one gallery in connection with the topic of money.

1 Does the speaker say that you need to pay to go into the National Gallery of Landscapes?
2 Does the speaker say that the National Gallery of Landscapes is very good?
3 Does the speaker say that you have to pay for the Ancient Arts Gallery?
4 Does the speaker say that it is worth paying to go into the Ancient Arts Gallery?

Exam tip

You may hear more than one item connected to a statement, but only one answer will be correct. The speaker may talk about the topic, but you must make a match to the exact meaning.

5 Which one of these questions 1–4 is similar to the phrase *value for money*?

ℹ️ **Exam information: Paraphrasing in matching questions**
The recording will use synonyms and paraphrases so you should think of other ways to express the information in the questions before you listen. You may hear some of the words from the questions on the recording and the speaker(s) may mention the options in the list more than once. You must listen carefully to match the correct ideas or information.

6 Read the audio script in exercise 3 again and write the part which paraphrases statement 1.

    1 **Statement 1 =** It is good value for money.

       Paraphrase = _____

7 Paraphrase statements 2–4.

    2 The app is free for students. _____

       _____

    3 The staff are knowledgeable. _____

       _____

    4 It's an excellent choice for families. _____

       _____

8 **Listen to the rest of the talk and answer the questions.**
🔊
20

    Question 1: What does the speaker say about the museums? Write the correct letter A, B or C.

    1 It is good value for money.   *C*

    2 The app is free for students.   _____

    3 The staff are knowledgeable.   _____

    4 It's an excellent choice for families.   _____

    A The National Gallery of Landscapes

    B The Gallery of Textiles

    C The Ancient Arts Gallery

Part 3: Practising matching questions

9 Listen and complete Parts 2 and 3.

Part 2

🔊 21

Match the films to the descriptions. Write the correct letters, A–E next to questions 1–4.

1 *Keep on Running* _____

2 *My Best Life* _____

3 *Out in the Sun* _____

4 *Good Times in Bridgetown* _____

A It is suitable for young people under 12.

B Both parents and teenagers will enjoy it.

C The storyline is based on real-life events

D It is popular with both men and women.

E The film won several awards recently.

Part 3

🔊 22

Questions 5–8

Who will prepare the parts of the students' presentation on disappearing languages?

5 The visual information. _____

6 The facts and figures. _____

7 Examples from different continents. _____

8 Some cultural issues and impacts. _____

A Oliver

B Caroline

C Nisha

D All of them

7 Completion questions 2

Aims | Understanding the question types (completion questions); **Answering completion questions** (understanding processes of flow charts, using layout and format, question layouts, speaker contradictions and common errors); **Practising completion questions**

Part 1: Understanding the question types

ⓘ Exam information: Completion questions

In completion questions, you have to complete gaps with words or numbers from the recording. You may need to choose the answer from a list (A, B, C, D, etc.) or write the answer. There is a word limit for each gap; for example, NO MORE THAN TWO WORDS AND/OR A NUMBER. Remember that any words you write must come from the audio script. These questions usually appear in Parts 1 and 2 of the Listening test.

1 Match sample questions A–D to question types 1–4. Write a short description for each type.

1 Form   2 Table   3 Flow chart   4 Notes

A _____

Residence name	Cost per month	Facilities	Number of people
Kings Court	**(1)** _____	Wi-fi Shared **(2)** _____	6
(3) _____ Close	$750	Wi-fi Gym	**(4)** _____

B _____

Test 1 _____

↓

Review test results

↓

Assess 2 _____

C _____

Delivery details

Name: Jenny **(1)** _____

Mobile: 06543 **(2)** _____

Email: jenny5@example.com

Address: 54 **(3)** _____, London.

Date: August **(4)** _____

D _____

Finding academic papers
- use reading lists, **(1)** _____

Time management
- set deadlines for reading, choose most **(2)** _____ articles

Writing tips
- get **(3)** _____, produce multiple drafts

Part 2: Answering completion questions

 Exam information: Understanding processes of flow charts

Flow charts show a process and order of information. Before you answer a flow chart completion question, try to think about what the arrows mean and what might happen in each step.

2 Look at the flow chart and answer questions 1–5.

1 What order will you hear the information in?
2 What is the first thing to happen?
3 If you identify an IT problem, what kinds of things might you attempt? Why is it useful to think of this?
4 Why are there two arrows after the second box?
5 What might you do if a problem continues? Why is it useful to think of this?

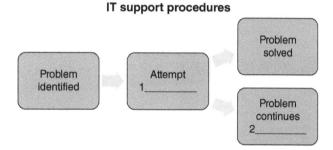

IT support procedures

 Exam information: Using layout and format

Table and flow chart completion questions both have layouts that can help you predict the answers. **Tables** have different labels (usually at the top and in the left corner). These labels tell you the type of information in each box. The format of the writing in a table can also tell us a lot about how to complete the gaps.

3 Look at the table below. What information would you find in 1, 2 and 3?

Beaufort Scale Wind Classification			
Category	**Description**	**Damage**	**Average Wind Speed (km/h)**
6	Strong breeze	Large branches move Umbrellas difficult to use	**(1)** _____
7	Moderate gale	**(2)** _____ Walking difficult	54
8	**(3)** _____	Branches can break Walking very difficult	65

4 Look at the table in exercise 4 again and answer questions 1–3.

1 Should words or numbers complete the space in question 1 in the table? How do you know? Should the numbers have decimal spaces? What is a more likely answer: 42 or 89? Why?
2 Look at the descriptions of damage. Do they use note form or complete sentences? How do you know? What does this tell you about how you should write your answer to question 2 in the table?
3 Look at the descriptions for categories 6 and 7. What parts of speech are used to form the descriptions? How does this give you an idea of what kinds of words you should write for question 3 in the table?

In all of these completion questions, looking at the format of the sentences or notes around the answers can give you important information about the kind of answer to write and how it should be written.

5 The note completion task is the same as the table completion but in a note format. Are the answers for this note format the same as the answers in exercise 5?

Beaufort scale –

Category 6: Strong Breeze (**(1)** _____ kmph average)

- Large branches move

- Umbrellas difficult to use

Category 7: Moderate gale (54 kmph average)

- **(2)** _____

- Walking difficult

Category 8: **(3)** _____ (65 kmph average)

- Branches can break

- Walking very difficult

It is quite common to hear changes to the details or spelling/numbers repeated wrongly on a booking form, so listen carefully to the whole extract.

6 Look at the form completion task and then read the start of the audio script. Underline where there is a contradiction or change in each audio script and circle the correct answer.

Exercise class booking form

Class name: Kickboxing – Intermediate

Date: Thursday 27th

Time: (1) _____

Name: John **(2)** _____

Telephone: (3) _____

> Assistant: There's two that day, which one are do you want to book? The one at 4.30 or the one at 8.15?
> John: I'll go for the 4.30 one.
> Assistant: Ooh, I'm afraid the last space has been taken.
> John: OK. 8.15 then.

> Assistant: OK … I just need a few details. What's your name?
> John: John Hayden.
> Assistant: How do you spell your surname?
> John: H–A–Y–D–E–N.
> Assistant: That's H–E–Y …
> John: No, H–A–Y …

> Assistant: Great, and what's your contact number?
> John: 0–5–double 6–4–3–double 1–2–8.
> Assistant: 0–5–double 6–4–3–double 1–8.
> John: No, double 1–2–8.

Exam tip

Make sure you are familiar with address formats in English-speaking countries, spellings of large cities, and the pronunciation of individual letters and long numbers.

Part 3: Practising completion questions

7 Listen and complete Parts 1 and 3.

Part 1

🔊 23

Questions 1–3. Complete the form below.

Write **ONE WORD AND/OR A NUMBER** for each answer.

FLIGHT BOOKING RESERVATION FORM	
Personal details	
First name:	Alison
Surname:	Russell
Email:	**(1)** _____
Date of birth:	10/02/1998
Flight information	
Place of departure:	**(2)** _____
Destination:	Singapore
Date and time:	20th December 10.40 p.m.
Flight number:	**(3)** _____
Price (per passenger):	$610

Part 3

🔊 24

Track 24 Questions 4–7. Complete the flow chart below.

Write **NO MORE THAN THREE WORDS AND/OR A NUMBER**.

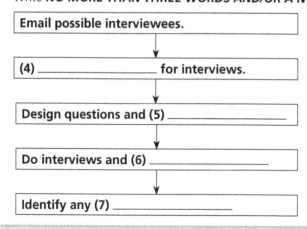

| Email possible interviewees. |
| ↓ |
| **(4)** _____ **for interviews.** |
| ↓ |
| **Design questions and (5)** _____ |
| ↓ |
| **Do interviews and (6)** _____ |
| ↓ |
| **Identify any (7)** _____ |

Aims | Understanding the question types (labelling plans, maps and diagrams);
Answering labelling questions (understanding the answer format, using visual clues,
understanding signposting and location language); **Practising labelling questions**

Part 1: Understanding the question type

ℹ️ Exam information: Labelling plans, maps and diagrams

These questions all have an image, which is either a plan or map of a place, or a diagram of an object. The image has
some written labels and some gaps. You must complete the gaps. Sometimes you have to write words and sometimes
you have to choose the correct labels from a list in a box. These questions test your ability to relate language
connected to location and description to details in visual information.

1   Match the example test questions A, B and C to the correct type of visual information in the box.

Plan _____   Map _____   Diagram _____

A   Write the correct letters next to questions 1–5.

1 _____   2 _____   3 _____   4 _____   5 _____

A	Massage room	B	Training area
C	Solarium	D	Dressing room
E	Office	F	Information desk
G	Dance room	H	Fitness classes

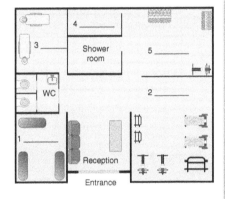

**B   Questions 1–4. Write NO MORE THAN TWO WORDS OR
A NUMBER.**

MICROSCOPE DIAGRAM

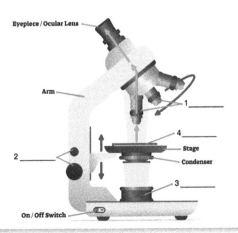

C **Questions 1–5. Write the names of the places. Write NO MORE THAN TWO WORDS.**

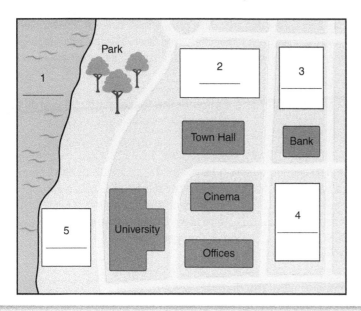

Part 2: Answering labelling questions

 Exam information: Understanding the answer format

Look closely at the instructions, the gaps and any other information about the format of the answers to help you chose the correct format for your own answers.

2 Answer the questions about the visual images in exercise 1.

1 What is the format of the answers for A?
2 What would happen if you wrote words for the answers in A?
3 Do you need to use all the letters in the box for A?
4 What is the format of the answers for question B?
5 Can you write a number in any of the answers for question B?
6 What is the format of the answers for question C?

 Exam information: Using visual clues

These question types all use images and labels, which means that there are some visual clues to help you as you listen. Firstly, it is important to think about where on the image the recording will start and then how the speaker will move around the plan, map or diagram.

3 Answer questions 1–3 about each task in exercise 1.

1 Where will the recording start?
2 How will the speaker move around the images?
3 What visual clues are there to help you?

ℹ️ Exam information: Understanding signposting and location language

You will hear synonyms and paraphrases of some of the labels that are on the plan, map or diagram. The speaker will also use words and phrases to help you follow the plan, map or diagram as you listen. This includes language to describe movement or the relationship between places or objects, as well as location and different parts of objects.

4 Read and listen to the description of the helicopter and complete the spaces with the words you hear. 🔊 25

*"Helicopters are much more versatile aircrafts than planes. They can move **1** _____ and **2** _____ and hover. They can also change direction from, say, **3** _____ to **4** _____ much more easily than a plane. The helicopter has a cockpit **5** _____ where the pilot sits and controls the aircraft. **6** _____ the body of the helicopter are the landing skids. The main rotor blade is **7** _____ and there is a smaller rotor **8** _____ the tail. The rotor blades **9** _____ and as the speed increases the helicopter gradually **10** _____ off the ground".*

5 Read the description in exercise 4 again and label the diagram below.

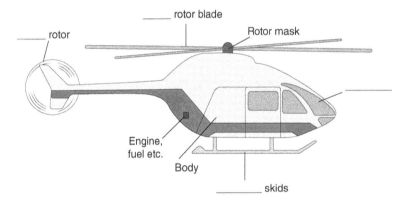

```
_____ rotor blade
_____ rotor          Rotor mask




Engine,
fuel etc.
        Body
              _____ skids
```

6 Now number the answers in the order that you heard them on the recording. What did you notice about the order of the answers and their location on the diagram?

7 Write the answers from exercise 4 in the correct column below.

Location	Phrases for direction	Geographical position	Verbs of movement

8 Add some more words and phrases to each column.

Part 3: Practising labelling questions

9 Listen and complete Parts 2 and 4.

Part 2

🔊 26

Questions 1–5. Label the plan below.

*Choose **FIVE** answers from the box and write the correct letters **A–H** next to questions 1–5.*

The Museum of Nature

A Great Hall
B Gift shop
C Sea Life Zone
D Cloakroom
E Reception
F The Mountain Zone
G Temporary exhibitions
H Lockers

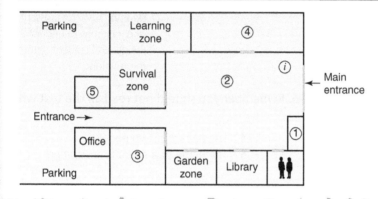

Part 4

🔊 27

*Questions 6–10. Label the diagram. Write **NO MORE THAN THREE WORDS AND/OR A NUMBER.***

Halley V1 Research Station

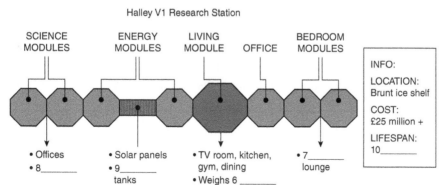

1 Locating answers in reading texts

Aims | Introduction to skimming and scanning; Locating answers using skimming and scanning; Skimming and scanning a reading text

Part 1: Introduction to skimming and scanning

Skimming and scanning are reading techniques. Skimming means reading parts of a text quickly so that you understand the general content. Scanning is used to look for specific details and it involves moving your eyes over the text looking for names, numbers and other factual information.

1 Look at the scenarios below. Which items would you scan and which would you skim?

1 bus timetable   2 newspaper article   3 information leaflet   4 index of books   5 Facebook page

2 Skim the four paragraphs below about Maria Mitchell and match them to the headings 1–4.

1   Her working life
2   Her contribution to science
3   Her early life
4   A role model for women

 **Exam tip**

In an exam, you can quickly skim the first and last sentences in paragraphs to understand the general content of the information.

3 Scan texts A–D to find the information in 1–5. Remember you should not read *all* the text when you are scanning.

1   Two planets
2   A year
3   A town
4   The names of two people
5   The name of a scientific instrument

A Few people have heard of the astronomer Maria Mitchell, yet she remains one of America's most influential astronomers. Author Amy Brill respects Mitchell for her perseverance as a woman in science and wrote a novel based on the astronomer's life. However, Professor Renee Bergland, who has written extensively about women in science, highlights that women were encouraged to become scientists in that period. She argues Mitchell should be seen as an example of what can be achieved by supporting women in science and not as someone who faced much adversity.

B The career of astronomer Maria Mitchell spanned several decades and included a variety of roles. Whilst still a teenager, she opened a school and then a year later went on to work as a librarian in Nantucket, a position that she held for over 20 years. During her free time in this period, she developed her fascination with and skills in astronomy. In 1847 she discovered a comet and, as a result of this, she became well known and highly respected throughout the scientific world. She went on to teach at Vassar College, New York.

C Several factors contributed to the development of Maria Mitchell's scientific capabilities. Although she showed considerable aptitude in mathematics, her upbringing was influential too. Her mother was a librarian and her father a teacher, and both believed strongly in educating all their children equally, irrespective of gender. In addition, the women in the fishing town of Nantucket, where the family lived, were accustomed to running their own lives independently while their husbands were at sea for long periods. This environment influenced Maria's development significantly.

D Maria Mitchell discovered a comet using a Dolland telescope and it was named 'Miss Mitchell's Comet'. As a result of this discovery, she became the first female member of the American Academy of Arts and Sciences. Her work mainly focused on photographing sunspots and the stars, which she did using observational equipment she had designed herself. She also studied planets, predominantly Saturn and Jupiter. She carried out a large amount of research, much of which was published in *Silliman's Journal*, a top scientific journal of that era.

Part 2: Locating answers using skimming and scanning

 Exam information: Skimming large texts

Skimming texts in the IELTS Reading paper can give you an idea of the structure of the text, which means you will be able to find the answers to the questions more quickly because you can go straight to the relevant sections.

4 Skim the text on the next page and choose the best summary A–D.

A The number of women astronomers has decreased since the professionalization of science.
B Many more women are entering the field of astronomy because of the legacy of Maria Mitchell.
C Astronomy has always been a popular science for women because they are better at observation than men.
D Female scientists have always had to work harder than male scientists to create a successful career in astronomy.

 Exam information: Scanning for specific answers

You can scan an IELTS text for names and numbers, but also for more uncommon or technical words which are unlikely to be paraphrased. Names, numbers and unusual words in the text and/or questions can help you identify where in the text the answers are.

5 Scan the text to find the answers to the questions. The questions are not in text order. Time yourself to try to do this in less than two minutes.

1 What was William Mitchell's profession?

2 What do women receive 26 per cent of?

3 Which gender was more involved in science in the 1800s?

4 What has the UIS started to do recently?

5 In what century was Maria Mitchell famous?

6 What is the full name of the UIS?

7 What were created in the 1870s?

8 How many scientists are women now?

The Changing Gender of Astronomy

Nowadays studying and working in the field of astronomy and almost all scientific fields, with the possible exception of medicine, is dominated by men. Currently, according to the UNESCO Institute for Statistics (UIS), approximately 30 per cent of the world's scientific researchers are women. Based on this figure for the 21st century, people perceive that this percentage has always been true. However, it has not always been the case and astronomy is an interesting example.

Contrary to popular belief, in the past science was often seen as an activity for women. For example, in the 1800s in the USA science was not a profession and, therefore, it was equally open to girls who showed aptitude, although they were almost always from educated, wealthy backgrounds. Maria Mitchell is an example of someone who benefited from this environment. Her father, William, was a teacher and encouraged her interest in the subject. As a result, she became a well-known and respected astronomer in the 19th century, eventually having a long career working as an academic at Vassar College in New York.

The gender divide in astronomy came about due to the creation of paid jobs in the 1870s. These jobs were taken by men, and this meant that the number of opportunities available to women interested in astronomy and science declined. Although Maria Mitchell campaigned for women in science throughout her career, the effects of the professionalization of the field can still be seen today. Only 26 per cent of astronomy PhDs are awarded to women, and many women do not see it as a viable career path despite having such a good role model in Maria Mitchell.

Although it is widely believed that women have less-fulfilling careers in science in general, it is difficult to know what is happening in specific countries or areas of the world. As a result, the UIS has started to conduct surveys to find out which factors prevent women from choosing careers in science. These surveys will ask men and women about topics such as family life, financial issues, culture, education and so on. The aim is to be able to better advise women about careers in scientific subjects in the future.

Part 3: Skimming and scanning a reading text

6 Skim the text and answer the questions.

1 Which is the correct summary of paragraph 1?
   a The throwaway culture is becoming less popular.
   b The effects of throwaway culture.

2 Which is the correct summary of paragraph 2?
   a The change in the way products are made.
   b The skills that people should learn nowadays.

3 Is this summary of paragraph 3 true or false?
   The ways technology companies make products is good for consumers.

4 Is this summary of paragraph 4 true or false?
   People are becoming increasingly dependent on throwaway culture.

The cost of throwaway culture

1 The throwaway culture of the late 20th and early 21st centuries changed the world beyond recognition. In this throwaway culture consumers dispose of or replace products such as clothes or gadgets with more desirable versions every one to two years. This could be due to an improvement in quality of the more recent product, but it is more likely that the replacement products fulfil an artificial need that has been created by global brands. However, there is a growing realization amongst many people that it is not compatible with the future of a thriving, diverse planet.

2 Up until the 1950s, many products were built to last, due to the fact that they were both durable and able to be repaired. For example, in the USA there were 60,000 shoe repairers until the 1940s, however, fewer than 6,000 remain because it is often cheaper to send shoes to landfill and purchase new ones. This situation is common in the garment industry due to changing ideas of fashion, which are driven by the industry itself, and the results are extremely damaging to the environment. For example, it is estimated that in the UK around 350,000 tonnes of clothing is sent to landfill each year. In addition, skills such as basic sewing and carpentry, which were common a generation ago, have not been passed on to the younger throwaway generations.

3 The problem is equally as serious in the technology sector because products are often manufactured with 'planned obsolescence'. This means that the product is designed to fail after a relatively short time or is unable to be repaired due to its design. Given that computers double in power every 18 months, as proved by Moore's Law, companies can easily convince consumers that innovation has made their latest smartphone or other devices obsolete. In addition, many manufacturers do not produce repair manuals, to prevent consumers from being able to repair devices themselves.

4 Despite the prevalence of throwaway culture over the last 50 years, there are signs that it may be losing its appeal. As issues of climate change become more important, people are keen to prolong the life of the things they own. An example of this is local repair shops that are non-profit organizations. One opened in Amsterdam in 2009, and since then over 1,300 have appeared around the world. Another innovation is a community 'library of things', where local residents can borrow machines and tools to repair their belongings. In London over 300 people raised £10,000 to establish a library of things for their community. Both of these ideas have the potential to transform people's dependence on throwaway culture.

7 Scan the text and complete the sentences. Write NO MORE THAN THREE WORDS OR A NUMBER.

1 There were _____ shoe menders in America in the mid-20th century.

2 According to Moore's Law computers become twice as powerful every _____

3 In 2009 a new type of shop for fixing objects opened in _____

4 People in the UK throw away approximately _____ of clothes every year.

5 Several hundred people contributed money to create a _____ in London.

6 The habit of throwing away products began in the late _____ century.

7 'Planned obsolescence' means companies design products so that they stop working after a _____

8 Manufacturers used to make long-lasting products until the _____

2 Reading for detail

Aims | Introduction to paraphrasing; Techniques for using paraphrasing; Reading for detail to complete a task

Part 1: Introduction to paraphrasing

Test questions use different language to the relevant part of the text, though the meaning is the same. This is called paraphrasing. After locating the part of text relating to the question, you must read carefully to ensure you answer correctly. This is called close reading or reading for detail.

ⓘ Exam information: Common paraphrasing techniques

Paraphrasing uses several different techniques. Words or grammatical structures are changed, or the information is presented in a different order. Paraphrasing will often use more than one of these techniques, which is why reading in detail is essential.

1 Read the two paragraphs that contain the same information but use different language. Look at the underlined sections (1–6) in paragraph B and compare with paragraph A. Then match the changes to paraphrasing techniques (a–f). The first one is done as an example.

1 Paragraph B — overconfident (adjective), Paragraph A — overconfidence (noun) = b, changes in word form (adjective — noun)

> **A** Overconfidence can have many negative effects. In business, it can be disastrous when people invest money in badly performing stocks or support new business ideas which have little chance of success. These kinds of poor choices happen more frequently than many people realize. Overconfidence can also create difficulties in education because teachers can easily mistake this high level of confidence for academic aptitude. Despite the fact that there are several theories on where overconfidence comes from, this characteristic has not been fully understood yet.

> **B** There are many issues associated with being (1) overconfident. (2) In the workplace, (3) businesspeople often make bad financial decisions due to overconfidence, which is something that happens more often than people think. In education, overconfidence (4) can be confused with academic ability, which can cause problems. There is still a lot for researchers to do (5) in order to completely understand (6) the origins of overconfidence, even though some theories do exist.

a synonyms – words with similar meanings
b changes in word forms – nouns, verbs, adjectives or adverbs
c changing the order of information
d active and passive forms
e positive and negative structures
f summaries – meaning over more than one sentence is reduced

Part 2: Techniques for using paraphrasing

 Exam information: Taking a step-by-step approach

Reading in detail requires a step-by-step approach. First, establish what kind of answer you are looking for (e.g. a type of job, an adjective describing a landscape). Then, scan the text to find the correct place where the answer is located. Remember that the language will be paraphrased. Finally, read these sentences in detail to decide on the correct answer.

2 Look at the text and Question 1. What kind of word do you think the answer is, e.g. noun, verb?

Interpersonal skills are a fundamental part of becoming successful in the modern workplace.[1] There are numerous books and online courses which claim to <u>increase our ability to</u> listen to others, demonstrate leadership or offer advice to colleagues. [2] However, studies have shown that confidence is regularly cited by employees across many fields of work as being highest on their list. [3] There is a belief among many people that this will lead to <u>improvements</u> in other areas of life, such as risk-taking or teamwork.

Question 1 Complete the sentence using NO MORE THAN TWO WORDS from the passage for the answer.

1   Most workers would like to <u>improve</u> their levels of _____.

3 Look at the underlined words and the coloured words and phrases in the task in Question 2. Find the following techniques of paraphrasing in these sections.

1   a passive sentence (text) changed to active (question)

2   two ways of writing 'get better'

3   two ways of writing 'people with jobs'

 **Exam tip**

Remember NOT to just match words that are the same in the text and the question. Word matching will often lead you to the wrong answer.

4 Read the text, the question and the answer. Use the three steps in the Exam information box to identify the correct answer.

In the workplace, confidence can be confused for reliability. When colleagues ask each other for advice, employees who give clear responses are usually more respected by their peers. This is because confident people tend to answer questions directly, whereas more cautious people can be vague in their responses and therefore less reliable. For example, it is seen as more helpful for someone to tell a colleague that they think a project will take one or two weeks rather than saying that it depends on a range of unknown factors. It takes courage to respond frankly, because many tough answers aren't always popular ones. However, too much confidence in these kinds of interactions can lead to others making important decisions based on faulty or misleading information.

Question 1 Write NO MORE THAN TWO WORDS from the passage for the answer.

In the workplace, _____ answers aren't seen as very practical or useful.

5 Read the following incorrect answers. Explain why they are incorrect.

1 In the workplace, _cautious_ answers aren't seen as very practical or useful.

2 In the workplace, _clear_ answers aren't seen as very practical or useful.

3 In the workplace, _tough_ answers aren't seen as very practical or useful.

Part 3: Reading for detail to complete a task

6 Read the text and answer the questions.

The Enduring Attraction of Lie Detectors

The polygraph machine or lie detector, as it is more commonly known, is a universally recognized object. In general, this is due to its constant use in popular culture, especially in American movies and on television crime series. Scenes where a suspected criminal is being interrogated by the police while a pen spikes up and down a chart are familiar to people all over the world. The rapid movement of the pen on the chart adds to the drama and suspense of the scene and has thrilled audiences for many years.

Psychologists have known for a long time that individuals show a range of physical signs when they lie. From increased heart rates to muscle twitches and tiny facial expressions, everyone is different. As a result, it is difficult to be sure when a person is being deceptive. Many studies have highlighted the fact that humans can distinguish between truth and lies in only 54 per cent of cases, which makes us extremely unreliable. For hundreds of years people have been trying to find a way to improve this. One attempt was the polygraph, a machine invented in 1921 by John Larson at the University of California. He was keen to introduce more science into policing and created the polygraph machine to use while interviewing suspects in criminal cases. The machine was connected to a person and it measured their blood pressure, breathing and sweat. Any changes in these measurements as suspects were answering questions were considered by the machine to be signs that they were not telling the truth.

John Larson worked with Leonarde Keeler, who made the device more commercially attractive by making it smaller and putting it inside a box so that it was portable. In the late 1920s, after the Wall Street crash, the polygraph became popular with financial organizations that wanted to interview employees they suspected of theft. Then the lie detector was commissioned by the American government, and by the 1950s thousands of government employees had taken lie detector tests to assess their suitability for certain kinds of work. During the 20th century about 25 per cent of corporations in the USA used polygraph tests on their employees, and by the 1980s there were over 10,000 trained examiners in the country. Interestingly, there was very little take-up in other parts of the world, so the lie detector remains very much an American phenomenon.

A surprising point about the lie detector is that it continues to be used today, despite the fact experts have long questioned its rate of success over time. Even today, over 2.5 million tests are conducted annually in the USA, yet there is little evidence from over 50 studies to suggest that the polygraph actually works. As Dr Andy Balmer from the University of Manchester notes, the popularity of the machine was based on the fact that people thought it was effective, not that it _was_ effective. In other words, its psychological effect is the key to the endurance of the lie detector.

QUESTIONS 1–4 Complete the sentences. Use NO MORE THAN TWO WORDS from the passage.

1 As a result of its long history in _____, the lie detector is widely recognizable.

2 Humans are very _____ because they notice the body language of deception only half the time.

3 Lie detectors used _____ in physical signals to identify people who were telling lies.

4 The polygraph machine was redesigned to be _____ to companies by Leonarde Keeler.

Questions 5–7 Complete the sentences. Use NO MORE THAN THREE WORDS from the passage.

5 In the mid-20th century _____ began using the lie detector.

6 Academics have repeatedly challenged the _____ of the polygraph machine.

7 Dr Balmer says the reason for the success of the polygraph machine is because of the _____.

7 Underline the sections of the text which contain the answers in exercise 6 and explain the paraphrase.

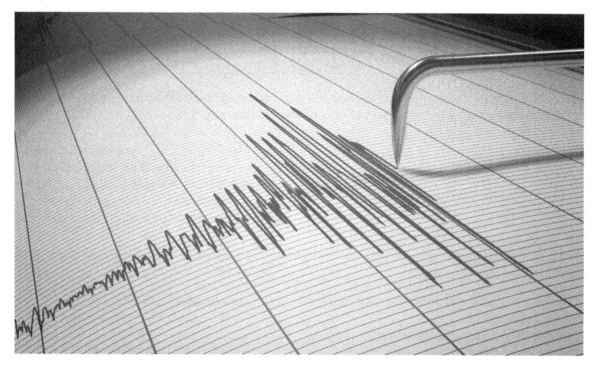

3 Completion tasks

Aims | Analysing completion tasks; **Techniques for completion tasks** (reading the instructions, noticing the language, locating answers, reading in detail); **Practising completion tasks**

Part 1: Analysing completion tasks

 Exam information: Using words from the text

In **Sentence, Summary, Note** and **Table completion** tasks, you must complete a gap with written information. This may be from a list of options or from within the text. If you need to write words, they MUST be from the text.

1 Read the information and decide if statements 1–4 are True or False.

1	Sentence and summary completion questions are in note form.	TRUE / FALSE
2	Summary completion questions have more than one sentence.	TRUE / FALSE
3	Notes are written information that highlight main and important points.	TRUE / FALSE
4	You must leave some words out of note and table completions.	TRUE / FALSE

Sentence completion tasks and **Summary completion tasks** are grammatically complete sentences. They require articles and prepositions. In a sentence completion you will see separate sentences, each with a gap that needs to be completed. In a summary completion, you will have a short paragraph summarizing the text or part of the text, and you need to complete the gaps.

Table completion tasks and **Note completion tasks** might not be grammatically complete sentences. When you think of notes or tables, often words that aren't completely essential (like articles) can be left out. Check the style of the notes or table to see if smaller words are left out and follow that style in your answers.

2 Look at tasks A–D and write the task type using the words in bold in the information in 1. Decide if they are grammatically / not grammatically complete sentences.

Habitat

Humpbacked whale
– Found in all major oceans
– Much _____ movement

Giant manta ray
– Usually found in _____ waters, e.g. the Sinai Peninsula

A Task type: _____

Many _____ have realized the value in using social media influencers over the last 20 years. A simple _____ from these individuals via their networks can increase sales significantly. While many …

B Task type: _____

Playing an instrument as a child may well impact upon _____.
Melodies affect _____ before they start to have a strong recognition of songs.

C Task type: _____

Jane Goodall – Life and research
– 1957: Started her career with animals in _____.
– 1965: Gained a doctorate in _____ patterns in chimpanzees.

D Task type: _____

Part 2: Techniques for completion tasks

 Exam information: Reading the instructions

For these task types the format of the answer is important. You may have to write a letter, a word, or several words and you must use correct spelling. The questions will always tell you what to write so make sure you read them carefully.

3 Read the test questions and the student's answer sheet and answer questions 1–3.

1 What has the student done wrong in each section? Find the mistakes.
2 Why do you think the student made these mistakes?
3 What would you do to avoid making these mistakes?

Questions 1–3
Complete the table below.
Use no more than TWO words from the passage for each answer.

Questions 4–7
Complete the summary using the list of words below. Write the correct letter, A–G, in boxes 4–7 on your answer sheet.

Questions 8–10
Complete the notes. Use no more than THREE words from the passage for each answer.

Student's answer sheet

1 *maximum number*
2 *intensive corses*
3 *to enquire online*

4 *F*
5 *B*
6 *E*
7 *reality*

8 *diferent colours*
9 *imagination*
10 *all the young children*

 Exam information: Noticing the language

You need to know what kinds of words complete the gap. It could be a verb, noun, adjective or adverb, or a 2–3-word phrase. The language around the gap can help you choose the correct answer.

4 Match the types of words given in the box to what is required for each gap in 1–4.

| adjective | noun | phrase | verb |

1 Safety is _____ for all airlines, and a lot of time and money is spent on this area.
2 The rail company will surely do a lot better _____.
3 People can experience _____ on any form of transport, but particularly on ships.
4 Formula one cars are _____ to be quick yet stable.

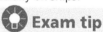 **Exam tip**
Not ALL content words are useful to locate the answer. For example, types of 'crew members' are mentioned throughout the text, so won't help us locate the answer.

 Exam information: Locating answers

You need to locate answers quickly in order to complete the IELTS test in time. Look for synonyms or paraphrases of content words then read carefully to find the words to complete the gap.

5 Look at the sentence and think of synonyms for the underlined words. Then scan the text to find where the answer is located.

Crew members were <u>well-respected</u> for their _____ and <u>interacted</u> with all other ranks.

A While there is a common belief that the life of a 19th-century sailor was a hard one, with men forced onto ships where a miserable life at sea awaited them, quite the opposite was true for the great majority of sailors. They were generally a proud group, who were skilled, well-paid and got to see far-flung places.

B Sailing also offered a way of job progression that was hard to find at this time. The first step of a life at sea was as a landsman, when they would learn about sailing by getting hands-on experience on deck. While this was a low-paid role, it would take only a few years for a landsman to become a seaman and finally an able seaman. This group were the elite of sailing – they could choose their boats and earn considerable money.

C The opportunities didn't stop there. While in many professions there was a clear division between each strata of society, on a ship these divisions were not so clear. The captain valued the expertise of seamen and able seaman and, because of the lack of space, some socializing between all individuals was inevitable. This also made promotion easier, even to the highest rank aboard and becoming captain. For example, Captain Cook had humble beginnings and worked his way up through the ranks.

6 Look at the differences highlighted between the question sentence and the text extract and answer questions 1–5.

1. What kind of word goes in the gap?
2. Which sentence is active and which sentence is passive?
3. What paraphrase for 'crew members' appears in the text?
4. How is the possessive form in the question (their) represented in the text?
5. What is the answer?

Question sentence:

Crew members were well-respected for their _____ and interacted with all other ranks.

🔆 Exam tip
Remember that completion questions are always in the order you will find the answers in the text.

Text extract:

The captain valued the expertize of seamen and able seaman and, because of the lack of space, some socializing between all individuals was inevitable.

7 Complete the summary for the text in exercise 5 with no more than THREE WORDS for each gap.

Being a seaman in the 1800s wasn't the tough and **1** _____ existence that many stereotypes lead us to believe. In fact, once they had some **2** _____ new sailors could progress quickly to well-paid positions. Sailing had a great deal of social mobility compared to other jobs at the time. Crew members were well-respected for their **3** _____ and interacted with all other ranks, sometimes leading to the opportunity of **4** _____ of their own ship.

Part 3: Practising completion tasks

8 Read the text and complete questions 1–8.

Permaculture: A Vision for Sustainable Living

The term permaculture advocates a sustainable approach to life through implementing a variety of concepts and practices. One of the key ideas is that of closed-loop systems, which means a system that is self-sufficient in terms of all its energy. An example of this is a farm that provides all the food for its livestock rather than buying any from an outside supplier. This could include using kitchen waste as animal feed as well as growing suitable crops. Unfortunately, closed-loop systems often rely on having a large space to produce all the resources required to close the system and, therefore, it is generally only a viable option for farmers or others with large areas of land.

Permaculture comes from the words 'permanent' and 'agriculture' and as such, attitudes towards selecting and growing specific crops feature heavily. Permaculture advocates perennial crops which, unlike crops that require harvesting and replanting, regrow every year without replanting. While this sounds sustainable, it must be highlighted that the quantity of perennial crops in the typical human diet is remarkably small compared to annuals. Much of permaculture is about innovative thinking and using resources sparingly, and stacking functions is another concept central to the movement. This is where built structures fulfil more than one function. For example, an animal shelter could have solar panels on the roof, or a rainwater collector could be used to grow aquatic plants. However, this approach has an inherent risk of doing both things badly if the secondary function does not logically fit with the primary one.

Permaculture has made some bold claims of success, yet as a theory it has been criticized because there is insufficient scientific research to categorically support such claims. While many people who work in the field are academics, countless others have a poor grasp of biology. However, its principles clearly point to a more thoughtful approach to life. The overarching theme is to work with nature rather than against it, which means observing the environment and adapting systems and processes to fit local environmental conditions. By noticing how plants, insects and mammals interact, a lot can be learned about how we can live in a more sustainable way and inflict less damage on our surroundings.

Questions 1–5 Complete the table. Choose NO MORE THAN TWO WORDS from the passage for each answer.

	Definition	Problems
Closed loop systems	supplies all (1) _____ required	only suitable for landowners or (2) _____
Perennial crops	Grow year on year	People eat a (3) _____ amount of perennials
Stacking functions	Multiple uses for (4) _____	Difficult to do well if the functions don't (5) _____

Questions 6–8 Write NO MORE THAN TWO WORDS from the passage for each answer.

6   The negative views of permaculture are due to a lack of _____.

7   Some people working in the industry do not understand _____ particularly well.

8   The goal of permaculture is to reduce human _____ to the environment.

4 Multiple-choice tasks

Aims | Analysing multiple-choice tasks; Techniques for multiple-choice tasks
(paraphrasing questions and options, comparing the options, eliminating wrong answers);
Practising multiple-choice tasks

Part 1: Analysing multiple-choice tasks

 Exam information: Multiple-choice tasks

In this question type, you need to select the correct option from a list of answers and write the letter (e.g. D) on your answer paper. There are different types of multiple-choice questions which often appear in the IELTS Reading test, but they might not all appear in one test.

1 Match the descriptions 1–4 to example tasks A–D.

1 A question with answer options (A–D).
2 A statement with ending options (A–D).
3 A list of five options with two answers to select (A–E).
4 A list of seven options with three answers to select (A–G).

A What TWO reasons does the writer give for the failure of the Stretch project?
  A lack of expertise
  B speed of technology
  C rising project costs
  D bad communication
  E quality of product

B What point does the writer make in the final paragraph about preservation of windmills?
  A They are expensive to use for generating power.
  B They are largely maintained by volunteers.
  C They can be used as a backup for other energy sources.
  D They are mainly too fragile to have any working function.

C What THREE groups does the writer consider benefit most from social networking?
  A the elderly
  B the self-employed
  C teenagers
  D disabled people
  E entrepreneurs
  F villagers
  G unemployed people

D The design and construction of the Amer Fort in India
  A was led by the necessity for strong defenses.
  B enabled a cool airflow for hotter weather.
  C mainly focused on aesthetic considerations.
  D focused on different levels for different residents.

 Exam tip

The order of the multiple-choice questions will be the same as the information in the text.

Part 2: Techniques for multiple-choice tasks

 Exam information: Paraphrasing questions and options

When you see a multiple-choice question, remember that you will not see all the same words in the text.

2 Look at the underlined words in the example question and answer questions 1 and 2.

1 Which underlined words are easy to find synonyms for?
2 Which underlined words are more difficult to find synonyms for?

> Male <u>cuttlefish</u> can use <u>colour</u> to
>
> A <u>warn</u> others of <u>threats</u>.
> B <u>scare</u> possible <u>competition</u>.
> C improve <u>mating</u> <u>chances</u>.
> D change their <u>sex</u>.

3 Match options A–D from the exam task in exercise 2 to sentences 1–4.

1 Male cuttlefish can change their colour to indicate potential hazards.
2 Male cuttlefish can attract the opposite sex better by changing colour.
3 Male cuttlefish can often change colour and with it transform from male to female.
4 Male cuttlefish can frighten other males who may be potential rivals.

 Exam information: Comparing the options

Focus on small differences between options, and between the options and the text to identify a correct and an incorrect option.

4 Underline the differences between each sentence and the one before, beginning with sentence 2. Do sentence 1 and sentence 5 have a similar meaning?

1 Cuttlefish can change their colour to indicate potential hazards.
2 Cuttlefish often change their colour to indicate potential hazards.
3 Cuttlefish often change their colour to indicate possible mates.
4 Male cuttlefish often change their colour to indicate possible mates.
5 Male cuttlefish often change their colour to attract possible mates.

 Exam information: Eliminating wrong answers

When you are looking for the right answer, it is important to discount wrong answers too. Most options will be referred to in the text, but only one option will have **no differences in meaning** from the text – discount wrong answers too.

5 Look at the text extract and the example question, then complete questions 1 and 2.

1 Underline where each option (A–D) is mentioned.
2 Do all parts of the options agree with the text? Why / Why not?

> Male cuttlefish can use colour to ...
>
> A warn others of threats.
> B scare possible competition.
> C improve mating chances.
> D change their sex.

> Many animals rely on visual communication methods to transmit basic emotions, warnings or attraction. One interesting example of this is the male cuttlefish, which can display two different colour signals from opposite sides of its body – a male pattern when facing a female to try and attract her, and a female pattern on the other side to trick other potential male rivals.

6 Follow steps 1–3 to complete the question.

Step 1 Think of synonyms and paraphrases for how words in the question might appear in the text.

Step 2 Think of what differences there are between options.

Step 3 Eliminate incorrect options and select the correct options. Focus on details to check your answers.

For which THREE purposes does the writer say animals use touch?

A locating food
B confrontations
C attracting others
D group integration

E locating others
F recognizing others
G rearing babies

Touch is also a key form of communication for some animals. The most obvious example is perhaps its use in challenge and submission in a fight. However, it also serves a more social function. Grooming is often used to reaffirm bonds and hierarchies amongst groups, which is common with mothers when rearing their young. This is common in mammals, but also birds and some insects. Many insects also use touch to round up a group when a food source has been sniffed out in order to bring it back to the colony. In addition to this, ants use chemicals for many very useful reasons, like sending messages to other ants. They can even identify whether another ant is a friend or foe by this method.

 Exam tip

Do not rely on your common sense to answer. You must find the answer in the text. For example, animals do use touch for cleaning others, but the answer is not in the text, so it is not right.

Part 3: Practising multiple-choice tasks

7 Read the text and complete questions 1–4.

Rap Music: Where it all started

Music is far more than just words, rhythms and chords, it's also an expression of culture, and never has that been so evident than in rap and hip-hop music. Rap, the lyrical style, and hip-hop, the musical genre behind rap, have been deeply interconnected for the last 50 years, and both combine to portray the emotions and sentiments of the rappers in a bare and often startling way. While rap often has strong associations with violence and aggression, and lyrics that can be quite confrontational, it is also a form of poetry that serves as an outlet to articulate the lives and culture of rappers.

While the story of rap and hip-hop as a form of music started in the 1970s, rapping as a spoken delivery style behind musical beats is much older. Rapping, in fact, goes back hundreds of years to places like West Africa and the Caribbean, where rhythmic stories were told over the beats of drums, and we can see further musical roots of rap in the Blues music of the 1920s and 30s. Compared to the hip-hop musical style, rap is its elder ancestor. 'Hip' has long been a term in English. It was used in the early 1900s to describe something fashionable or current, but it was only coined in the term 'hip-hop' more than 50 years later, in the late 1970s, when it was appropriated by DJs at parties in New York City to describe the kind of music they were producing in clubs.

The musical style at that time was based on manipulating records or songs to make longer sections with drumbeats. Soon DJs realized that they needed to keep people entertained during these drumbeats and inspired the introduction of rapping. Rappers would come on and talk and rhyme along with the beat during these sections, to keep the audience moving and energized. As the audiences started enjoying these sections, rappers became better and better, and it didn't take long for them to find fame in the parties and clubs of the area. Although this was something localized to the New York area at first, it soon caught on both nationally and internationally. In fact, by the end of the decade *Rapper's Delight* by The Sugarhill Gang was a hit in over ten countries, and it's still a widely known rap anthem today.

In those early days, the musical genre of hip-hop was relatively simplistic, however during the 80s and 90s the genre developed in terms of complexity and inventiveness, to become what is known as the 'Golden Era' of hip-hop. In this era, some of the most famous hip-hop groups, like Run DMC and Public Enemy, were formed and more females, like Salt n Pepa and Queen Latifa, emerged on the hip-hop scene. The lyrical style also changed around this time, moving away from the party feel of the late 70s and becoming more political and even aggressive at times. This did not stop the rise of hip-hop and rap, though, and by the early 2000s rap had become one of the dominant genres in the charts, with acts like Eminem and 50 Cent having hit after hit both in the USA and throughout the world, despite the majority of rap still originating from the US. There was also another lyrical change at this time too. Because of rising sales and a wider audience, some of the lyrics tailored their words to a wider audience, reducing anything too confrontational. Now, rap is one of the most popular genres in the world and its success shows no sign of stopping.

1 In paragraph 1, how does the writer describe rap music?
   A It can sometimes be quite sentimental.
   B It's an expression of life experience.
   C It's not as violent as people think.
   D It has always been connected to hip-hop.

2 The earliest examples of rap came from
   A fashions in the early 1900s.
   B local parties in New York.
   C storytelling practices.
   D the Blues musical style.

3 Rapping in clubs mainly came about
   A from crowd pressure for different entertainment.
   B to give the DJ time to work on longer drum sections.
   C as a way of attracting more famous people to parties.
   D as a way to maintain the momentum of the crowd.

4 Name TWO ways in which the writer thinks hip-hop and rap has changed.
   A It has become more mainstream.
   B It lost its authenticity in the 2000s.
   C The music has become more innovative.
   D It has become increasingly violent.
   E Acts have become more international.

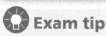 **Exam tip**

Look at the question numbering carefully. A question where you have to select two or three options may just be one question (for example question 4 above). In this case, write all the letters for that question in one box on the answer sheet.

5 Identification tasks

Aims | Analysing identification tasks (understanding the *Not Given* option); **Techniques for identification tasks** (checking information corresponds, identifying facts and views); **Practising identification tasks**

Part 1: Analysing identification tasks

Identifying information tasks take the form of ***True / False / Not Given*** questions. Answer TRUE if the information corresponds with the text, FALSE if the information contradicts the text and NOT GIVEN if the sentence neither agrees nor contradicts.

Identifying writer's views tasks take the form of ***Yes / No / Not Given*** questions. Answer YES if the information corresponds with the views in the text, NO if the information contradicts the views in the text and NOT GIVEN if the sentence neither agrees nor contradicts.

1 Read the information then look at the photo and answer questions 1–5 with True / False / Not Given.

Understanding the *Not Given* option

Although this task is a reading task, one of the best ways to understand the concept of *Not Given* is through an image.

1 The man standing up is wearing glasses.
2 The old man is cutting a fish.
3 The photo shows a family having dinner.
4 The woman standing up is holding a glass.
5 There is orange juice on the table.

 **Exam tip**

Don't spend too long on one sentence. You may spend a lot of time trying to find an answer which is not there, so if you can't find the exact same information, it could be because the answer is **NOT GIVEN**.

Part 2: Techniques for identification tasks

 Exam information: Checking information corresponds

To answer TRUE or YES, each part of the sentence must correspond with the text. If one part is not mentioned in the text, it is NOT GIVEN. If one part is contradictory in the text, it is FALSE or NO.

2 Compare each corresponding part of sentences 1 and 2. Do all the parts of each sentence mean the same thing?

1 Most people / only choose taking the stairs rather than a lift or escalator / when they think about / its long-term advantages.

2 Taking the stairs instead of the lift or escalator / is mostly done by people / who have the ability to think of / the long-term benefits.

3 Read the text and answer TRUE / FALSE / NOT GIVEN to each statement. Look at the underlined parts of the text in detail.

1 People do not do things that appear to be hard work.

2 Focusing on enjoyment could be a way to motivate people to do more difficult things.

3 During the experiment, the stairs became a more popular choice than the escalator.

Sometimes changing habits can be influenced by many things. Often when things seem hard work or unpleasant, we're less inclined to do them. For example, taking the stairs instead of the lift or escalator is mostly done by people who have the ability to think of the long-term benefits. However, making something fun might also encourage us to take the harder road. In one subway station in Sweden, they put this into practice by replacing the traditional stairs with piano stairs. This involved decorating the stairs in the form of a piano, with each stair playing a different note. In the experiment, researchers watched how many people took the stairs and how many took the escalator next to the stairs. 66 per cent more people than normal chose to take the stairs.

 Exam information: Identifying facts and views

Answering True / False / Not Given questions is sometimes easier because they are based on fact. In Yes /No / Not Given questions the answers are based on views or claims given in the text, so it is useful to separate the facts and views.

 Exam tip

Often quantifiers are used to give different meanings, so look for words like *most* or *enough* and what they refer to. For example, see sentence 3 in exercise 3.

4 Look at the next paragraph of the article. Decide which sentences 1–4 are fact and which are the writer's views.

> **1** Of course, this kind of experiment needs to be replicated a great many times before it can be definitively stated that fun makes us change, but the results are encouraging. **2** Injecting fun into daily habits, especially when it is organized at a governmental level, can have great benefits on the overall health of the population. **3** Obesity levels are rising in most countries around the world, especially in young people according to recent data, and it is common knowledge that this is largely due to a lack of nutritional foods and exercise. **4** Therefore, initiatives like this could be the perfect way to turn the tide around.

5 Look at sentences 1–3: one agrees with the text, one contradicts the text and one is not given. Mark each sentence with YES, NO or NOT GIVEN, based on the writer's views.

1 We cannot conclusively state that fun changes our habits.

2 Governments can't make positive changes to the habits of individuals.

3 Young people must urgently change their eating and exercise habits.

Part 3: Practising identification tasks

6 Read the text and answer the questions.

Read the following passage. Do the statements agree with the views of the writer? Write

YES   if the statement agrees with the views of the writer.

NO   if the statement contradicts what the writer thinks.

NOT GIVEN   if it is impossible to know what the writer's point of view is.

1 The progress of early cities would be surprising to many people.

2 Early cities were often dangerous and violent compared to towns and villages.

3 4,000 years ago, cities had all the same characteristics as other urbanizations.

Read the following passage. Do the statements agree with the information below? Write

TRUE   if the statement agrees with the information

FALSE   if the statement contradicts the information

NOT GIVEN   if there is no information on this

4   People cannot agree on what the oldest city in the world is.

5   All the earliest cities were formed in the Middle East and Asia.

6   Early urbanizations had few features that we associate with modern cities.

7   The city of Uruq had a basic public transport system.

8   Mohenjo-Daro was one of the most advanced cities of its time.

The Emergence of Cities

Many academics and governments debate what the oldest city might be, but this often depends on the definition of a city, for early cities bore little resemblance to the skyscraper-filled metropolises of today. Perhaps it is more interesting and informative to chart the developments of these early cities rather than giving them labels, as the evolution we can note in early cities is far more advanced than most people would expect. Another fascinating area lacking study is why cities came into existence. Remembering that conditions in early cities were anything but luxurious and often cramped and unhygienic, the pull to move to cities is still an unanswered question.

But where did it all start? Most large urbanizations formed from towns about 4,000 years ago. This happened in different regions at different times. In places such as modern-day Pakistan we can trace cities back to around 4,000 years ago, in China to around 3,000 years ago and in the Middle East and Turkey as long as 10,000 years ago. However, whether the earliest urbanizations could be called cities is doubtful; they often had only a few thousand residents – not enough to make a town these days – and they lacked public space and infrastructure. These are elements which, in my view, are essential ingredients of a city as they imply a common life and ways of self-governance and organization that distinguish them from other urbanizations.

Around 4,000–5,000 years ago we can see the emergence of urbanizations with these features that we cannot doubt can be defined as cities, and these were surprisingly advanced. Take Uruq, in modern-day Iraq, a city no longer in existence but which at its peak had around 50,000 inhabitants. This city had some of the first examples of public architecture, like temples, as well as early writing and a canal system to transport goods to the nearby river. But no city as far back could offer such exceptional examples of engineering and planning as Mohenjo-Daro, in modern Pakistan. It was a revelation in engineering for a city so far back in history, with a water drainage and heating system, as well as urban planning, with central marketplaces and a grid system for the streets.

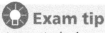 **Exam tip**

Answer in the format shown in the instructions. Do not answer Yes to a True question.

6 Matching tasks

Aims | Analysing matching tasks; **Techniques for matching tasks** (matching paragraph content to a description, using paraphrase and synonyms to match features and information); **Practising matching tasks**

Part 1: Analysing matching tasks

1 Read the information about the different task types and match them to tasks 1 and 2.

> You may need to **match information**, which tests your ability to identify which paragraph contains specific information. The paragraphs are normally lettered (e.g. A, B) and this is how you should write your answer.

> You may need to **match features**, which tests your ability to read more carefully. This involves matching sentences or statements to a list of options. The options will be listed by letters (e.g. A, B), and this is how you should write your answer.

1 Match each sentence with the organization A–D. Write the correct letter A–D on your answer sheet.

A The World Health Organization   C The United Nations

B The Red Cross   D UNESCO

1 _____ is under increasing criticism from some governments.

2 _____ is formed of three separate organizations.

3 _____ needs to expand to remain relevant in today's climate.

2 The passage has seven paragraphs A–G. Which paragraphs contain the following information? Write the correct letter A–G on your answer sheet. You may use any letter more than once.

1 a comparison of different power systems

2 an analysis of power use per country

Part 2: Techniques for matching tasks

🛈 Exam information: Matching paragraph content to a description

Matching information questions often describe specific details from the text. This is usually a combination of a type of information and a topic. There are many different types of information, such as reasons, explanations, problems, processes, comparisons or examples. The topic can help you locate the relevant section of the text.

2 In sentences A–C circle the type of information and underline the topic in each statement.

A Factors which contribute to foods becoming 'super foods'.

B The response to recommendations from doctors.

C Explanations for the increase in coconut oil consumption.

ⓘ Exam information: Using paraphrase to match features

You will not see the same words in the text as in the question. Think of other ways this information might be stated.

3 Match texts 1–3 to sentences A–C in exercise 2. Explain the paraphrases using the underlined words.

1 The <u>guidance</u> is based on recent research and covers many different types of foods. <u>This information tends to be well received</u> because it is based on <u>solid evidence</u> on foods that constitute a healthy diet.

2 The <u>main reasons</u> for this <u>rise</u> are advertising and online health advice from diet advisers. Sales have been <u>going up</u> steadily in recent years.

3 They have <u>several things in common</u>. <u>Firstly</u>, <u>they usually contain a lot of</u> nutrients. <u>They are also likely to be</u> vegetables <u>and</u> tend to be protein based.

4 Match ONE of the statements A–C from exercise 2 to the paragraph below. Underline the section of the text which contains the answer.

A large number of scientific studies have examined claims made about some healthy foods in recent years. Even though many of these claims have been challenged by scientists, people still believe in these so-called miracle foods. This problem has many causes but is mostly due to the way in which society processes information nowadays. Many people follow suggestions about diet online from non-experts and tend to ignore the advice that they receive from medical professionals. An example of this can be seen with coconut oil. The American Health Association has specifically advised people not to eat coconut oil in large amounts due to its high fat content, yet people continue to consume it, believing that it protects the human body from a range of diseases.

5 Explain how the other TWO statements in exercise 2 are not the same as the information in the paragraph. Underline the section of the text which helped you.

 Exam tip

Matching information and feature questions are not in text order, so you might find the answer to the first question near the end, and the answer to the second question before that.

ⓘ Exam information: Using paraphrase to match information

In Matching tasks, the statements are paraphrased, but the options are usually the same as in the text. The items are often places, names of people, types of buildings or inventions. Scan the text to find them, then read the text around the items carefully, looking for synonyms and paraphrases of the language in the statements.

6 Look at statements 1–3 and options A–C. Do you expect the statements or the options to be paraphrased in the text?

1 An advantage which <u>depends on specific behaviour</u>.	A coffee
2 An example of research with <u>unexpected results</u>.	B chocolate
3 A case where the positive effects are <u>not universal</u>.	C oily fish

 Exam tip

There are many words in statements that can be similar (e.g. effects, results; advantage, positive), so it is important to focus on the differences between the sentences.

7 Look at the underlined words in the statements 1–3 in exercise 6 and match them to the paraphrases a–f. Then think of other ways to paraphrase these sections.

a only apply in some cases

b the outcome was surprising

c cannot be broadly applied to all

d relies on a particular routine

e the effects were not what was predicted

f certain actions must be taken

8 Follow steps 1–3 to complete the task.

Step 1 – Read the text below and find the words A–C in exercise 6.

Step 2 – Look at the underlined words in exercise 6 and match them to the underlined sections of text.

Step 3 – Read these sections carefully and choose your answers.

Scientists can only be sure of the effectiveness of foods on our health by conducting research. An interesting case where science has been useful is oily fish. There have been numerous reports that oily fish can help brain function as people get older, and many people have started to think that this information is true. However, a systematic review of many studies was surprised to find no conclusive evidence to support the claim. Chocolate is another food which is supposed to benefit the brain but may not be as beneficial as people think. In order to have a positive effect, people must only eat dark chocolate in small quantities. Additionally, there are situations that are more complicated. Research into the effectiveness of coffee to prevent diabetes and heart disease is controversial. Some studies suggest coffee can reduce the risk of developing diabetes. The problem is that some people are sensitive to it and therefore the benefits do not apply to everyone.

Part 3: Practising matching tasks

9 Read the text and answer the questions.

Which paragraphs A–G contain the following information?

1 An explanation of universal basic income. _____

2 How views supporting those less fortunate have evolved. _____

3 The possible economic drawbacks of universal basic income. _____

4 The fundamental reason people disagree about the issue of universal basic income. _____

The End of Poverty?

A Our way of thinking about poverty has changed greatly over the past few hundred years. Initially, poverty was seen as a harsh fact of life that some people had to endure, without help. In fact, some early thinkers believed that poverty was a necessary part of life, and that the incentive hunger gave people to work led to economic progress. This perspective, while still present in many schools of thought, has been challenged by many governments, who now provide financial assistance, healthcare and education to their populations, and it has been further challenged most recently by proponents of universal basic income.

B A universal basic income is a self-explanatory term that is used to describe a regular amount of money for citizens provided by their government. There are different ideas of how this may work. Some thinkers believe that every single citizen should receive this, while others think it should go to sections of society that fall below a certain minimum level. The common factor however is that it should be automatic. People shouldn't need to apply and go through a multitude of bureaucratic processes to receive it. It is, put simply, their right.

C These kinds of schemes may seem too good to be true, and indeed, there are many people who disagree with universal basic income as a concept. Critics have asserted that such a scheme would be financially disastrous, because there would be such an increase in demand for goods and services that prices would rise and, consequently, people would get less for their money. This would, in turn, negatively impact upon standards of living. Additionally, many detractors believe that giving people essentially 'free money' would disincentivize them to get jobs or get on in life.

D However, initial studies have shown some very positive effects of such an income. Probably the most famous of these studies was undertaken in Finland, where they ran a two-year study with the government paying 20,000 unemployed people around €560 per month. The payment was automatic and those selected couldn't opt out of the scheme. They found that these people selected, in comparison to people on normal welfare benefits, reported better financial well-being and better levels of mental health and confidence.

E Trials also indicate that rather than demotivate people from working, schemes like this increased motivation to find employment, or stay in employment or get further training. This was suggested by a study in Canada, which saw increased study and employment figures during the study, as was also found in the Finnish study. The Canadian experiment, however, did not reach its full term as there was a change of government, with the incoming government cutting the trial short citing it as an expensive and unsustainable effort.

F Another study commenced in Madhya Pradesh in India in 2010, which also reported positive results. School performance improved and the villages involved saw a sudden and large growth in entrepreneurship, with many people setting up their own enterprises. The study also indicated that there was a large increase in all-round community well-being, with improved sanitation and greater inclusion. Quatinga Velho is a more unusual study of this kind, because it is entirely run by public donations. Based in Brazil, this initiative has been running since 2008 and the results of the initiative show that people used their money for basic needs and there was no increase in anti-social behaviour or unemployment; in fact, most recipients reported increased self-esteem and less social insecurity.

G This just reinforces what a dividing issue universal basic income is. People's opinion of it can often be centred around whether they believe it is a basic responsibility to help people on the poverty line, or whether that responsibility solely lies upon those in poverty. One fact is almost certain, though – we will need to think of other economic models soon. As the rise of technology continues to grow, so do the job losses as more and more machines do what we humans used to. We need to now think of a new way to provide for rising unemployment and a rising population – universal income could be just that.

Match each sentence with the country, A–D. You may use any letter more than once.

5 An example of an abandoned trial of universal basic income. _____

6 A trial that showed people were spending their money carefully. _____

7 A trial which was mandatory for participants. _____

8 A trial that relies on the generosity of individuals. _____

9 A trial which resulted in more small businesses. _____

A Finland	B Canada	C India	D Brazil

7 Matching headings

Aims | Analysing matching headings tasks; **Techniques for matching headings tasks** (identifying main and supporting ideas, using the language of headings, avoiding wrong headings); **Practising matching headings tasks**

Part 1: Analysing matching headings tasks

 Exam information: Matching headings

This task tests general understanding of each paragraph and the ability to understand the main points of the text. There is a list of headings labelled (i, ii, iii, etc.) to match to each paragraph. **Matching heading** questions include an example and additional headings than you do not need to use.

1 Read headings i–v and decide if statements 1–5 are True or False.

> i   Training kindergarten teachers well
> ii   How young children make friends
> iii Social skills development in children under five
> iv The best time to start school
> v   Choosing a good kindergarten

 Exam tip

Because headings are short summaries of the paragraphs in a text, it can be possible to predict the type of information that might be in the text just by looking at the headings.

1	Headings contain lots of details.	TRUE / FALSE
2	Some headings can be quite similar.	TRUE / FALSE
3	Headings are like short summaries.	TRUE / FALSE
4	This question type is about main ideas.	TRUE / FALSE
5	You should use all the headings you see.	TRUE / FALSE

2 Match the paragraph descriptions 1–3 to the headings i–v in exercise 1 they describe.

 **Exam tip**

You must answer by writing the roman numeral on your answer sheet.

   1 Ideas about the age when children should socialize with other children and begin formal classes.

   2 A paragraph that looks at different methods that are effective in making early years teachers ready to teach.

   3 Descriptions of how very young children interact with one another and how this changes as they get older.

Part 2: Techniques for matching headings tasks

 Exam information: Identifying main and supporting ideas in paragraphs

Understanding paragraph structure can help you identify main ideas and therefore the correct headings. Paragraphs usually have a topic sentence that introduces the main subject or topic near the beginning, then continue by explaining this main idea further with examples, reasons or explanations. The last sentence is often a conclusion of the main idea in the paragraph.

3   Underline the main idea and TWO supporting ideas in paragraphs A and B.

A

Research has shown that removing road signs and markings can significantly reduce accidents. Although it sounds like a strange idea, towns and cities that have introduced these measures have far fewer accidents than before. The idea came from a Dutch engineer called Hans Monderman during the 1980s, who noticed that when roads had fewer markings and signs, many drivers reduced their speed and drove more carefully. More recently, a study in Wiltshire in the UK found that removing road markings reduced accidents by 35 per cent. This approach appears to be much more effective than increasing the amount of traffic-calming ideas.

B

However, these traffic measures can give us many insights. Psychologists are interested in the effectiveness of these different measures because they help to understand people's relationship with authority. Road markings display driving laws which people know that they should follow. However, removing road markings and traffic signals means that people have to take responsibility for their own decision making rather than just following driving rules. Psychologists have noticed that people respond differently to these changes in how roads look. Many people begin to drive more responsibly when there are fewer signs to follow, but for others not having official rules to follow makes them more nervous drivers. This gives psychologists an insight into which people value authority and independence.

 Exam information: Using the language of the headings

The headings are short summaries of the main idea and the language uses synonyms and paraphrases of the text. When you read each paragraph, you should ask yourself if the headings *completely* match the main idea in the paragraph. It is important to focus on some of the grammatical words in the headings as well as the content words.

4   Read sentences 1–4 carefully and choose the TWO sentences with the same meaning.

   1   The best idea for making roads safer.
   2   Excellent ideas for making roads safer.
   3   The most effective idea for making roads less dangerous.
   4   How to make all roads safer.

5   Read the headings i–iv and paragraph A again and answer questions 1–4. Pay attention to the underlined words.

   i   The latest idea for making roads safer
   ii   Doing less to improve road safety
   iii How to reduce accidents by 35 per cent
   iv   Improving all drivers in a UK town

   1   Does the main idea explain the <u>latest</u> idea for making roads safer?
   2   Does the main idea explain how <u>doing less not more</u> can improve road safety?
   3   Does the main idea explain <u>the way</u> to reduce accidents by <u>35 per cent</u>?
   4   Does the main idea describe improving <u>all</u> drivers in a UK town?

6 Read the first and last sentences of Paragraph A again. Choose the correct heading i–iv from exercise 5.

 **Exam information: Avoiding wrong headings**

In the paragraphs above, the details in the paragraphs are in the supporting ideas NOT the main ideas. These details can be in the extra headings that you do not need to use. Remember that a supporting idea is usually an example or a solution or comparison or other detail.

7 Match the supporting ideas from Paragraph A to the type of information. What clues were in the text to help you decide?

1 An example
2 A problem
3 A change
4 An opinion

8 Now, look at the headings below for Paragraph B, what is the correct heading based on the main idea, and what heading is incorrect as it focuses on detail?

i How different people react to laws.
ii How to give drivers more responsibility.

Part 3: Practising matching headings tasks

Exam tip

You can read the headings first and then the text, or you can skim read the text and then focus on the headings Match the headings you are most sure of first.

9 Read the text and answer the questions.

> **The reading passage below has six paragraphs, A–F.**
>
> **Choose the correct heading for each paragraph from the list of headings below. Write the correct number, i–viii, in boxes 1–6.**
>
> **List of headings**
>
> i   A near-depleted land
> ii   The initial challenges
> iii   Locating asteroids
> iv   A different idea of space
> v   A controversial idea
> vi   Solving Earth's problems
> vii   The value of asteroids
> viii   Managing the future

1	Paragraph A	iv
2	Paragraph B	
3	Paragraph C	
4	Paragraph D	
5	Paragraph E	
6	Paragraph F	

In the Abundance of Space

A When many people think of space, they think of exciting developments like space tourism or living on planets, but one key potential use of space is for a much more mundane process. Mining of the Earth's resources has been done over hundreds of years, and as a result some resources are rapidly running out. The next step for this activity could be mining in space – to be exact, the mining of asteroids. For many people this is not the glamourous idea of space exploration, but it is becoming more likely.

B Asteroids offer us so much more than is readily available on earth. Asteroids, which are essentially small chunks of potential planets, are full of resources that human beings use plentifully. They contain a huge amount of minerals and rare earth metals, as well as water, ice and other liquids and vapours like methane and ammonia. These resources are currently used in many ways and in many products, so being able to mine them in asteroids would be extremely useful. What's more, they are near the surface of these asteroids and so extraction might not be too challenging.

C Many of these resources have been mined heavily in all areas of the world to the extent that they will be depleted if we continue to use them at the current rate. Mining takes a toll on land, and the exponential growth of the population has rapidly increased the amount of resources required. In addition, many of the resources that remain are very costly to extract, which means that other options must be found. Without alternative sources for these resources, it will be difficult to guarantee our survival on this planet.

D While it may seem that asteroid mining is the perfect answer there are potential barriers, the most pressing of which is the cost and difficulty of undergoing such a complex operation in space. At the moment, NASA are exploring the feasibility of mining in space using conventional technology. While there are companies who are planning on doing this, the cost of actually sending the technology and equipment into space is extremely high and the endeavour is extremely difficult. However, moving between asteroids is relatively simple and with processing carried out in space these rare materials could be transported back down to the Earth.

E For some people, asteroid mining raises some ethical questions. Given that people have already nearly depleted the natural resources of the Earth, it is questionable whether we should be looking to start mining in space and depleting the resources on other planets. In fact, it may be beneficial for the international community to discuss the situation in more detail before any mining starts. Two eminent professors in astrophysics and theology have questioned the ethics of asteroid mining and concluded that limits must be put on such use of bodies in space.

F The professors outline a system for controlling the amount of resources mined on asteroids. It uses a one-eighth rule, where humans are only allowed to use an eighth of the resources in the solar system, which is still more than a million times more than the Earth's resources combined. However, following our population and resource growth rate since the Industrial Revolution gives us only 400 years before we reach the one-eighth. While this may help people recognize the rate of our resource depletion, and by implementing it so far in advance we will be able to plan for our next depletion of resources, we still have the question of whether space should be used for such activities.

8 Matching sentence endings

Aims | Analysing matching sentence ending tasks; **Techniques for matching sentence ending tasks** (analysing the questions, locating answers); **Practising matching sentence ending tasks**

Part 1: Analysing matching sentence ending tasks

ℹ️ Exam information: Matching sentence endings

In this question type, you need to match sentence halves using the text. The sentence beginnings will be in text order and you will always have more sentence endings than you need. You should write the letters (A, B, C, etc.) as your answer. This task tests your ability to understand points in the text.

1 Look at the task and answer questions 1 and 2.

    1 Which ending A–D does NOT grammatically match sentence 1? Why?

    2 Which endings A–D grammatically fit with sentence 2? Why?

🔆 Exam tip

In matching sentence endings questions, the sentence endings must match grammatically as well as matching the information in the text.

Complete each sentence with the correct ending A–D below. Write the correct letter A–D on your answer sheet.

    1 The Roman Empire became   A more expensive to maintain than defend.

    2 The Roman border was   B founded by Augustus Caesar.

                             C a political system ruled by one individual.

                             D significantly weaker after various attacks.

Part 2: Techniques for matching sentence ending tasks

ℹ️ Exam information: Analysing the questions

The sentences in this question type are separated at different points, such as after the subject, after the verb or after a preposition. Having a good understanding of sentence structure can help you because you can reject endings that do not fit grammatically.

2 Match the words in bold in sentences 1–8 to the grammatical terms. Then write the types of words that could follow on.

    ~~modal verb~~   present simple *to be*   present simple negative   conjunction

        plural noun   preposition   past simple *to be*   future form

1 Schools that float **can** <u>*modal verb; followed by infinitive verb without to*</u>

2 River **schools** _____

3 One of the key aspects of these schools **is** _____

4 Floating schools depend **on** _____

5 In Colombia floating schools are successful **because** _____

6 These schools **were** _____

7 Traditional schools **are not** _____

8 It is possible that floating schools **will** _____

3 Match the sentence endings a–h to the sentence beginnings in exercise 2. There may be more than one possible answer.

a opened by the mayor of the local town.
b the need to provide education for all.
c provide education in remote places.
d suitable for remote areas with low populations.

e flexible teaching staff.
f they can respond to local needs.
g are popular in places which flood often.
h funding from central government.

 Exam information: Locating answers

In some **Matching sentence endings** tasks, more than one sentence ending may grammatically fit the sentence beginnings. Use the content of the sentences to help you locate the answers in the text. Look for any names, dates, numbers, places or other words which you can scan the text for and find easily.

4 Underline the words in a–d that could be easy to find in the text (e.g. names, numbers).

1 Young children
2 Teachers
3 Parents
4 Teenagers

a work on average 3 hours per night.
b received a grant of $500.
c are the main focus of the Ministry of Education.
d in Bangladesh work very hard.

5 Look at the sentence beginnings 1–3 and endings A–G and answer questions 1 and 2.

1 The success of floating schools is
2 In Sempegua, the floating school is
3 Two of the world's famous floating schools

A was destroyed during some extreme weather conditions.
B become popular with many local children.
C due to recent improvements in the way they are built.
D made to cope with heavy rains of the monsoon.
E the result of financial help from governments.
F were selected to take part in a competition.
G will be rebuilt soon.

1   Which endings A–G grammatically fit the sentence beginnings 1–3. _____

2   Which options from A–F did you discount for questions 1–3? Why? _____

6   Scan the text *Floating schools: A success story in education* for the answers to the task in exercise 5. Then answer questions 1 and 2.

1   In which paragraphs are the answers for each question? _____

2   What clues did you use to help you locate the answers? _____

Floating schools: A success story in education

Floating schools are used in areas of the world which suffer from flooding or experience rainy seasons. Typically, these extreme weather events prevent children from attending school, sometimes for long periods of time. Until recently it was extremely expensive for governments to try to provide education for these communities, but developments in architecture and technology have produced some innovative solutions. The result is that in countries such as Bangladesh, Nigeria and Colombia these floating schools have been extremely effective in providing poor children with an education.

In Bangladesh various charities provide over 100 floating schools, which are large boats equipped with solar panels on the roofs. These supply energy to the lights and computers on board. The schools are well built, with the roof able to withstand heavy rain from the monsoons. The schools can accommodate up to 30 students, and as part of the fleet of floating schools one charity also operates other floating organizations, such as libraries and adult education centres. Similarly, the town of Sempegua in the north of Colombia has a floating school in order to provide continuous education during the rainy season. This school is also able to function on the ground in the dry season and has benefited over 400 underprivileged families.

These floating schools are constantly exposed to extreme weather and therefore sometimes they have to be replaced. This was the case with the floating school that served the community of Makoko, which is located on the Lagos lagoon in Nigeria. After it had been in service for three years, the school collapsed during heavy rains. It had served the community well and, like the floating school of one of the charities in Bangladesh, was shortlisted for a design award. A replacement school will be built in the future and will continue to serve the Makoko community, who live in constant fear of flooding. It is likely that more floating schools will be created as the need to provide this kind of infrastructure is not going to disappear in the near future.

Part 3: Practising matching sentence ending tasks

7   Read the text and answer the questions.

Complete each sentence with the correct ending A–H below. Write the correct letter A–H on your answer sheet.

1   One key problem of music streaming is that
2   The great majority of musicians don't
3   World-famous musicians
4   A way we can help little-known artists

A complete with major artists like U2 or Rhianna.
B they are paying increasingly smaller amounts as competition grows.
C have much earning potential anymore.
D suffer the most from the move from physical albums to streaming.
E the payment has to be divided between everyone who created the song.
F is to keep buying their physical album copies and sharing their songs.
G usually make money through touring or merchandizing.
H is to invest in their creativity and watch their videos.

How do musicians make money?

The entire landscape of the music business has changed dramatically over the last 30 years. From what was once a business based on sales of records, cassettes and CDs, now streaming has become the norm, and musicians have had to adapt to the fact that traditional album sales are not their main income stream.

Internet streaming of music has had a large effect on income for artists. Famous music-streaming services pay usually about $0.007 per song played. This sum then has to be split between everyone who has a stake in the copyright, which includes the artists, the songwriters, the producers and the music label, meaning that, at the end of the day, the artist's proportion is minuscule.

This has also led to a polarization of the music industry, where there are world-famous chart-topping artists like Rhianna or Bruno Mars, who are streamed so frequently and are so famous that they can monetize their success in other ways, and the other 95 per cent of artists, who make almost nothing and have much fewer monetizing opportunities.

One example of this is the rock group U2. In 2017, they made around $55 million, but of that less than 4 per cent came from streaming and album sales. The large majority (around 95 per cent) of their income came from touring. If we compare the touring potential of U2, who can fill stadiums around the world, with the average groups, who fill much smaller capacity spaces at much cheaper rates, we can see how this disparity exists.

An additional way that musicians now make money is through merchandizing and deals promoting other brands. This is, yet again, an option only for the super-famous. Some have their own successful brands as a result of their fame. One example of this is Beyoncé, who has made over $400 million in sales from her perfume, Beyoncé Heat. These kinds of income streams can really only be generated by best-selling artists, as they need to capture a wide audience in order to generate sales.

So this leaves the question of how the smaller-selling artist can survive in this kind of industry. While it is incredibly tough, revenue from streaming has slightly increased for most artists, although not sufficiently to sustain a career. However, advertising on video sites has seen an increase in revenue as a larger share of this money goes to the artists and those that made the songs. As well as this, crowdfunding is becoming more popular, so perhaps, if you support a less-well-known artist, you need to help fund them before they make an album, rather than buy the traditional product after it is made.

9 Flow-chart and diagram completion

Aims | Analysing flow-chart and diagram completion tasks; Techniques for flow-chart and diagram completion tasks (understanding process and order, using visual clues, the language of movement and location); **Practising flow-chart and diagram completion tasks**

Part 1: Analysing flow-chart and diagram completion tasks

 **Exam information: Flow-chart and diagram completion**

In flow-chart and diagram completion tasks, you must complete a gap in a flow chart or diagram with written information from the text. The instructions will tell you how many words to write.

1 Decide if statements 1–4 are True or False. Check your answers in the key on page 185.

1	A flow chart shows a sequence of actions.	TRUE / FALSE
2	Arrows can help you understand which action is most important.	TRUE / FALSE
3	Both diagrams and flow charts can show processes.	TRUE / FALSE
4	Flow charts have more specific images than a diagram.	TRUE / FALSE

Part 2: Techniques for flow-chart and diagram completion tasks

 **Exam information: Understanding process and order**

First, look at the flow chart or diagram to understand what is happening. To describe a process, give an overview and then describe it from the first step to the last step in the process.

2 Read the sentences A–G about a shipping process and put them in order from first step to last step.

A This then starts an order execution process, where the computer either indicates that the product is in stock or orders it.

B Once this order is on the packaging table, a packer checks it and seals it for shipping.

C The online shopping delivery process has been refined over years and it's now rapid and extremely efficient.

D When the product is available, the computer assigns a warehouseman to collect it.

E When the order is finally shipped, the customer can track its progress.

F Customers first trigger the process when they choose their product, make their order and pay for it.

G All packages are then placed in a specially designated zone to be shipped to the customer.

3 Complete the flow chart with words from the process description in exercise 2.

| The process begins with an order from a 1_____. | → | The order is either 2_____ or is ordered. | → | A warehouseman collects the package. | → | The package is prepared for 3_____. | → | The customer can monitor the status of the package. |

 Exam information: Using visual clues

Diagram completion questions often have a lot of visual information that you need to understand in order to answer the question. This can show you what the topic is, and whether it is a process or static image.

4 Look at the following diagrams. Which one is a process? Which one is static?

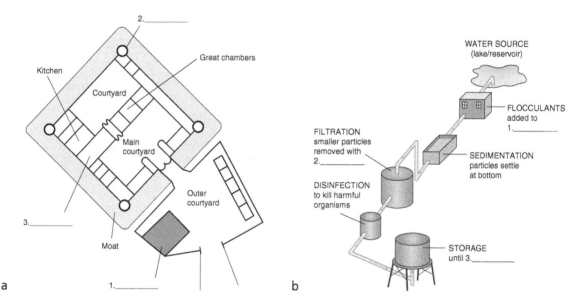

a

b

Exam tip

You will often see diagrams described in the passive form. For example, the water treatment diagram is likely to be passive because the actions happen to the water.

 Exam information: The language of movement and location

Static information will use words that describe positioning and location (e.g. a moat *surrounds* the castle). A process will use language of movement and order (e.g. *At this stage*, the water is *purified* ...).

5 Read the Exam information. Then mark the words 1–10 used to describe a static image with S and those used to describe a process with P.

| 1 adjoining | 2 either side of | 3 after that | 4 dissolves | 5 in the far corner |
| 6 the final step | 7 prior to this | 8 cleans | 9 at this point | 10 on the outer edges |

6 Complete the text describing the water diagram using the verbs below.

collected   deposited   disinfected   filtered   join   remove

Water is generally **1** _____ from a source such as a lake or reservoir to start the treatment process. The water firstly has flocculants added to it in order to **2** _____ together dirt and large particles so they can be **3** _____ out of the water, which happens during sedimentation. Filtration then helps **4** _____ smaller particles still left in the water. Lastly, water is **5** _____ in order to be clean and safe for use, and then **6** _____ in large tanks for later use.

 **Exam tip**

Your answers may be written words, or you may have to choose from options (labelled A, B, etc.).

Part 3: Practising flow-chart and diagram completion tasks

7 Read the text and answer the questions.

The Science of Surfing

Even though it is possible to learn to surf without fully understanding the science of waves, experienced surfers say that having this basic knowledge can make a significant difference. Many people think that water moves in waves, but in fact energy is transmitted through water. Although we only see waves on beaches, they are formed out in the open ocean, often many kilometres from the shore. They are mainly caused by the interaction between the wind and water but can be caused by other factors, such as volcanoes or earthquakes.

Ripples are produced by the friction between the wind and the water in the open ocean and they start to move through the sea. Without any obstacles to interrupt their movement, the speed of these ripples gradually increases, but they don't start to increase in size so they are still very small waves. As they approach the shoreline they begin to slow down. At this point, the reduction in speed causes the wave to start to take its shape. If surfers can learn how to recognize when a wave is starting to form, they can position themselves better in order to 'catch' a wave. As the wave moves towards the shore it rises up and curls over. The top part of a wave is called the crest and as this continues to roll over it forms a lip. The lip is the part of the wave which breaks, and a hollow section is created, which is what surfers are interested in. Surfers want to position themselves in this tube or barrel to ride the wave towards the shore.

Surfing is known as an extremely difficult sport to master because it is physically demanding, but also because of the changing nature of the sea. Natural elements such as wind, temperature and the seasons all impact on the oceans in different ways and mean that surfers must pay attention to their surroundings at all times. The key to surfing for people new to the sport is observation. Rather than just catching the first wave they see, surfers should sit on their boards and take a few minutes to observe the way the waves are moving. After picking a wave to surf, it is important to get yourself ready. Surfing is all about balance and weight distribution; being too far forward or back on the board will make catching a wave very difficult.

The next stage is to catch the wave, and to do this the surfer must be in the correct place. As the wave starts to rise they must start to paddle with their hands. The aim is for the surfer to maintain the same speed as the wave and then, as the crest forms, to swiftly jump up into a standing position. One aspect which novice surfers forget is to look over their shoulder a few times as they paddle to keep an eye on the progress of the wave. Without checking the wave's location, it can be easy to miss it. Finally, there are some techniques for beginners to ensure they can jump smoothly onto the board and maintain their balance long enough to ride the wave. This mostly involves pushing the body up and jumping onto the board in one fast motion and remaining in a low, crouching position because this is more stable than standing upright. Although mastering these techniques can be time-consuming, people who repeatedly practise them are likely to learn to surf within a relatively short period of time.

Questions 1–4. Label the diagram below using words from the text. Use NO MORE THAN THREE WORDS for each answer.

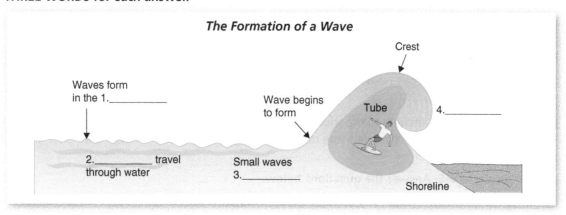

The Formation of a Wave

Crest

Waves form in the 1._____

Wave begins to form

Tube

4._____

2._____ travel through water

Small waves 3._____

Shoreline

Questions 5–8. Complete the flow chart with words from the passage. Write NO MORE THAN THREE words.

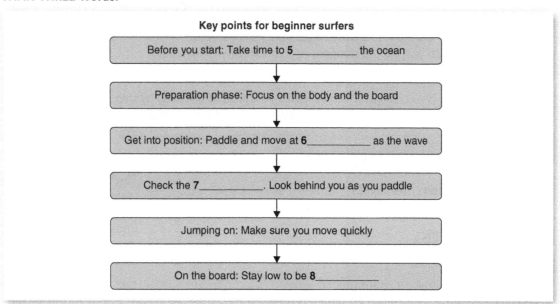

Key points for beginner surfers

Before you start: Take time to 5_____ the ocean

Preparation phase: Focus on the body and the board

Get into position: Paddle and move at 6_____ as the wave

Check the 7_____. Look behind you as you paddle

Jumping on: Make sure you move quickly

On the board: Stay low to be 8_____

10 Short-answer questions

Part 1: Analysing short-answer questions

 Exam information: Short-answer questions

These questions are designed to check your understanding of factual information and specific details in a text. The answers can be words or numbers such as times, years or amounts of money. The instructions will tell you how many words to write. It is important to check exactly what the question is asking and pay careful attention when writing the answers in order to avoid making simple mistakes.

 Exam tip

Short-answer questions may be written as a direct question or an instruction (e.g. Name THREE ...).

1   Read a candidate's answers to the short-answer questions below and identify the mistakes. Why might the candidate have made these mistakes?

> **Questions 1–6. Answer the questions below.**
>
> **Write NO MORE THAN TWO WORDS OR A NUMBER.**
>
> Direct question
> 1   What TWO factors caused problems for sea travel in the 18th century?
> 2   Which group of people were most interested in explorations?
> 3   Where did the first Orient Express from Paris travel to?
> 4   In which year did the company open an office in Singapore?
>
> Instruction
> 5   Name TWO changes which increased the speed of travelling by ship.
> 6   Name the company that was the most successful in the 1960s.

1   Storms, pirates, diseases
2   Engineers, biologists
3   Paris to Romania
4   May 1953
5   Cheap fuel
6   A technology company

 Exam tip

Remember that these answers would all be marked as incorrect, so it is very important to pay attention to small details in short-answer questions.

Part 2: Techniques for short-answer questions

i Exam information: Locating specific information

You don't always need to read <u>all</u> the text carefully before you can answer the questions; it's better to scan the text for the specific information needed. Look for names or dates, because the capital letters and numbers stand out. If the question doesn't ask for or contain things like dates, numbers or names, look for unusual words related to the question.

2   Read questions 1–6, then scan the text on page 71 of Unit 8 to find the answers. Give yourself 90 seconds to do this.

1   Three physical music formats used in the past: _____, _____, _____
2   The amount of money paid out to stream a song: _____
3   The year U2 earned $55 million: _____
4   The percentage of earnings U2 made from concerts: _____
5   The name of Beyoncé's fragrance: _____
6   Two ways less-known artists can make money: _____, _____

i Exam information: Focusing on question words

It is important to think about what the question is asking you. This will tell you what kind of information is needed. For example, if the questions asks for *How*, then you are looking for the way or manner something was done; if the question asks *What year* you have to write the year, not the exact date or month.

3   Rewrite items 1–6 in exercise 2 using the question words.

How   How much   In what   What (x3)

i Exam information: Paraphrasing questions

You won't see the same words in the text as you see in the questions, so it is important to identify paraphrases of the questions in the text.

4   Find words and phrases with the same meanings as 1–6 in the text on page 71 of Unit 8:

1   formats used in the past (para 1)
2   amount of money (para 2)
3   earned (para 4)
4   earnings U2 made from concerts (para 4)
5   fragrance (para 5)
6   to make more money (para 6)

i Exam information: Avoiding incorrect answers

There may be more than one answer that looks correct. Therefore, it is important to read carefully around the answer to check it. Look at the example in exercise 5.

5 Look at the question below. Underline all the possible answers in the text scanning for the information. DO NOT read the text.

> **Question:** How much does Andrew Lloyd Webber earn per day?
>
> One of the world's richest musicians, Andrew Lloyd Webber, has spent his career composing music rather than playing on stage. Famous for his musicals, including The Phantom of the Opera, which brought in $550,000 in its first week alone in Broadway, he made around $150,000 a week in the 1980s, an amount which he now makes every 24 hours. This brings his money-making power to around $1 million a week and gives him a net worth of over $1 billion.

6 Match the numbers in 1–4 to what they refer to in the text A–E. Use all the letters. Notice the small differences between each option.

1 $550,000
2 $150,000
3 $ 1 million
4 $ 1 billion

A The amount Andrew Lloyd Webber earns per week
B The amount Phantom of the Opera made in its first week
C The amount Andrew Lloyd Webber earns per day
D The amount Andrew Lloyd Webber is worth
E The amount Andrew Lloyd Webber earned per week

7 Which number in exercise 6 is the correct answer to the question in exercise 5?

 **Exam tip**

Noticing small differences between statements and being exact with matching meanings can help throughout the exam.

Part 3: Practising short-answer questions

8 Read the text and answer the questions.

The Fascination of Circumnavigation

Ever since Ferdinand Magellan set off to travel the globe in search of new trade routes in 1521, humans have been fascinated by circumnavigation. The sight of a sailing ship setting off on a round-the-world journey into the unknown has always caused feelings of both fear and admiration in those people watching from the land. In the 16th century, circumnavigation pioneers such as Magellan and Francis Drake were seen as heroes and celebrated for their bravery. Even nowadays, sailors such as Ellen McArthur, who in 2001 was the first woman to sail solo around the world, are considered role models for their qualities such as determination and endurance.

In the 16th and 17th centuries circumnavigation was a dangerous activity. The first expeditions set off without knowing what kinds of weather, sea conditions or other difficulties they would face. In the very first attempt by Ferdinand Magellan only 18 sailors from the original crew of 260 returned, and Magellan himself was one of those who died. Most died from starvation or scurvy, a disease which is caused by not having enough vitamin C. At that time transporting the types of fruit and vegetables required to provide a healthy diet was impossible. In fact, it was not until 1768 that a circumnavigation was completed without anyone dying from scurvy. This was James Cook's first expedition in the ship HMS *Endeavour*.

There are many intriguing stories associated with travelling around the world, since it can be done on any number of different types of transportation or none at all. The first woman to journey around the world was American journalist Nellie Bly, who completed her trip in a remarkable 72 days. She travelled by steamship, omnibus and train. The person who holds the world record for circumnavigating the world only on foot is American Dave Kunst. He started the trip in 1970 and finished it four years later having covered over 23,000 km and used 21 pairs of walking boots. These stories show how circumnavigation has been influenced by both human characteristics and human inventions.

In more recent years, circumnavigation has taken on a more space-age approach. As a result of the developments in space travel, astronauts started to circumnavigate or orbit the Earth in space. The Russian Yuri Gagarin successfully achieved this first on 12 April 1961. This extraordinary feat of engineering and scientific knowledge made Gagarin an international celebrity overnight, and the following edition of *Time* magazine featured his photo on the front cover. His achievement made various American organizations such as NASA increase their commitment to the space race, which resulted in the moon landings and created a lot of new technological advances in the world. This just highlights how pivotal circumnavigation has been to our history, from the first seafaring navigators to the latest space-age explorers.

 Exam tip

For instruction short-answer questions (*Name TWO ...*), check the scoring. You may receive one point for each answer, or you may need to write both answers to score one point.

Questions 1–6. Answer the questions below.

Write NO MORE THAN THREE WORDS AND/OR A NUMBER for each answer.

1   What aspect of their personality were 16th-century explorers praised for?   _____

2   Which common illness was the result of a lack of vitamin C?   _____

3   When was the first expedition to have no deaths from poor diet?   _____

4   Name TWO land vehicles used in the first female world circumnavigation.   _____

_____

5   How long did an American man take to circumnavigate the world using no transport?   _____

6   What organization made Yuri Gagarin famous all over the world?   _____

1 Writing assessment criteria

Part 1: Understanding writing test instructions and assessment criteria

Exam information: Writing task types

The IELTS writing test consists of two tasks:

Task 1: assesses your ability to describe, summarize and explain data presented in a chart, diagram, graph or table.

Task 2: assesses your ability to write an essay about an opinion, argument or problem.

Each task is assessed independently, and Task 2 carries more weight in marking than Task 1.

1 Read the sample test and decide if statements 1–5 are TRUE or FALSE.

1 Task 1 requires you to describe and give your opinion about the data presented in the figure. TRUE / FALSE
2 The more information you include in your Task 1 response, the higher you are likely to score. TRUE / FALSE
3 You should write no fewer than 150 words for you Task 1 response. TRUE / FALSE
4 You will score higher marks for your Task 2 response if you strongly agree with the statement in the question. TRUE / FALSE
5 You should aim to spend twice as long on Task 2 than for Task 1. TRUE / FALSE

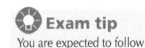

Exam tip

You are expected to follow instructions carefully.

WRITING TASK 1

You should spend about 20 minutes on this task.

> *The chart below shows the average final exam results for four different subjects over a three-year period.*
>
> *Summarize the information by selecting and reporting the main features, and make comparisons where relevant.*

Write at least 150 words.

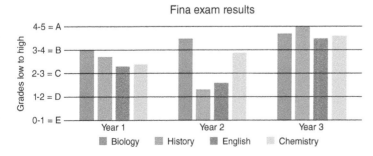

Fina exam results

WRITING TASK 2

You should spend about 40 minutes on this task.

Write about the following topic:

> *Children these days are not given enough opportunities to take risks and learn from their mistakes.*
>
> *To what extent do you agree or disagree with this opinion?*

Give reasons for your answer and include any relevant examples from your own knowledge or experience.

Write at least 250 words.

2 Match the criteria 1–5 to the descriptions a–e.

Each task is assessed against four equally weighted criteria:

1 Task Achievement (for Task 1)

2 Task Response (for Task 2)

3 Coherence and cohesion

4 Lexical resource

5 Grammatical range and accuracy

a Organize ideas and information in a logical way within each paragraph and through the text, making the links between elements clear to the reader.

b Use a wide range of sentence structures accurately and appropriately.

c Select and summarize the relevant information presented in the task prompt using your own words, full sentences and the correct minimum number of words.

d Select appropriate vocabulary for the context and use it correctly.

e Present your point of view on a subject, and support it with relevant reasons and examples using your own words, full sentences and the correct minimum number of words.

> **⚙ Exam tip**
>
> Avoid copying whole phrases from the question or using words from a published text that you have memorized. This is referred to as plagiarism and considered to be a form of dishonesty. It is heavily penalized in the marking.

Part 2: Applying assessment criteria

3 Read the student's response to Writing Task 1 in exercise 1. Then, considering the four assessment criteria in exercise 2 (1, 3, 4 & 5), answer questions 1–3.

> The bar chart shows the average final exam results for four different subjects over a three-year period. According to the chart, history was the easiest subject, except in the second year, when the students did badly in their final exams. In fact, year two wasn't a good year for any of the subjects because most students got Ds or Cs.
>
> Biology results got better and better over the three years, not like English which dropped down in the second year. That was also what happened for history. Chemistry results were more like biology.
>
> In conclusion, the chart shows that science teachers were getting better at preparing students for the exams. History and English teachers also did well except in the second year. The reasons for that should be looked into.

1 Has the student followed the instructions?

2 What do you think the student has done well?

3 What aspects do you think could be improved?

4 Read the teacher's feedback and indicate how the teacher would rate the student's performance against the four criteria by ticking the relevant boxes in the table.

> *Not a bad first attempt. You have a rough structure with a brief introduction and conclusion and two body paragraphs. You have linked some of the information and used some complex grammatical structures (e.g. the paragraph beginning 'According to the chart' contains two well-formed complex sentences). There are relatively few grammatical or lexical errors, but your style is a little too informal.*
>
> *You should focus on task achievement and following instructions carefully. Your response is too short (add 20+ words). Use your own words in the introduction. You have also speculated about the reasons for the trend in your conclusion and made a recommendation – remember, you should only summarize and describe.*
>
> *The other areas to develop are coherence and lexical range. To improve the coherence, focus on one key trend in each body paragraph and include more details from the graph. To improve your lexical range, look for more formal synonyms for words that you repeat, e.g. get better – improve.*

	excellent	good	needs work	poor
Task achievement				
Coherence and cohesion				
Lexical resource				
Grammatical range and accuracy				

5 Look at the teacher's feedback in exercise 4 again and underline the suggestions for improvement.

Part 3: Evaluating and improving written work

Task 1

6 Redraft the Task 1 response following the suggestions given in the feedback. Then compare your draft to the sample response on page 186.

Task 2

7 Read the student's response to Writing Task 2 in exercise 1 on page 186. Then complete the table by indicating what the student has done well and what needs to be improved for each of the four assessment criteria in exercise 2 (2, 3, 4 & 5).

Assessment criteria	Good aspects	Aspects requiring improvement
Task response		
Coherence and cohesion		
Lexical resource		
Grammatical range and accuracy		

8 Now check your evaluation against the teacher's evaluation on page 187 in the answer key.

9 Read the student's first draft with the teacher's annotations. Redraft the response. Then compare your response with the revised draft on page 187.

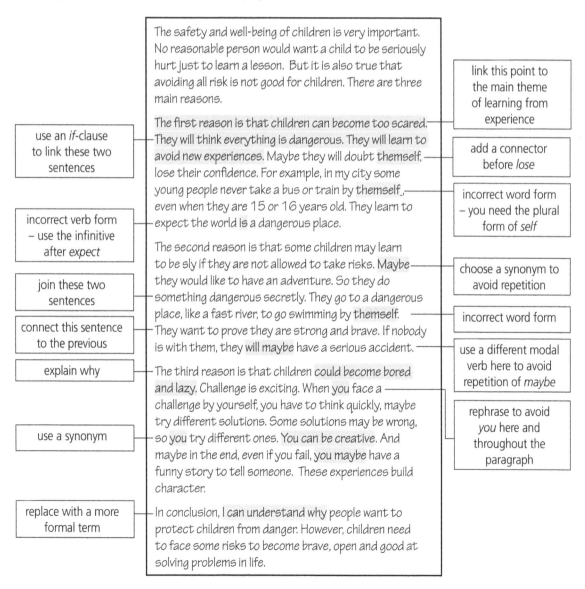

use an *if*-clause to link these two sentences

incorrect verb form – use the infinitive after *expect*

join these two sentences

connect this sentence to the previous

explain why

use a synonym

replace with a more formal term

The safety and well-being of children is very important. No reasonable person would want a child to be seriously hurt just to learn a lesson. But it is also true that avoiding all risk is not good for children. There are three main reasons.

The first reason is that children can become too scared. They will think everything is dangerous. They will learn to avoid new experiences. Maybe they will doubt themself, lose their confidence. For example, in my city some young people never take a bus or train by themself, even when they are 15 or 16 years old. They learn to expect the world is a dangerous place.

The second reason is that some children may learn to be sly if they are not allowed to take risks. Maybe they would like to have an adventure. So they do something dangerous secretly. They go to a dangerous place, like a fast river, to go swimming by themself. They want to prove they are strong and brave. If nobody is with them, they will maybe have a serious accident.

The third reason is that children could become bored and lazy. Challenge is exciting. When you face a challenge by yourself, you have to think quickly, maybe try different solutions. Some solutions may be wrong, so you try different ones. You can be creative. And maybe in the end, even if you fail, you maybe have a funny story to tell someone. These experiences build character.

In conclusion, I can understand why people want to protect children from danger. However, children need to face some risks to become brave, open and good at solving problems in life.

link this point to the main theme of learning from experience

add a connector before *lose*

incorrect word form – you need the plural form of *self*

choose a synonym to avoid repetition

incorrect word form

use a different modal verb here to avoid repetition of *maybe*

rephrase to avoid *you* here and throughout the paragraph

2 Task achievement (Task 1)

Aims | Understanding task achievement band descriptors; Evaluating a Task 1 response; Improving task achievement

Part 1: Understanding task achievement band descriptors

 Exam information: Performance levels

IELTS examiners use a nine-band scale to assess the test taker's level. Each level of performance is defined in detail for each of the four assessment criteria.

1   Read Writing Task 1 instructions and visual prompt and answer questions 1–6.

   1   What do the numbers on the left-hand side of the graph represent?

   2   How many different species of birds are represented in the graph?

   3   Which two species follow a similar trend?

   4   Which details from the graph would you highlight to emphasize this trend?

   5   How is the trend for coastal bird sightings different?

   6   Which details from the graph would you highlight to emphasize this contrasting trend?

 **Exam tip**

Before writing your response, take a few minutes to study the visual prompt. Look for patterns in the data so that you can give a meaningful summary.

WRITING TASK 1

You should spend about 20 minutes on this task.

> *The graph below shows bird sightings in the first week of May at a national park between 1975 and 2020.*
>
> *Describe the information by selecting and reporting the main feature and make comparisons where relevant.*

Write at least 150 words.

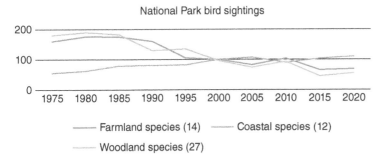

National Park bird sightings

Farmland species (14) Coastal species (12) Woodland species (27)

2 Show how the student's response meets the band 7 requirements by completing 1–3 with information from the band descriptor below (You may use the same phrase more than once.)

Band descriptor

Band 7: *The test taker covers the requirements of the task, presents a clear overview of main trends, differences, or stages, clearly presents and highlights key features / bullet points but they could be more fully extended*

Student's response

> The graph shows sightings of three types of birds at a national park in early May over a 45-year period beginning in 1975.
>
> Two categories of birds, woodland species and farmland species, experienced a dramatic decline, especially during the first half of the study period. **[presents a clear overview of a main trend]** This was particularly evident for sightings of the 27 woodland species, which nearly halved between the years 1975 and 2000, falling from 180 to 95. Thereafter their numbers fluctuated but for the most part remained significantly below the 2000 figure. **[highlights key features]**
>
> Sightings of farmland species showed a very similar mainly downward trajectory to that of the woodland species. The number of farmland birds seen also rose slightly in the first five years of the study then fell significantly (from 160 to 100 sightings) until 2000, but ended slightly stronger at approximately 70 per cent of the 2000 figure. **[1_____]**
>
> Sightings of the 12 coastal species of birds, in contrast, show a rising pattern but with more moderate changes overall. **[2_____]** Figures nearly doubled and then fluctuated around 100. By 2020, only sightings of coastal birds exceeded the figure for 2000. **[highlights key features but 3 _____]**

3 Complete the Task achievement description for bands 6 and 5 with a–f.

Band	Fulfils requirements	Clear overview	Key features
7	covers the requirements of the task	presents a clear overview of main trends, differences, or stages	clearly presents and highlights key features / bullet points but could be more fully extended
6			
5			

a   presents and adequately highlights key features / bullet points but details may be irrelevant, inappropriate or inaccurate
b   presents an overview with information appropriately selected
c   recounts detail mechanically* with no clear overview; there may be no data to support the description
d   addresses the requirements of the task
e   presents, but inadequately covers, key features / bullet points; there may be a tendency to focus on details
f   generally addresses the task; the format may be inappropriate in places

*without selecting the most relevant detail

Part 2: Evaluating a Task 1 response

4 Read Writing Task 1 instructions and visual prompt and answer questions 1–5.

1   What trend can you see if you compare the five figures across the bottom row?
2   Which figures in the bottom row stand out?

3   What trend can you see if you compare the figures from top to bottom in the five columns?
4   What relationship can you see between the first trend (subject preferences) and the second trend (preferred mode of instruction)?
5   Students who enrolled for Art and Art History showed a very strong preference for one mode of study (face-to-face instruction). Which students were more open to different modes of study?

WRITING TASK 1

You should spend about 20 minutes on this task.

> *The table below shows course enrolment figures for five subject areas taught in three different ways.*
>
> *Describe the information by selecting and reporting the main features, and make comparisons where relevant.*

Write at least 150 words.

COURSE ENROLMENT FIGURES 2018

	Art & Art History	Creative Writing	Modern Languages	Literature	Philosophy
Face-to-face	67	52	89	21	17
Online	8	14	17	17	14
Blended	17	20	24	16	14
TOTAL	92	86	130	54	45

 Exam information

Task 1 required you to achieve a balance between summarising general trends and referring to selected information in the prompt. You are not expected to describe all of the information in detail.

5   Read the student's response and the teacher's annotations highlighting the aspects that need to be improved. Then redraft the answer. Compare your answer with the sample answer on page 188.

Student's response

> The table shows the number of people who enrolled on five different types of courses that were taught in three different ways. [inappropriate format – the first introductory sentence should be separate from the rest of the paragraph and further developed] Modern languages were very popular. Eighty-nine people wanted to study languages face-to-face, 17 wanted online and 24 wanted blended course. Next was Art and Art History. Sixty-seven enrolled for the course face-to-face, eight for the online and 17 for the blended. After that was creative writing. Fifty-two people chose it for face-to-face, 14 for online and 20 for blended. [this paragraph recounts detail mechanically with no clear overview – give an overview of the main trend and select key details to highlight]

The more serious academic subjects – Literature and Philosophy – were less popular. But there was not such a big difference in the number of people who chose the face-to-face, online and blended options, especially for Philosophy. [provide data to support the statement about Philosophy]

The table shows that some courses were more popular than other courses and some people liked online learning, but others did not. [provide a clearer overview relating subject preference and preferred mode of study]

(140 words) [increase the word count to 150 minimum]

Part 3: Improving task achievement

6 Read Writing Task 1 instructions and visual prompt. Make notes about the information that stands out.

WRITING TASK 1

You should spend about 20 minutes on this task.

The diagram below shows the process of building a new house.

Explain the information by selecting and reporting the main features, and make comparisons where relevant.

Write at least 150 words.

Stages	Scheduled weeks															
	Preparation								Building							
	1	2	3	4	5	6	7	8	9	10	11	12	13	14	15	16
Assess site	■															
Draw up plans		■	■													
Obtain approval				■	■											
Hire builders						■										
Purchase insurance						■										
Prepare site							■									
Pour concrete foundation									■	■						
Construct frame											■					
Install walls & roof												■	■			
Fit windows														■		
Install plumbing & electricity															■	■
Paint exterior & interior																■

7 Write your response, including an introduction and two body paragraphs, then compare your text with the sample answer in the key on page 189.

3 Task response (Task 2)

Aims | Interpreting Task 2 questions (meeting task requirements); **Developing a Task 2 response** (stating your position, qualifying your position and developing your position); **Improving a Task 2 response**

Part 1: Interpreting Task 2 questions

ⓘ Exam information: The task response descriptor

The task response descriptor applies to the second writing task. It includes three main components: *meeting task requirements, taking a clear position* and *developing your position with reasons and supporting evidence or examples*.

ⓘ Exam information: Meeting the task requirements

To *meet the task requirements*, you must answer the set question. This means reading it carefully to identify not only the topic but also the approach you are expected to take. There are four main approaches commonly required for IELTS Task 2 questions.

1   Match the Task 2 questions 1–4 on the topic of education with the most appropriate approach a–d.

  1   Art and music are normally included in the school curriculum. What is the value of learning about art and music in school?

  2   Young people are not always able to reach their full potential at school. What are the most effective ways of improving pupils' educational attainment?

  3   The best way of dealing with poor motivation for learning is to allow young people to choose which subjects they wish to learn from an early age. To what extent do you agree or disagree?

  4   Some parents believe that boys and girls should be educated separately, whereas for others the preferred approach is to teach boys and girls together. What are the advantages and disadvantages of each approach?

  a   propose a solution to a problem
  b   compare and contrast opinions or arguments
  c   evaluate an opinion or argument
  d   present and justify an opinion

Part 2: Developing a Task 2 response

 Exam information: Stating your position

You should use your introductory paragraph to establish your position – that is, state clearly your point of view and/or approach to the question. There is no 'right' or 'wrong' position for Task 2 questions.

2 The introductory paragraphs 1–4 have been written in response to the questions in exercise 1. Underline the part of the paragraph where the writer states their position.

> 1 Many educational systems have become increasingly focused on training young people for successful careers and neglected subjects that are considered non-essential, such as music and art. In my view, this approach can be very limiting. Exploring the arts can have many benefits for pupils, no matter what their intended career.

> 2 Low educational achievement can be the result of many factors, not all of which are directly related to schools. However, schools can undoubtedly do a great deal to raise educational attainment. There are three main initiatives that I believe could be effective.

> 3 The causes of low motivation for learning may be diverse and complex. Giving young learners more responsibility for choosing what they learn could certainly increase their motivation, but only up to a point.

> 4 There have been many attempts to find evidence in favour of both co-educational and single-sex education. I believe that both types of schools can be effective and it is up to parents to decide which would be most suitable for their child.

 Exam information: Qualifying your position

You should take a clear, but not extreme, position. Most position statements are qualified by expressions such as *to some degree* or modals such as *could*, because Task 2 often deals with complex topics that don't have simple answers.

3 Read each introduction in more detail and answer questions 1–3.

1 In each of the introductions in exercise 2, the writers express their positions in the second half. What does each writer do before that?

2 The words *very* and *many* in the first introduction express a strong position. Which adverbs in introductions 2 and 3 indicate a strong position?

3 The modal verb *can* in the first and second introductions expresses a softer or more tentative position. Which words or phrases in introductions 3 and 4 also express a tentative position?

Exam information: Developing your position

For a better understanding of what IELTs examiners are looking out for when you present and develop a position, study the band descriptors. Notice the emphasis on maintaining a consistent position.

4 Complete the table below with the specific descriptions a–d for each band 5–7.

Band	Meets requirements	Presents a position	Develops the position
7	addresses all parts of the task	presents a clear position throughout the response	
6	addresses all parts of the task although some parts may be more fully covered than others		
5	addresses the task only partially; the format may be inappropriate in places		presents some main ideas but these are limited and not sufficiently developed; there may be irrelevant detail

a   expresses a position but the development is not always clear and there may be no conclusions drawn
b   presents a relevant position although the conclusions may become unclear or repetitive
c   presents relevant main ideas but some may be inadequately developed / unclear
d   presents, extends and supports main ideas, but there may be a tendency to over-generalize and/or supporting ideas may lack focus

5 The two paragraphs below follow Introductory paragraph 2 in exercise 2 on the topic of educational attainment. Which paragraph develops the writer's position more effectively?

… There are three main initiatives that I believe could be effective.

The first initiative would be to focus on the pupils' early years and identify problems at an early stage. The first years of schooling are particularly important because this is when children learn to read and do arithmetic. Good reading skills make it possible to learn the other school subjects. Basic numeracy is essential for further development in maths and many sciences. If pupils have any problems with reading and maths at this stage, they should be given extra individual help immediately so that they do not fall behind with their other learning.

Another could be to help teachers develop their teaching skills. Some teachers are not as effective as they could be because they do not have the right skills. Helping them to improve their skills would make them better teachers and better able to help their pupils learn.

6 Redraft the second body paragraph and add a third paragraph of your own.

7 Read the concluding paragraph and compare it to the introduction. What are the similarities and differences?

Introduction

Low educational achievement can be the result of many factors, not all of which are directly related to schools. However, schools can undoubtedly do a great deal to raise educational attainment. There are three main initiatives that I believe could be effective. ...

Conclusion

These three measures may not be necessary for every child, but they could help children who would have particular needs. Although schools may not be able to directly address all of the causes of low attainment, it is important that schools are given the support they need to educate all children, not just those who find learning easy.

8 Read the Task 2 response, focusing on the development of ideas in paragraphs 2 to 4 and the effectiveness of the conclusion. Use marginal notes to indicate where and how the essay could be improved.

What is the value of learning about art and music in school?

Many educational systems have become increasingly focused on training young people for successful careers and neglected subjects that are considered non-essential, such as music and art. In my view, this approach can be very limiting. Exploring the arts can have many benefits for pupils, no matter what their intended career.

When young people do something like painting a picture, they need to consider many aspects. First, they need to plan the design. Then, if the painting is not looking good, they have to think about what the problem is and decide how to change it. If they play a musical instrument, for example in an orchestra, they may have problems playing together with the other players. They need to work out how to solve those conflicts.

Art and music are aspects of culture and take many different forms in different parts of the world. Maths and science are the same everywhere. If you want to understand people from different parts of the world, you should study their culture, including their art and music. This will give you broader understanding and help you connect with diverse people. This is one of the reasons travelling is so valuable.

Another benefit of education in art and music is that it instils discipline and can lead to increased self-confidence. Becoming better at these skills requires a great deal of practice and repetition. The individual can develop the ability to receive criticism and try harder next time. Overcoming these difficulties repeatedly over time can help the person to develop genuine self-confidence.

These points show that exploring the arts can have many benefits for pupils, no matter what their intended career.

Part 3: Improving a Task 2 response

9 Redraft the essay in exercise 8. Then compare your essay with the sample answer on page 190.

4 Coherence

Part 1: Understanding coherence

Coherence

Coherence is a key aspect of the second performance descriptor. It refers to the logical sequencing of ideas and information.

1   Read the extracts from the descriptors a–c and rank them from band 7 to 5. Underline the key words that help you distinguish the levels.

   a   The response arranges information and ideas coherently and there is a clear overall progression

   b   The response logically organizes information and ideas; there is clear progression throughout

   c   The response presents information with some organization but there may be a lack of overall progression

 Exam information:

In the IELTS writing test, a key aspect of coherence is progression. This means that ideas and information lead to a logical conclusion and are sequenced in a way that is easy for the reader to follow.

Part 2: Focusing on coherence

Rhetorical patterns for Task 1

To make your writing more coherent, learn how different types of writing in English are typically organized. Different types of Task 1 prompts require different *rhetorical patterns*.

2   Match the rhetorical patterns a–d to the Task 1 visual prompts 1–4.

   a   Process description – to explain a series of natural changes or how something is done
   b   Classification – to group information into categories and compare and contrast
   c   Chronological description – to describe trend(s) over time
   d   Spatial description – to describe a place

1 Electric car sales

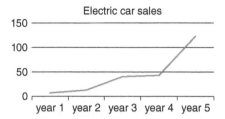

2 Distribution of deer

3 Children's television viewing preferences

Children's television viewing preferences 1= favourite 5 = least favourite					
Age	Cartoons	Factual	Comedy	Drama	Music
3–4	1	4	2	5	3
5–6	1	2	3	5	4
7–8	3	1	2	4	5
9–10	5	1	4	2	3

4 Product design process

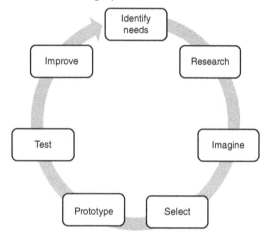

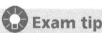

3 Match the rhetorical patterns a–d in exercise 2 to the explanations 1–4 below.

1 This pattern is usually used to describe maps. State in general terms what the map illustrates, then highlight key features from most important to least important, or moving in a sequential manner, e.g. from right to left, top to bottom or clockwise.

2 This pattern is typically used for line graphs. State the general nature of the trend (e.g. rising, falling, u-shaped, bell-shaped or irregular), then describe key features in sequence from beginning to end.

3 This pattern is generally used for diagrams which illustrate a sequence of steps or events. State the overall purpose or nature of the sequence, then describe it in detail, beginning with the first stage and ending with the last.

4 This pattern is appropriate for tables, charts or line graphs showing more than one trend. Indicate the general pattern, e.g. whether the data sets are broadly similar or different, then describe the key points using either a **block pattern** – describe one data set and then the other – or a **point-by-point pattern** – identify key points for comparison and compare the data sets point by point.

> 🔧 **Exam tip**
>
> One of the most common ways of organizing writing in English is **general-to-specific**. Whichever rhetorical pattern you are using, you should generally give main points before specific examples, reasons or details.

4 Reorder the sentences 1–5 so that the text follows a coherent chronological pattern.

1 There is a peak in passenger numbers of approximately 250,000 between 8.00 a.m. and 9.30 a.m. _____

2 There is then another bigger peak of nearly 300,000 passengers between 5.00 p.m. and 6.30 p.m. _____

3 From 10.00 a.m. onwards there is a small but steady number of passengers for several hours, followed by a small rise at about midday. _____

4 The number of travellers then falls sharply. _____

5 The graph shows average public transport passenger numbers over a typical 24-hour weekday in a large metropolitan area. _____

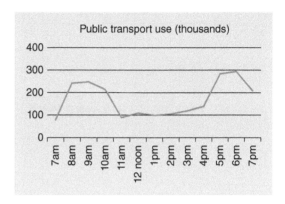

Rhetorical patterns for Task 2

Different types of Task 2 questions also require different rhetorical patterns.

5 Read the Task 2 questions 1–4 and summarize the task type, e.g. propose a solution to a problem, present and justify an opinion. Then match questions 1–4 with the most appropriate rhetorical pattern a–d.

1 Why have mobile phones become indispensable for so many?

2 Would a tax on single-use plastic reduce plastic pollution?

3 How can health inequality be addressed?

4 Some believe that zoos are unethical. Ohers consider them essential for conservation. What is your view?

a Begin with a comment on the context. Evaluate the weaker opinion or argument, highlighting the weaknesses. Then evaluate the stronger opinion or argument, highlighting the strengths. Finally, state your position.

b State your opinion and give your reasons along with evidence and examples. The sequence of reasons can be from strongest to weakest or weakest to strongest.

c If you agree, state how strongly you agree and give reasons for your position. If you disagree, show you understand the opinion or argument given, then state that you disagree. Give reasons for your point of view.

d If you have one solution, state your proposal and give reasons in support. If you have more than one solution, give each one in turn along with supporting reasons. The sequence of solutions can be from strongest to weakest or weakest to strongest.

Part 3: Improving coherence

6 Name the type of rhetorical pattern attempted in the Task 1 extract below. Identify the problem with coherence. Rewrite the paragraphs in a more coherent way. Compare your answer with the model.

The pie charts show the average household expenditure of families living in urban areas and families in rural areas. Rural households spend 18 per cent of their income on transport in comparison to 14 per cent for urban households. They also spend more on housing and fuel (32 per cent of income vs 27 per cent). Urban families spend more of their income on restaurants and recreation (9 per cent vs 7 per cent and 13 per cent vs 8 per cent). People living in the countryside allocate 12 per cent of their income to groceries and people in the city only 10 per cent.

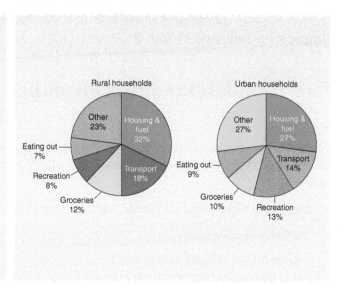

7 Read the Task 2 exam prompt below and identify the question type. Rewrite the test taker's outline to ensure a more coherent response.

Task 2

For a more environmentally sustainable future, cities should be smaller and more people should be encouraged to live in the countryside.
To what extent do you agree?

Introduction: *Many people are concerned about the environment and looking for ways to live sustainably. I agree that sustainable living is important but disagree that this can be achieved by displacing population from cities to the countryside.*

Body paragraph 1: Main point: Reasonable to associate sustainability with rural life
Reason 1: close contact with nature = valuing nature
Reason 2: opportunity to take action, e.g. grow food

Body paragraph 2: Main point: rural living not actually more sustainable
Reason 1: more fuel needed for transport
Reason 2: more fuel needed for heating

Body paragraph 3: Reason 1: less travel, more access to public transport
Reason 2: flats more efficient to heat
Reason 3: better access to sustainably produced goods
Main point: city living is more sustainable

Conclusion: *Although we do not always associate urban living with environmental sustainability, urban populations can often live in a way that is better for the environment. Environmentally friendly city living should be encouraged.*

8 Write the three body paragraphs. Then compare your answer with the sample on page 192.

5 Cohesion

Part 1: Understanding cohesion

Cohesion

Cohesion is the other key aspect of the second performance descriptor. Whereas *coherence* refers to the logical sequencing of ideas and information, *cohesion* refers to the words, phrases and other elements that hold a text together.

1   Match the highlighted components of cohesion in the band 6 descriptor to definitions a–c .

> **Band descriptor**
>
> **Band 6:** Uses cohesive devices effectively, but cohesion within and/or between sentences may be faulty or mechanical; may not always use referencing clearly or appropriately; uses paragraphing, but not always logically.

a   words such as pronouns that are used to substitute for or refer to nouns
b   divisions within a text that indicate a change in topic
c   words or phrases that show the connection between parts of a sentence or text

2   Write CD next to the cohesive devices and RW next to the reference words.

1   however _____ 　　2   which _____ 　　3   firstly _____
4   in contrast _____ 　　5   they _____ 　　6   whereas _____

Part 2: Focusing on cohesion

Cohesive devices

Different cohesive devices signal different types of logical connections or transitions.

3   Look at the five types of cohesive devices 1–5 and categorize the expressions below accordingly.

> also   as a consequence   but   finally   for instance   in addition
>   in contrast   next   secondly   so   therefore   whereas

1   Additive transitions when one point is in addition to another, e.g. *and*
2   Adversative transitions when one point is in contrast or opposed to another, e.g. *nevertheless*
3   Causative transitions for cause-and-effect relationships, e.g. *because*
4   Sequential transitions when listing points, e.g. *firstly*
5   Example transitions to signal examples, e.g. *for example*

4 Read the Task 1 answer extract below. Underline the cohesive devices and indicate the type of relationship expressed by annotating each with a number from 1 (Additive) to 5 (Example).

> *The two youngest age groups (aged 3–4 and 5–6) rated cartoons as their favourite, ranked drama as their least favourite and gave comedy and music middle rankings. The older children (7–8 and 9–10) also identified the same category, factual programmes, as their top choice; however, their other preferences were ranked quite differently. For example, children aged seven to eight chose music programmes as their least favourite, while those in the older age bracket liked cartoons least.*

The grammar of cohesive devices

Different cohesive devices connect different grammatical components of the text.

5 Look at the three main types of cohesive devices. Then identify the cohesive device in each sentence a–c and add them to the correct category 1–3.

1 Devices that introduce a noun phrase, e.g. *as a result of*
2 Devices that connect clauses, e.g. *and, but, because*
3 Devices that show how one sentence relates to the previous, e.g. *as a consequence, finally*

a Children aged seven to eight liked music programmes least, while those in the older age bracket liked cartoons least.
b The older children (7–8 and 9–10) preferred factual programmes. However, their other preferences were ranked quite differently.
c In contrast to older children, younger viewers preferred playful television content.

6 Complete 1–4 in the text with the cohesive devices below.

> in comparison to   whereas   also   on the other hand

> Rural households tend to spend more of their income on essentials, **1** _____ urban households spend a higher percentage of their money on non-essential items. Rural households spend 18 per cent of their income on transport **2** _____ 14 per cent for urban households. They **3** _____ spend more on housing and fuel (32 per cent of income vs 27 per cent). People living in the countryside allocate 12 per cent of their income to groceries and people in the city only 10 per cent. Urban families, **4** _____, spend more of their income on restaurants and recreation than rural families (9 per cent vs 7 per cent on eating out and 13 per cent vs 8 per cent on recreation).

7 Answer questions 1–5 about the text in exercise 6.

1 Which transition word or phrase connects two clauses?
2 Which show the relationship between two sentences?
3 Which introduces a noun phrase?
4 Which of these cohesive devices is additive?
5 Which are adversative?

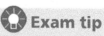 **Exam tip**

Overuse of transition words or phrases is just as problematic as underuse. If your text is coherent, that is if the ideas and information are logically sequenced in a recognizable rhetorical pattern, you should not need to use a transition signal for every sentence or clause.

Referencing

Use reference words, such as *they or them*, to avoid repetition, e.g. When **young people** do something creative, ~~young people~~ **they** need to consider many aspects.

8 Look at the three types of reference words 1–3 and categorize the words below according to their type.

that   she   his   which   him   their   her   he   them

1 personal pronouns, e.g. *they*
2 relative pronouns, e.g. *who*
3 possessive adjectives, e.g. *her*

9 Fill the gaps with suitable reference words. Draw an arrow between each reference word and the noun phrase to which it refers.

City dwellers may have less contact with nature, but (1) _____ tend to have a lower average carbon footprint. (2) _____ are more likely to live near (3) _____ workplace and have access to good public transport. (4) _____ also commonly live in flats, surrounded by other flats, (5) _____ can help to retain heat and reduce fuel consumption. City dwellers have easier access to services and often have more choice as consumers, so it is often easier for (6) _____ to buy sustainably grown food and products (7) _____ have been made in a sustainable way.

Paragraphing

Good paragraphing helps the reader see how the essay is organized. Well-formed paragraphs have a topic sentence, which indicates the main point developed by the other sentences. The gap between paragraphs signals to the reader that the writer is moving to a new main point.

10 Identify the topic sentences in the paragraphs in exercises 6 and 9.

11 Look at the Task 2 question and the first half of the essay and answer the questions 1–3.

> **Task 2**
> To tackle the problem of poor health, governments should provide free healthcare to all their citizens, even those who can afford to pay. Do you agree or disagree?

Healthcare is essential for well-being but expensive to provide. While some people would argue that individuals should pay for their own healthcare in order to incentivize healthier lifestyle choices, I believe that the state should bear this responsibility. The first argument in favour of this approach is that it would reduce health inequality among the population. All people would have access to the same level of care regardless of income. Equal access to healthcare is particularly important for children in lower-income families, whose well-being should not be compromised because of their parents' lack of income. Universal government-funded healthcare would also help to protect all people from certain harms, even those who can easily afford to pay for care themselves. Many infectious diseases, such as flu, can easily pass from one person to another. Vaccination programmes paid for by the government can help to protect the whole population, rich and poor alike.

1 Divide the text into three paragraphs: the introduction and two body paragraphs.
2 Underline the cohesive devices.
3 Highlight the reference words and indicate with an arrow the noun to which they refer.

Part 3: Improving cohesion in Task 2

12 Look at the Task 2 question and the essay. Then redraft the essay by dividing it into paragraphs, adding cohesive devices, and replacing nouns with pronouns to reduce unnecessary repetition.

> **Task 2**
> Lifestyle factors such as poor diet and smoking have a significant impact on health. How can people be encouraged to take responsibility for their own health?

Rising living standards in many countries around the world have been accompanied by an increase in health problems associated with more affluent lifestyles. The problems include the consumption of tobacco and high-calorie processed foods. In this environment, people need help to look after themselves more responsibly. There are three main ways this can be achieved. Public health campaigns could be used to educate the population about the dangers of smoking and excessive consumption of unhealthy foods. Public health campaigns should point out the long-term consequences. The consequences are not always obvious in the short-term. If possible, real people should be invited to talk about their experiences. The public can relate personally to the message. Public health messages could be reinforced by legislation. A higher rate of sales tax could be imposed on products that are unhealthy to discourage consumers from buying them. Supermarkets and shops could be required to limit the quantity of certain products that can be purchased at one time to discourage excessive consumption. On a more positive note, parents should be encouraged to model healthy lifestyles for their children by cooking and eating together. Schools could be involved in helping children to develop the necessary knowledge and skills by providing practical lessons in an interesting and fun way. Children can learn about healthy food choices and develop cooking skills from an early age. Children are more likely to maintain these habits as adults. There is no simple or easy way to address the problem of unhealthy lifestyle choices and their consequences. Together, these three approaches could help to reduce unhealthy behaviours and encourage healthier alternatives.

6 Lexical resource 1: range

Aims | Understanding the components of lexical resource; Focusing on lexical range (flexibility and precision, collocations, common collocations in Task 1); **Improving lexical range in Task 1**

Part 1: Understanding the components of lexical resource

 **Exam tip**

To score well in the third assessment criterion, lexical resource, you must show that you have a wide range of vocabulary and that you can use words accurately.

1 Read the band 7 descriptor. Underline the parts that refer to range and highlight the part that refers to accuracy.

> **Band descriptor**
>
> **Band 7:** uses a sufficient range of vocabulary to allow some flexibility and precision; uses less common lexical items with some awareness of style and collocation; may produce occasional errors in word choice, spelling and/or word formation

2 Read the Task 2 question and two versions of an extract written in response. Decide which extract demonstrates better lexical resource and explain why.

> **Task 2**
> The loss of wild animals and wild places is an inevitable consequence of progress. To what extent do you agree or disagree?

a People have damaged nature in order to prosper. Prosperity has helped the population to grow and go further into areas of the natural world where wild animals once lived.

b People have exploited natural resources in order to prosper. Prosperity has enabled the population to grow and expand further into areas of land where wildlife once thrived.

Part 2: Focusing on lexical range

 Exam information: Flexibility and precision

To demonstrate both flexibility and precision, you need to go beyond the most common words in English and learn words and phrases with more precise meanings.

3 Synonyms for the verb *give* are listed below. Match each synonym 1–4 with the closest definition a–d.

1	award	a	to give a quantity of something essential, often for a specific purpose
2	donate	b	to give something such as a medal or honour based on the decision of officials
3	provide	c	to make something that is wanted or needed available to others
4	supply	d	to give something to help a person or an organization

4 Complete sentences 1–4 with the most appropriate word from exercise 3.

1 Charitable agencies such Oxfam _____ essentials such as food and water to people affected by war or natural disasters.

2 People should be encouraged to _____ unwanted clothing and household goods to organizations that serve the poor.

3 To encourage altruistic behaviour, schools should _____ prizes to children who help others, not just children who achieve academically or in sport.

4 For a more just society, governments must strive to _____ equal opportunities to all.

5 Group the words a–l into two categories:

1 words that are related to *like*
2 words that are related to *say*

a	state	e	appreciate	i	claim
b	insist	f	cherish	j	enjoy
c	admire	g	announce	k	confirm
d	argue	h	approve of	l	savour

6 Underline the word in bold that is most appropriate for the context in sentences 1–6. Check your dictionary if you are not sure of the precise meanings.

1 Working parents often have little time for themselves; when they do have free time, they really ***approve of / savour*** it.

2 People often save things that are no longer useful, such as old toys and letters, because they ***cherish / admire*** the memories associated with them.

3 Even children who do not ***appreciate / enjoy*** school, can ***appreciate / enjoy*** the help they receive from a kindly teacher.

4 Many people ***argue / announce*** that young people are more interested in popular entertainment than the arts, but this is not always true.

5 Astronomers have never been able to ***insist / confirm*** that life exists on planets other than Earth.

6 In a job interview it is unethical to ***claim / announce*** that you have more experience and qualifications than you actually have.

7 When you take the IELTS speaking test, you have to ***claim / state*** your name.

Collocations

Collocations are common word combinations. The phrases *cherish a memory* and *state your name* are examples of one type of collocation: verb + noun.

7 Look at the types of collocation below and add expressions a–e to the correct category 1–4.

1 verb + adverb, e.g. *increased sharply*
2 adverb + adjective, e.g. *densely populated*
3 adjective + noun, e.g. *dramatic fall*
4 noun + noun, e.g. *survey data*

a rapid expansion
b decreased gradually
c gender stereotype
d commonly accepted
e steep rise

 Exam information: Common collocations in Task 1

Certain **adjective + noun** and **verb + adverb** collocations are common in Task 1 descriptions of line graphs. For example, *There was a **steep rise** in prices.* (adjective + noun) and *Prices **rose steeply**.* (verb + adverb). Using both patterns correctly demonstrates flexibility.

8 Rewrite sentences 1–4 using the pattern indicated in brackets.

1 There was a sharp fall in consumer confidence from January to March.

(verb + adverb) _____

2 Consumer confidence then increased marginally over the next three months.

(adjective + noun) _____

3 There was a slight dip in confidence in July.

(verb + adverb) _____

4 After that, confidence rose rapidly until December.

(adjective + noun) _____

Exam tip

To make the best use of your time, focus on building your vocabulary around key concepts such as quantity, scale and quality. When choosing less common words, make sure they are formal or semi-formal in style.

9 For sentences 1–8, replace the less precise expressions in bold with the more precise and formal word or expression a–h that is most similar in meaning.

a concerted   c a great deal of   e significant   g widely
b convincing   d marginal   f broad   h beneficial

1 There has been *a lot of* debate around racial equality.
2 Government should make a *big* effort to tackle poverty.
3 There was *a little bit* of growth in food exports.
4 The graph shows that there has been a *big* increase in international trade.
5 A *big* range of initiatives have been tried, but none have been successful.
6 No one has put forward a *really good* argument for a national living wage.
7 Reducing the cost of food would have a *good* effect.
8 The number of people out of work fluctuated *a lot* in the first half of the century.

Part 3: Improving lexical range in Task 1

10 Redraft the Task 1 response so that it demonstrates better lexical range. Then add a further 40–50 words to complete the text. Compare your answer to the model on page 193.

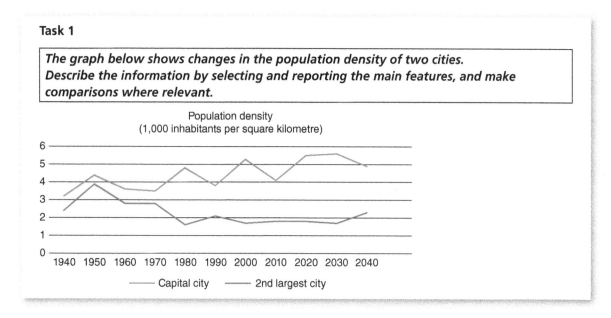

Task 1

> *The graph below shows changes in the population density of two cities.*
> *Describe the information by selecting and reporting the main features, and make comparisons where relevant.*

The graph shows how the population density of the capital city and the next-largest city changed over a 100-year period. There were big differences between the two cities, especially from 1970 onwards.

Between 1940 and 1970, the pattern of change was very similar. Population density in both cities grew a lot between 1940 and 1950 then fell sharply over the next ten years. Then population density grew sharply in the capital city and fell sharply in the second city. Between 1980 and 2000 the population density in the capital city fluctuated a lot, between about 45,000 and 55,000 inhabitants per square kilometre. Over the same period, density in the second city ...

7 Lexical resource 2: accuracy

Aims | Understanding the lexical resource descriptor; **Focusing on lexical accuracy** (word choice, dependent prepositions, spelling, word formation (suffixes and prefixes), countable and uncountable nouns); **Improving lexical accuracy** (Tasks 1 and 2)

Part 1: Understanding the lexical resource descriptor

1 Read the band 7 lexical resource descriptor and identify three types of mistake IELTS examiners look out for.

Band descriptor

Band 7: uses a sufficient range of vocabulary to allow some flexibility and precision; uses less common lexical items with some awareness of style and collocation; may produce occasional errors in word choice, spelling and/or word formation.

2 Identify the type of lexical error in sentences 1–3. Correct the mistakes, replacing each problem word or phrase with a suitable alternative.

1 When applying for a new job, it is unethical to exagerate your qualifications.
2 It is very benefit to start learning a language at an early age.
3 The rule of law is an important principal.

Part 2: Improving lexical accuracy

Word choice

Mistakes in word choice often occur when you choose lexical items that are inappropriate. Avoid using old-fashioned or literary terms, informal expressions or clichés. Be careful with words that are similar to words in another language you know, but that have a different meaning.

3 Replace the incorrect word choice in each sentence with a more appropriate expression. Use your dictionary to help you.

1 Many people are nervous when they face new situations but to succeed in life you have to be brave and dip your toe in the water.
2 It is rubbish to think that only the lucky few can really succeed in life.
3 A schoolmistress who is very strict can inhibit a child's creativity.
4 Travellers to Antarctica are likely to see many wondrous things.
5 Before approving a new medicine, scientists should assure that it is safe.

Dependent prepositions

Dependent prepositions are words such as *in* and *for* that are commonly found with particular words to form a common phrase. Often there is no logical reason for particular pairings, so it is best to learn these phrases as a single lexical item.

4 Choose the correct dependent preposition for each sentence 1–5.

1 The problem **about / with** recent attempts to combat climate change is that they do not go far enough.
2 There is no easy solution **to / for** this problem.
3 Not everyone is aware **of / with** the changes that have taken place already.
4 Children are naturally curious **for / about** how things are made.
5 People who are wealthy are not always interested **in / to** the problems faced by those who are less well off.

5 Find the seven incorrect dependent prepositions and correct them.

There has been a significant increase of social media platforms designed to appeal for young people. This can pose a risk to children. Parents often disapprove against their children's online viewing habits, but they are not always as familiar about new platforms as the younger generation. There is a need of more regulation of social networking sites. These measures could prevent young people against accessing unsuitable online content. As a society, we are all responsible with protecting children from harm.

Spelling
Many English words are difficult to spell because they are not always pronounced as they are written.

6 What is the correct spelling of the words in bold? Why do you think they have been misspelled?

There have been **severel exellent sugestions**.

7 Underline the silent letters in words 1–6 and add the missing silent letters to words 7–12.

1 doubt   2 condemn   3 receipt   4 island   5 reign   6 guess

7 gover___ment   8 ___sychology   9 debri___   10 g___ilty

11 de___t   12 ex___ellent

8 In each sentence 1–5 find and correct two spelling mistakes.

1 The mass media often places too much importence on apearance and success and not enough on values.
2 If everyone had the same acess to oppertunity, people from humble backgrounds could achieve as much as those born into wealth.
3 Aggresive advertising can encourage people to spend more than they can aford on products they do not really need.
4 In the past, it was comon practice to educate children seperately; nowadays, it is more common to teach them together.
5 The information in the chart can be catagorized into three main themes: education, care for the elderly, and envirenmental initiatives.

Word formation (suffixes)

Many root words exist in a variety of forms, e.g. *difference* (noun), *differ* (verb), *different* (adjective). You can often recognize the word form by suffixes. Adverbs, for example, often have the suffix *-ly*, e.g. *luckily.*

9 Underline the suffixes in the words and place them in the correct column of the table.

abolish   beneficial   business   clarity   construction   fearless
government   likelihood   negative   organize
relationship   spontaneous   static

Nouns	Verbs	Adjectives
democra<u>cy</u>	demonstr<u>ate</u>	avail<u>able</u>
confid<u>ence</u>	strength<u>en</u>	grate<u>ful</u>
teach<u>er</u>	classi<u>fy</u>	diff<u>erent</u>

Prefixes

Prefixes can be added to many root words to create words with a different meaning, e.g. *re* + *write* = *write again*. Take care not to confuse prefixes with similar meanings, for example: *un-, non-, il-, im-, in-, ir-* and *dis-,* which all denote 'not', and *de-* and *dis-,* which denote reversal or removal.

10 Add the correct prefix to the words in bold in the paragraph below.

Regions that have been **1** ___**industrialized** often suffer high
2 ___**employment**. Often the only work available is **3** ___**regula**r and
4 ___**secure**. Land in such areas is often **5** ___**suitable** for other
purposes because it needs to be **6** ___**contaminated**. Residents often
feel **7** ___**regarded** and **8** ___**important**.

 **Exam tip**

Some prefixes can have more than one meaning, for example *dis-,* which can mean 'not' (e.g. *dislike*) as well as 'reversal' or 'removal' (e.g. *disengage*).

Countable and uncountable nouns

It is important to remember that uncountable nouns, e.g. *knowledge*, do not have a plural form or take plural verb forms or modifiers.

11 Look at the types of nouns 1–3 and add examples a–h to the correct type.

a solution   b weather   c idea   d analysis
e wife   f attention   g medium   h equipment

1   countable and regular in the plural form (e.g. *teacher**s are** ...*)
2   countable and irregular in the plural form (e.g. *child**ren are** ...*)
3   uncountable (e.g. *education **is** ...*)

Exam information

Uncountable nouns often express abstract concepts or states and so are commonly found in academic writing, including IELTS writing tasks, e.g. *understanding, knowledge*. Other uncountable nouns refer to topics often addressed in Task 2 questions: *justice, education, health*.

Part 3: Improving lexical accuracy (Task 2)

12 Read the introduction and first body paragraph written in response to the Task 2 question. Identify and correct the errors. Then check the Answer key and explanations on page 194.

> **Task 2**
> *Large corporations will inevitably take over smaller family-run businesses because they can provide goods and services more efficiently and thereby improve quality of life. To what extent do you agree?*

In many parts of the world, big corporations have caused smaller companies to go out of business. To be honest, the big brands can be seen everywhere, and they have been successful to capturing the market for many products. They may be more efficiency at selling products, but they do not necessary improve living standards.

In some countries, independent shops have almost disapeared, and shopping districts are becoming the same everywhere. Consumers can buy products more cheaply, but they often have less choice. When small traders close down, a town can loose its caracter, and possibly part of its history. People may feel sad and empty because money doesn't buy happiness.

 Exam tip

As you are preparing for the test, keep a note of the types of mistakes you make in your writing, especially those that you make repeatedly.
In the test itself, remember to leave enough time to check your writing carefully for spelling and grammar mistakes.

8 Grammatical range

Aims | Understanding grammatical range; Focusing on grammatical range
(subordinating conjunctions; relative clauses, cleft sentences, the passive voice); **Improving grammatical range** (Task 1)

Part 1: Understanding grammatical range

1 Read the band 6 and 7 descriptors for grammar and decide if sentences 1–3 are TRUE or FALSE.

Band descriptors

Band 7: uses a variety of complex structures; produces frequent error-free sentences; has good control of grammar and punctuation but may make a few errors

Band 6: uses a mix of simple and complex sentence forms; makes some errors in grammar and punctuation but they rarely reduce communication

1   You will score a 7 for grammar as long as most of your sentences contain no errors. TRUE / FALSE
2   The main difference between band 6 and band 7 is the complexity of grammar structures and the frequency of errors. TRUE / FALSE
3   The clarity of your sentences is not as important as the complexity and accuracy of the grammar. TRUE / FALSE

 **Exam tip**

Examiners will look for good use of complex sentence structures. Learn when to use complex sentences and how to form them accurately. Good writers normally use a mixture of simple sentences as well as a variety of complex sentences, choosing whichever structures convey their points most clearly.

2 Read the extract from the essay on educational attainment from Unit 3. The first sentence is complex and the second is simple. Study both sentences and the remainder of the paragraph, then answer questions 1–4.

[1] The first years of schooling are particularly important because this is when children learn to read and do arithmetic. [2] Good reading skills make it possible to learn the other school subjects. [3] Basic numeracy is essential for further development in maths and many sciences. [4] If pupils have any problems with reading and maths at this stage, they should be given extra individual help.

1   What are the essential components of a simple sentence?
2   What makes a sentence complex?
3   Is sentence 3 simple or complex?
4   What about sentence 4?

Part 2: Focusing on grammatical range

Subordinating conjunctions

Using a wide range of subordinating conjunctions allows you to show the precise relationship between ideas and information, e.g. *because* and *if* in the paragraph in exercise 2.

3 Read sentences 1–4 and select from a–d the type of relationship between the clauses.

a cause and effect   b condition   c comparison   d concession

1 Male respondents preferred full-time study whereas female respondents preferred part-time study.

2 Although electric cars are more expensive on average than conventional cars, electric car sales have risen at a faster rate.

3 Podcasts have become very popular because they are easily accessible.

4 As long as you keep practising your language skills, you will improve.

4 Complete the table with the conjunctions below.

as   even though   if   since   provided (that)   unless   while

comparison	concession	cause and effect	condition
whereas	*although*	*because*	*as long as*

5 Complete sentences 1–6 with appropriate subordinating conjunctions from exercise 4 (for most sentences more than one conjunction is possible).

1 _____ the government does more to alleviate poverty, civil unrest is likely to continue.

2 Many people chose to study subjects such as medicine and law _____ they are not really interested in the subject.

3 Young girls often start wearing make-up _____ they feel pressurized to look like the models they see in the media and online.

4 _____ some employees are motivated by pay, others are more concerned about recognition and respect.

5 Retirees can look forward to a comfortable retirement _____ they have a good pension and savings.

6 _____ nearly everyone has a mobile phone, people can be reached anywhere, day or night.

Relative clauses

You can combine two simple sentences which give information about the same noun by replacing one reference to the noun with a relative pronoun (e.g. *who, that*) or adverb (e.g. *where, when*).

6 Read the sentences a–c and answer questions 1–4.

a The graph shows that there was accelerating population growth in some regions. In those regions, the government had invested in infrastructure and jobs.

b   The graph shows that there was accelerating population growth in regions where the government had invested in infrastructure and jobs.

c   The graph shows that there was accelerating population growth in the southern coastal regions, where the government had invested in infrastructure and jobs.

1   Which noun is repeated in the two sentences in sentence a?
2   What word in sentence b replaces the repeated noun?
3   What additional information is given in sentence 3 and how does this change the punctuation?
4   What are the other relative pronouns and adverbs and what type of word do they replace?

7   Combine the sentence pairs below using the correct relative pronoun or adverb and making any other necessary changes.

1   The chart shows there was a significant difference between the male respondents, who preferred full-time courses, and female respondents. Female respondents expressed a preference for part-time study.
2   Electric vehicle sales rose significantly unlike conventional car sales. Conventional car sales increased only slightly.
3   Young children benefit a great deal from playing in the countryside. In this setting, they can learn about wildlife and develop an appreciation for nature.
4   According to the chart, the youngest athletes ran the fastest times in the trial races. Most of the youngest athletes were between 16 and 18.
5   Some countries plan to be carbon neutral by 2040. They have to work hard to achieve this target.

The passive voice
Passive sentence structures can also be used for emphasis.

8   Read sentences a and b and answer questions 1–4.

a   People built high-density housing on contaminated land.
b   High-density housing was built on contaminated land.

1   Which sentence is in the passive voice?
2   How is the passive voice formed?
3   Why is the word *people* omitted from the passive sentence?
4   Which sentence conveys the important information more effectively?

9   Rewrite sentences 1–5 using the passive voice and making any other changes necessary.

1   People often break their promises.
2   Countries should ban the production of single-use plastic items.
3   It is possible to teach children to read before they start school.
4   They have cut down ancient forests and planted cash crops instead.
5   The government encouraged people to move out of crowded cities and into the countryside.

 **Exam tip**
Overuse of the passive voice can result in writing that is difficult to understand. As a general rule, only use the passive voice when the subject of the sentence in the active form is unknown or not the focus of the sentence.

Part 3: Improving grammatical range

10 The table below gives information about beach quality around Seal Island. Redraft the response summarizing data from the table. Use the suggestions in the boxes to improve grammatical range.

SEAL ISLAND BEACH QUALITY

	North	East	South	West
Bathing water	excellent	good	poor	sufficient
Litter removal	excellent	good	sufficient	poor
Lifeguard provision	sufficient	sufficient	poor	good
Safety notices	good	poor	poor	good
Changing facilities	excellent	sufficient	good	sufficient

> **rewrite the sentence using the passive voice**

> **combine the last two sentences in the paragraph using a subordinating conjunction**

The table displays data in relation to beaches around Seal Island. People rated beaches in the north, east, south and west against five criteria relating to cleanliness, safety, and the provision of facilities. There were significant differences among the four areas.

Beaches in the north were most highly rated overall. Beaches in the north received excellent scores in three categories. Beaches in this area were particularly strong in terms of water quality, absence of litter and facilities for changing.
They did not score well in the lifeguard category. Their provision in this area was still regarded as sufficient.

Beaches in the east and west of the island had similar overall ratings but had different strengths and weaknesses. Eastern beaches scored well in terms of cleanliness but poorly in terms of safety. Western beaches had good safety provision but were not very clean.

The beaches with the lowest ratings were those in the south. The poor ratings in safety related categories – water quality, the presence of lifeguards and signage – is the most worrying thing about these beaches.

The beaches on Seal Island all have some room for improvement. However, the beaches in the south require urgent attention.

> **turn the second sentence in this paragraph into a relative clause and embed it within the first sentence**

> **combine the last two sentences in the paragraph using a subordinating conjunction**

9 Grammatical accuracy

Aims | Understanding grammatical accuracy; Focusing on grammatical accuracy (articles, subject-verb agreement, tense and aspect, complex sentences and punctuation, relative clauses); **Improving grammatical accuracy**

Part 1: Understanding grammatical accuracy

1 Read the band descriptors 5–7 and decide if statements 1–3 are TRUE or FALSE.

Band descriptors

Band 7: uses a variety of complex structures; produces frequent error-free sentences; has good control of grammar and punctuation but may make a few errors

Band 6: uses a mix of simple and complex sentence forms; makes some errors in grammar and punctuation but they rarely reduce communication

Band 5: uses only a limited range of structures; attempts complex sentences but these tend to be less accurate than simple sentences; may make frequent grammatical errors and punctuation may be faulty; errors can cause some difficulty for the reader

1 The most important thing is to make as few grammatical errors as possible, so the best strategy is to keep your writing simple. TRUE / FALSE
2 To achieve a score of 7 in the grammar descriptor, you must not make any grammatical errors. TRUE / FALSE
3 All errors of a particular type will be regarded in the same way regardless of whether they result in confusion or not. TRUE / FALSE

Part 2: Focusing on grammatical accuracy

 Exam tip

Take care when writing simple as well as complex sentences. Many of the most common errors include problems with articles (*a, an, the*), subject-verb agreement and tenses.

Articles

The rules of article use are detailed and complex. When preparing for the IELTS test begin by focusing on the most frequent mistakes.

2 Read the information about articles and then find the errors in sentences 1 and 2.

1 There is an evidence that children who play outdoors are healthier than those who do not.
2 Generally speaking, the politicians should work on behalf of the people they represent.

3 Complete sentences 1–4 with *a, an, the* or ø (indicating no article is required).

1 _____ table shows _____ number of people who enrolled on five different types of courses that were taught in three different ways.

2 _____ two youngest age groups (aged 3–4 and 5–6) both ranked cartoons as their favourite and drama as their least favourite.

3 _____ rising living standards in many countries around _____ world have been accompanied by an increase in health problems associated with more affluent lifestyles.

4 There is no simple or easy way to address _____ problem of _____ unhealthy lifestyle choices and their consequences.

Subject-verb agreement

Another common error to look out for is lack of subject-verb agreement. The basic rule is simple: the subject of a sentence must agree in number with the verb, e.g. *The pie chart shows* … (singular noun + singular verb form); *The pie charts show* (plural noun + plural verb form).

4 Why do you think the writers of sentences 1–4 made the errors in bold?

1 International cooperation, even among countries with different priorities, ~~are~~ is √ essential.
2 People who live in overcrowded accommodation ~~is~~ are √ often disadvantaged.
3 Most of the respondents were employed, and most of the money ~~were~~ was √ spent.
4 Six per cent of the items were never returned, and six per cent of the food ~~were~~ was √ wasted.

Tense and aspect

A third type of error you should avoid is incorrect choice of tense and/or aspect. English has two tenses: present and past, each of which can be divided into four subcategories referred to as aspects (simple, continuous, perfect and perfect continuous). Whereas tense refers to time, aspect conveys additional information about an action or state; for example, whether it is ongoing or completed.

Future time is expressed most commonly in IELTS writing using the auxiliary verb *will* to make predictions, e.g. *Investing in clean energy will benefit future generations*.

> **ⓘ Exam information: Using the correct tenses in Task 1 responses**
>
> An IELTS Task 1 response may require you to use more than one tense. Use the present simple tense when the subject of the sentence is the visual prompt (*The diagram shows* …). If specific times are shown in the data, use the relevant tense (*Between 2015 and 2020, respondents preferred* …)

5 Write the verbs in sentences 1–4 in the correct tense.

1 Unless governments set ambitious targets and invest the necessary funds, the goal **is** not **going to be** met. _____

2 The international community should take further action on climate change because individual countries **had** not **been** _____ able to address the problem so far.

3 The graph **is showing** _____ enrolment trends for different academic subjects over a ten-year period.

4 People who **are speaking** _____ several languages often have an advantage over people who are monolingual.

ⓘ Exam information: Using the correct tenses in Task 2 responses

For IELTS Task 2 essays, it is common to use the present tense (simple, continuous and perfect aspects) and future *will*, because you are usually required to discuss current concerns or abstract issues.

Complex sentences and punctuation

To achieve a good score in IELTS it is important to attempt complex sentences. To achieve good accuracy, make sure you understand the grammar of complex sentences and how they are punctuated.

6 Read the two complex sentences 1 and 2 and explain the rule for the use of the comma in sentence 1.

1 Unless the government does more to alleviate poverty, civil unrest is likely to continue.
2 Civil unrest is likely to continue unless the government does more to alleviate poverty.

7 Match five additional rules for the use of commas 1–5 to the examples a–e.

1 Relative clauses that provide extra information should be separated by commas.

2 Defining relative clauses should not be separated by commas.

3 If a sentence begins with an introductory word or phrase, it should be followed by a comma.

4 If you use a coordinating conjunction (*and, or, but, so*) to join long independent clauses, you should place a comma before the conjunction.

5 If you use a conjunctive adverb (*nevertheless, furthermore*) to join independent clauses, you should use a full stop or semicolon between the clauses and a comma after the adverb.

a In many regions around the world, new agricultural techniques are being developed to improve efficiency.

b New techniques can have many benefits. However, there can also be unforeseen consequences.

c New techniques can have many benefits, but there can also be unforeseen consequences.

d International agencies that promote world peace are commendable.

e The United Nations, which promotes world peace, is commendable.

Part 3: Improving grammatical accuracy

8   Correct the errors in the student's essay written in response to the question:

> *Travelling to exotic natural environments has become increasingly popular in recent years. Should ecotourism be encouraged?*

Look for one error in article use and one error in punctuation

Increased awareness of the environmental issues has led some people to look for opportunities to travel to places, where they can engage with nature. This is understandable, particularly when it involves conservation work. However, ecotourism may have undesirable consequences.

Look for errors in article use, subject-verb agreement, tense, relative clause formation and punctuation

Many of most exotic natural landscapes can be found in parts of the world where there have been little development. People who lived in these places, they may be relatively poor. They might welcome tourists who bring income, however, the difference in wealth between the local people and visitors could make it difficult for locals to defend their interests.

Look for errors in punctuation, relative pronoun use and subject-verb agreement

The issue of power can be a particular problem, when tourism is controlled by large companies who are not local. Tourism require infrastructure: hotels, transport and other facilities. To attract visitors, developers may build these in the most desirable locations. Local people may be cut off from their own environment, even forced to leave their homes.

Look for errors in conjunctions, punctuation and article use

Natural environments can be fragile, and may be damaged by visitors who do not understand how to behave with unfamiliar plants and animals. A wildlife may be harmed if it is handled or fed unsuitable food. Too much interaction with wild animals may cause them to change their behaviour. So they could become domesticated. Visitors could also damage the environment by taking things they have found and keeping them as mementos, pieces of coral, for example.

Look for an error in punctuation

For all of these reasons, we should discourage mass ecotourism. There are many ways that people can interact with natural environments closer to home. There is no need to travel. If people wish to know more about exotic locations they can learn about them through books and films.

10 Review

Aims | Reviewing the assessment criteria (fairness in marking); **Reviewing key components of assessment** (task achievement, coherence, cohesion and lexical range, task response, cohesion and grammatical range, lexical accuracy, grammatical range); **Exam practice**

Part 1: Reviewing the assessment criteria

1   Assess your understanding of IELTS Writing assessment criteria. Read sentences 1–8 and decide if they are TRUE or FALSE.

1   The Task achievement / Task response criteria are the most important. TRUE / FALSE
2   Include whatever you like in your Task 1 and 2 responses as long as you make some reference to the question. TRUE / FALSE
3   To achieve good coherence, state your main point before giving more detailed information. TRUE / FALSE
4   The more cohesive devices you use, the higher your score will be. TRUE / FALSE
5   You should use formal or semi-formal vocabulary in IELTS writing. TRUE / FALSE
6   Show that you have a broad vocabulary, but avoid using words that are very uncommon. TRUE / FALSE
7   Grammatical range is just as important as grammatical accuracy. TRUE / FALSE
8   You are only allowed a specific number of grammatical mistakes for each band. TRUE / FALSE

ⓘ Exam information: fairness in marking

All IELTS writing examiners are carefully trained and monitored to ensure consistent and fair marking. Test takers can apply to have their test re-marked by a senior examiner if they feel the mark allocated does not match their performance.

Part 2: Reviewing key components of assessment

Task achievement (Task 1)

2   Redraft the introduction for the Task 1 question below so that it gives a better overview of the trend and uses fewer words from the rubric.

> **Task 1**
>
> The chart shows the results of a 2015 survey of respondents' preferred means of accessing news by age group. Summarize the information by selecting and reporting the main features, and make comparisons where relevant.

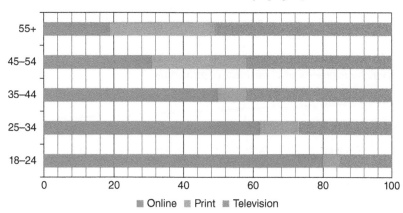

Preferred source of news by age group

■ Online ■ Print ■ Television

Coherence

The second IELTS writing descriptor relates to the logical sequencing and linking of information.

3 To complete the first body paragraph following on from the introduction in exercise 2, select three of the sentences a–j. The first 'topic' sentence is given in italics.

The most striking finding is that people under 35 years old have a preference for online news sources.

a   The percentage of those who chose television news tended to decline by age.
b   The oldest group was over five times more likely to access news via print media.
c   Fewer than 20 per cent of the oldest respondents preferred online news.
d   Eighty per cent of 18- to 24-year-olds preferred online news.
e   The next most obvious feature is the difference between the older and younger groups in how they rated print news.
f   Just over 40 per cent of respondents in these age categories preferred television news.
g   Over 60 per cent of 25- to 34-year-olds preferred online news.
h   Preference for television news shows a similar pattern.
i   Only 5 per cent of the youngest participants preferred news in this format.
j   The exception to this was the two groups 35–44 and 45–54.

4 Group the remaining seven sentences into two further body paragraphs. In each paragraph, sequence the sentences following the general-to-specific rule.

Cohesion and lexical range

5 Read the whole text in exercise 3. Add cohesive devices to the text and replace repeated expressions with appropriate alternatives.

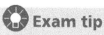 **Exam tip**

In the IELTS writing test, demonstrate good cohesion by linking ideas and information and good lexical range by using a range of cohesive devices and varying your language to avoid repetition.

Task response (Task 2)

6 Read the Task 2 question and the introduction. Answer questions 1 and 2.

> *Many sports clubs have become big businesses. To what extent do sports clubs serve the interests of their local communities?*

Introduction

The advent of televised sport and sponsorship deals with famous sporting figures has changed the role that sport plays in people's lives. It is not surprising that many sporting organizations have become increasingly businesslike in how they operate.

1 What key element is missing from the introduction?

2 Which of the two sentences below would you choose to complete the introduction?

    a Nevertheless, many sporting clubs continue to serve the wider interests of the ordinary people who support their local teams.

    b As money brings opportunities for corruption, tighter regulation of sporting organizations is needed.

Cohesion and grammatical range

7 The first body paragraph lacks cohesive devices and complex sentences. Improve the paragraph by following the suggestions (sentences are numbered for convenience).

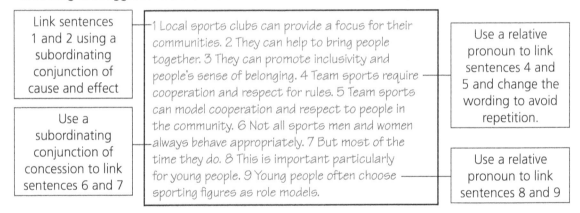

Link sentences 1 and 2 using a subordinating conjunction of cause and effect

Use a subordinating conjunction of concession to link sentences 6 and 7

1 Local sports clubs can provide a focus for their communities. 2 They can help to bring people together. 3 They can promote inclusivity and people's sense of belonging. 4 Team sports require cooperation and respect for rules. 5 Team sports can model cooperation and respect to people in the community. 6 Not all sports men and women always behave appropriately. 7 But most of the time they do. 8 This is important particularly for young people. 9 Young people often choose sporting figures as role models.

Use a relative pronoun to link sentences 4 and 5 and change the wording to avoid repetition.

Use a relative pronoun to link sentences 8 and 9

Lexical accuracy

8 Correct the errors in word class, spelling and dependent prepositions in the second body paragraph.

> Another way local sports clubs contribute to their communities is by providing training facilities and oppertunities to aspiring sports women and men. Sports programes encourage young people to maintain healthy and activity lifestyles and can help to divert them out of anti-society behaviour. Partisipants can learn not only sporting skills but also skills such as refereeing and coaching.

🔅 Exam tip

Develop an awareness of the type of errors you tend to make. During the exam, manage your time so that you have a few minutes at the end to check for errors.

Part 3: Exam practice

9 Complete Writing Task 1.

Now practise writing a complete test paper under timed conditions.

WRITING TASK 1

You should spend about 20 minutes on this task.

> *The chart below shows the breakdown of respondents' social media activity by income group.*
>
> *Summarize the information by selecting and reporting the main features, and make comparisons where relevant.*

Write at least 150 words.

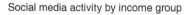
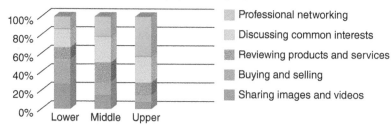

Social media activity by income group

- Professional networking
- Discussing common interests
- Reviewing products and services
- Buying and selling
- Sharing images and videos

100% 80% 60% 40% 20% 0%   Lower   Middle   Upper

10 Complete Writing Task 2

WRITING TASK 2

You should spend about 40 minutes on this task.

Write about the following topic:

> *Online platforms that enable consumers to share reviews of products and services have become increasingly popular.*
>
> *To what extent do these platforms serve the best interests of the people who use them?*

Give reasons for your answer and include any relevant examples from your own knowledge

or experience.

Write at least 250 words.

1 Speaking assessment criteria

Aims | Understanding the Speaking test format and assessment criteria; Evaluating and improving sample responses to Part 1, 2 and 3 questions; Practising speaking (Parts 1, 2 and 3)

Part 1: Understanding Speaking test format and assessment criteria

The test format

Having a clear understanding of what to expect in the Speaking test will help you prepare for the test and perform as effectively as you can on the day.

 Exam information: Speaking test format

The speaking test is 11–14 minutes long and consists of a three-part face-to-face oral interview with an examiner. The interview is recorded.

Part 1: introductions and general questions (4–5 mins)

Part 2: individual long turn (3–4 mins)

Part 3: two-way discussion (4–5 mins)

1 Match Parts 1–3 of the exam in the Exam information box to the task descriptions a–c.

   a This part of the test focuses on the ability to express and justify opinions and to analyse, discuss and speculate about issues. _____

   b This part of the test focuses on the ability to communicate opinions and information on everyday topics and common experiences or situations by answering a range of questions. _____

   c This part of the test focuses on the ability to speak at length on a given topic (without further prompts from the examiner), using appropriate language and organizing ideas coherently. _____

The assessment criteria

A good understanding of the assessment criteria will help you evaluate your current speaking skills and identify the skills you need to focus on to improve.

2 Complete the key indicators 1–4 with a relevant word or phrase from the box a–f.

a lexical resource   **b** fluency   **c** grammatical range

d coherence   **e** pronunciation   **f** grammatical accuracy

   1 The key indicators of _____ are speech rate and speech continuity. The key indicators of _____ are logical sequencing of sentences, clear marking of stages in a discussion, narration or argument, and the use of cohesive devices (e.g. connectors, pronouns and conjunctions) within and between sentences.

2 The key indicators of _____ are the variety of words used, the adequacy and appropriacy of the words used and the ability to circumlocute (get round a vocabulary gap by using other words) with or without noticeable hesitation.

3 The key indicators of _____ are the length and complexity of the spoken sentences, the appropriate use of subordinate clauses and the range of sentence structures, especially to move elements around for information focus. The key indicators of _____ are the number of grammatical errors in a given amount of speech and how these errors affect communication.

4 The key indicators of _____ are the amount of strain caused to the listener, the amount of the speech which is unintelligible and how noticeable the speaker's first language is.

3 **For each question 1–8 below indicate whether the statement is TRUE or FALSE and explain the reason for your answer.**

1 You will be given a few minutes to prepare for each section of the test. TRUE / FALSE

2 For the individual long turn in Part 2 you must speak for at least three minutes. TRUE / FALSE

3 The questions in Part 3 are related to the topic in Part 2. TRUE / FALSE

4 A good way to prepare for Part 2 long turn is to memorize set speeches on common topics. TRUE / FALSE

5 The faster you speak, the higher you will score for fluency and coherence. TRUE / FALSE

6 If you don't know a particular word to answer a question, it is acceptable to use another expression instead, as long as you don't hesitate too much. TRUE / FALSE

7 Your score for grammar will be based on the number of errors you make, so it is a good idea to stick to simple, clear sentences. TRUE / FALSE

8 It is an advantage to be able to use different sentence structures to emphasize key points. TRUE / FALSE

Part 2: Evaluating and improving sample responses

Speaking Test Part 1: Introductions and general questions

4 Listen to the speaker practising Part 1 of the Speaking test with his teacher and answer questions 1–3.
🔊 Listen a second time to check your answers.
28

1 What are the two questions asked?

2 Why does the teacher interrupt the speaker's response to the first question?

3 What strategy does the speaker use when he cannot remember the word to describe the aspect of fitness he would like to improve?

5 Listen a third time and answer questions 1 and 2.

1 Circle the linking words the speaker uses when describing his experience of fishing and improving his fitness.

| so | but | or | also | and | nor |

2 In this section, the speaker makes three grammatical errors. Listen and identify two errors in verb form and one error with articles.

6 Read the Part 2 prompt below and the student's notes. Listen to the speaker practise his response
🔊 and answer questions 1–3.
29

Candidate Task Card

Describe a person who has helped you at an important time in your life.

You should say:

- who it is – *my Uncle Jae; I'm his nephew & best friends with his son*
- what that person is like – *kind, sincere, hard-working teacher*
- what the circumstances were at the time – *year before my college entrance exam*
- how that person helped you – *encouraged me & helped me study*
- what happened as a result – *better exam results*

and explain why this person is important to you. – *changed the course of my life*

You will have to talk about the topic for 1–2 minutes.

You have one minute to think about what you're going to say.

You can make some notes to help you if you wish.

1 Has the speaker covered all of the points in the task?
2 What has the speaker done well?
3 What aspects of his response could be improved?

7 Now listen to the teacher's feedback to check your answers to exercise 6. What suggestions does the
🔊 teacher make to improve:
30

1 task achievement, fluency and coherence?
2 lexical resource?
3 grammatical range and accuracy?
4 pronunciation?

ℹ️ Exam information: Part 3 questions

For Part 3 of the Speaking test, the examiner will ask you 4–6 further questions on the topic from Part 2 and give you the opportunity to discuss more abstract issues or ideas.

8 Tick the questions 1–5 that the examiner may ask following the
Part 2 task in exercise 6.

1 Do you think it is possible to help someone too much?
2 How do you decide when it is appropriate to help someone who appears to be in need?
3 How did your cousin Chul feel about your uncle helping you?
4 Why do you think people find it difficult to ask for help?
5 Do you think young people today are more or less likely to ask for help than people in previous generations?

💡 Exam tip

Part 3 of the Speaking test is expected to last 4–5 minutes, so you may need to speak for up to one minute in response to each question. It is helpful to have a structure in mind to produce an extended response.

9 Read the response below to the question: *Do you think it is possible to help someone too much?* The response has been divided into sections a–c. Match the extracts from the speaker's response 1–3 to the relevant section a–c.

> **a** an example **b** statement of opinion **c** reasons for the opinion

1 *"I believe that sometimes you can help someone too much. Assistance is not helpful in every circumstance."*

2 *"Some people have a tendency to become too dependent on others. Maybe because they don't have confidence in themselves, or they don't want to make the effort to learn new skills. Maybe they're just looking for attention."*

3 *"My little sister, who is five years younger than me, used to ask me to do things for her all of the time – tie her shoelaces or comb her hair. After a while, I realized that she was capable of doing these things herself. She was asking me to help because that was the only way she could get my attention. When I realized that, I decided to spend more time talking to her rather than giving her help that she didn't really need."*

Part 3: Practising speaking (Parts 1, 2 and 3)

10 Record yourself giving short answers to the two Part 1 questions in exercise 4:

> • How did you spend your free time when you were a child?
> • If you could improve your health or fitness in one way, what would that be?

Listen to your recording and evaluate your answers against the four assessment criteria. Identify any improvements you could make. Try the task again.

11 Practise giving a Part 2 long turn answer.

- Look again at the Part 2 long turn prompt on page 122.
- Prepare notes.
- Record yourself speaking for at least one minute.
- Listen to your recording and evaluate it against the four criteria.
- Repeat the task.

12 Practise answering the Part 3 question:

> Do you think it is possible to help someone too much?

Record yourself, listen, evaluate and repeat.

2 Fluency

Aims | Understanding how fluency is assessed; **Focusing on fluency** (predicting topics and questions, mind mapping, expanding your response, using set phrases and structures); **Improving fluency** (Part 1 questions)

Part 1: Understanding how fluency is assessed

ℹ️ Exam information: Speaking test band descriptors

IELTS examiners use a nine-band scale to assess the test taker's level in the Speaking exam. Each level of performance is defined in detail for each of the four assessment criteria. This unit focuses on the **fluency** aspect of the first descriptor.

1   Read the extracts from band descriptors for fluency and coherence listed below. For each question 1–3 indicate whether the statement is TRUE or FALSE and give reasons for your answer.

> **Band descriptors**
>
> **Band 7:** The test taker speaks at length without noticeable effort or loss of coherence; may demonstrate language-related hesitation at times, or some repetition and/or self-correction.
>
> **Band 6:** The test taker is willing to speak at length, though may lose coherence at times due to occasional repetition, self-correction or hesitation.
>
> **Band 5:** The test taker usually maintains flow of speech but uses repetition, self-correction and/or slow speech to keep going; produces simple speech fluently, but more complex communication causes fluency problems.

1   To score a band 7, it is essential to speak at length without making any errors. TRUE / FALSE
2   It is acceptable to hesitate occasionally in order to think about what to say, but you could be marked down for fluency if you stop speaking to recall grammar or vocabulary. TRUE / FALSE
3   It is generally acceptable to give short answers as long as your speech is clear and rapid. TRUE / FALSE

2   Listen to the sample response from Part 1 of the test. Which of the three band descriptors for
🔊 31   fluency – 5, 6 or 7 – best describes the response?

Part 2: Focusing on fluency

There is no exam technique that can guarantee a fluent performance as fluency is the product of many hours of practice and preparation. To be effective, your preparation should focus on both **content** and **language** – what you will say as well as how you will say it.

💡 Exam tip

Thinking ahead of time about topics and questions that might arise in the exam can help you identify more quickly what you will say and therefore allow you to focus more on how you will say it.

Predicting topics and questions

3   The questions below are typical of the kind of questions that appear in Part 1 of the Speaking exam. Group the questions a–p into four topics.

Topic 1 _____   Topic 2 _____   Topic 3 _____   Topic 4 _____

a   What is the benefit of having hobbies?
b   What was your favourite teacher like?
c   What is a common snack food in your country?
d   What do you like most about where you live?

e What sort of restaurants are popular in your country?

f What do you remember about the house you grew up in?

g What was your least favourite subject at school?

h Can you describe your primary school for me?

i Is there anything you would want to change about the place you live?

j What can you remember about your first day at school?

k How have people's hobbies in your country changed over time?

l Do young people in your country have a healthy diet?

m What sort of hobbies did you have when you were a child?

n What is your favourite dish?

o What is your neighborhood like?

p What do you do in your leisure time?

 Exam information: common themes for IELTS Speaking

It is not possible to predict specifically what questions you will be asked in your exam. However, all of the questions will have some connection to you – your life experiences, your country, your thoughts, feelings and beliefs about a variety of topics.

Mind mapping

Mind mapping is a form of notetaking that can be used to organize your thoughts and record relevant vocabulary. It allows you to fit a lot of content onto one page and show how elements are connected.

4 The example below is based on the theme of school. Complete the mind map by adding the points in the box to the relevant categories on the mind map.

> janitor – always helpful, e.g. for lost & found   visual arts – enjoyable, esp. painting
> gym – too small   library – peaceful   chemistry – tiresome
> playing fields – dusty   head teacher – distant & strict

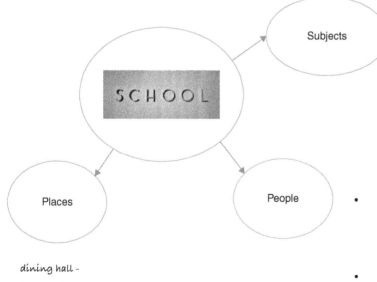

Expanding your response

Notice some of the elements in the mind map have been developed with additional information. For example, the information about the student's favourite teacher follows the pattern introduced in Unit 1:

OPINION (favourite) **+ REASONS** (creative, fun) **+ EXAMPLES** (classroom cinema, games)

Adding more detail to your mind map in this way can help you to plan for more extended responses.

5 A more complex pattern is given below. Fill the gaps using information about languages from the mind map.

OPINION (_____) **+ REASON** (_____) **+**

EXAMPLES (_____) **+ COUNTER OPINION** (_____) **+**

REASON/EXAMPLE (_____)

6 Create a mind map about the area in which you live using the questions below to help you structure the content.

1   What are the key facts, e.g. location, size of population?
2   What are the most important landmarks or places to visit?
3   What are the main industries?
4   What key events and/or historical figures are associated with the area?

7 Create a mind map on the subject of food using the questions in exercise 3 to develop sub-headings. Note 2–3 additional sub-headings, e.g. your favourite dish, and make connections between elements that are meaningful to you.

Exam tip

Including information about what you think and feel in your mind maps will prepare you for the more abstract questions in Part 3, e.g. *Do teachers need to be strict to be effective?* The student in our example would be prepared to respond as he has already reflected on his experience as a learner.

Using set phrases and structures

Exam tip

Using techniques such as mind mapping will help you develop both content and vocabulary for the Speaking test. Learning common set phrases and sentence frames, which you can adapt for a variety of contexts, will help you produce extended responses more fluently.

8 Listen to the Part 1 question and response and complete the gaps in the transcript below. Then listen a second time and underline the opinion + reason(s) + example(s).
🔊 32

Examiner: *Who was your favourite teacher?*

Test taker: *The teacher _____ was my history teacher in secondary school, Miss Yao. She was very creative, and her lessons were fun. At the end of term she used to make the classroom into a cinema so we could watch a film. We could bring snacks to eat, like in a real cinema.*
   _____ her was the way she used games to make lessons more enjoyable.

These phrases can be adapted for responses to any question related to a favourite person, place or thing. Using these phrases would allow you to demonstrate lexical resource because you avoid repeating the word *favourite* in the question, and to demonstrate grammatical range because you use the reduced relative clauses *(that) I liked the most* and *(that) I liked about*.

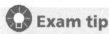 **Exam tip**

To develop fluency, practise set phrases and sentence frames with different content, adapting them as required. For example, to answer the question *What is your favourite dish?* you will need to say *The dish that I **like** the most **is** ...* because the question is in the present tense.

9 Respond to each question below using the phrases *The ... that I like the most is ...* and *Another thing that I like about ... is ...* making all necessary changes.

1 Tell me about your favourite restaurant?
2 What were your favourite television programmes when you were a child?
3 Who is your favourite writer?
4 What are your favourite films?
5 What was your least favourite subject at school?

Part 3: Improving fluency (Part 1)

10 Listen to the Part 1 questions on the recording. Pause the recording after each question and record your answer. Listen and identify elements to improve and/or expand on. Practise responding to the questions two further times to develop confidence and fluency.

3 Coherence

Aims | Understanding how coherence is assessed; Focusing on coherence (sequencing information logically, signposting extended responses, using cohesive devices appropriately); **Improving coherence** (Part 2)

Part 1: Understanding how coherence is assessed

Coherence is paired with fluency in the first of the assessment criteria.

1   Complete the gaps 1–3 in the coherence descriptor below with examples a–c.

> a *Next, it's important to consider ...*   b *while, she, and*   c chronological order

The key indicators of coherence are logical sequencing of sentences, e.g. **1** _____, clear marking of stages in a discussion, narration or argument, e.g. **2** _____, and the use of cohesive devices, e.g. **3** _____ within and between sentences.

ⓘ Exam information: coherence in the IELTS Speaking test

Coherence is assessed in all parts of the Speaking test; however, it is particularly important to maintain coherence in Parts 2 and 3 of the test, when you are required to speak at length.

2   Read the Part 2 long turn prompt below and listen to the first part of the speaker's response. Then
🔊 34   answer questions 1–3.

> Describe a problem experienced by young adults in your country.
> You should say:
>   - the cause of the problem
>   - what effect it has on young adults and others
>   - what could be done to address the problem.
> Explain why you think this issue is important.

1   The speaker begins this section by naming the problem and ends by giving a brief summary. What does the speaker do in the middle part of the extract?
2   What phrase has the speaker used to introduce the problem?
3   The speaker uses six words and expressions to link ideas and information within and between sentences, for example *if* or *and if* to introduce conditions. Which words or expressions:

a   introduce an example _____   c   introduce a reason _____

b   introduce a contrast _____   d   refer back to the problem? _____

Part 2: Focusing on coherence

Logical sequencing of information

In Units 1 and 2, you have seen examples of two common patterns for sequencing information:
OPINION + REASON + EXAMPLE
OPINION + REASON + EXAMPLE + COUNTER OPINION + REASON/EXAMPLE
These patterns are useful for presenting arguments.

 Exam information: rhetorical functions in the IELTS Speaking test

In the Speaking exam, you may also be required to: describe a person, place or thing; narrate a sequence of events; explain causes and effects; discuss problems and solutions. These *rhetorical functions* should also be approached in a logical way.

3 In exercise 2, the speaker is talking about cause and effect. After describing the problem and its causes, she explains how the lack of graduate jobs affects young people. The speaker's explanation includes sentences 1–7 below. Reorder the sentences so that they form a logical sequence. Then listen to the recording to check your answers.

1   But even after post-graduate studies, there is still no job for them in the end.
2   So they go back home and live with their parents.
3   That means parents have to continue working hard in low-paid jobs to support their adult children at home.
4   The effects of this problem are complex.
5   They keep working and encouraging their children to apply for good professional positions, because they don't want their university-educated children to do the kind of low-paid work they have always done.
6   When middle-ranking university students graduate, they can't find a graduate-level job, but they don't want to take low-paid work either.
7   If their children still cannot find a good graduate-level job, families may go into debt to pay for their children to do further studies.

4 Read the audioscript extracts below from the Unit 2 Exam Practice model answer. Identify which extract follows a *chronological* pattern and which follows a *large-to-small description* pattern. Use key words to illustrate the sequence.

1   *"I went to a large primary school, with about, let me think, maybe three or four hundred pupils. There were about 25 or 30 girls in my class. The building was new, modern. I remember we had a beautiful library and that the classrooms were very bright. We each had a box with our names on to put our things in, like our pencils and crayons."*

2   *"I don't remember very much, to be honest. I know I walked there with my mother and my big sister. There were crowds of children and their parents in front of the school. I was very excited, but also nervous and a little shy. Then we went in and I met my teacher. She was tall and slim, with a long nose. I didn't like her at first. I don't think I spoke at all that day, except to say my name."*

Signposting stages in an account, discussion or argument

Speaking coherently also involves giving information about how you are organizing your response and marking or *signposting* the different parts.

5 Listen to the third part of the long turn about problems faced by young adults and answer questions 1–3.

1 What is the main focus or *rhetorical function* of this section?
2 How is this section organized?
3 What signposting expressions does the speaker use?

6 Different rhetorical functions use some of the same signposting expressions, e.g. firstly. Others are more likely to use specific expressions. Place the signposting expressions 1–15 in the appropriate column in the table.

Describing a person, place or thing	Narrating	Explaining cause and effect	Describing problems and solutions	Expressing an opinion	Making a prediction

1 The best approach to solving …
2 From the outside …
3 In the middle …
4 In my opinion …
5 At first …
6 There are several factors that could lead to …
7 After that …
8 It's likely that … will …

9 The main reason … occurs is that …
10 There are a couple of reason I disagree with …
11 In the end …
12 In my view …
13 There are two way of dealing with …
14 It's inevitable that …
15 One of the consequences of …

Using cohesive devices

7 Good speakers also use cohesive devices to make the relationship between points clear to the listener. Two types of cohesive device are listed below along with examples. Place the further examples in the box into the correct category.

because   if   who   when   so   although   and
unless   as soon as

1 Use **coordinating conjunctions** to connect two or more equally weighted grammatical elements:
words (You can have *fruit **or** ice-cream*)
phrases (You can study *at home **or** in the library*)
or clauses (*I went to university, **but** my brother stayed at home.*)

Other coordinating conjunctions: _____

2 Use **subordinating conjunctions** to connect a main clause and a subordinate clause:
I've been much happier [main clause] ***since*** my sister joined me [subordinate clause].
Whenever we go out [subordinate clause], we have a great time [main clause].

Other subordinating conjunctions: _____

8 Listen again to the second part of the speaker's long turn and complete the gaps in the audio script with cohesive devices.

> The effects of this problem are complex. **1** _____ middle-ranking university students graduate, they can't find a graduate-level job, **2** _____ they don't want to take low-paid work either, **3** _____ they go back home and live with their parents. That means parents have to continue working hard in low-paid jobs to support their adult children at home. They keep working and encouraging their children to apply for good professional positions, **4** _____ they don't want their university-educated children to do the kind of low-paid work they have always done. **5** _____ their children still cannot find a good graduate-level job, families may go into debt to pay for their children to do further studies. **6** _____ even after post-graduate studies, there is still no job for them in the end.

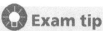 **Exam tip**

Some cohesive devices that are commonly used in writing, such as *therefore, consequently, however, nevertheless* and *moreover*, sound unnatural in speech. When speaking it is generally better to use simpler alternatives, such as *so, but, anyway* and *also*.

9 Another technique for maintaining cohesion in a long response is to use *this/these* + a summary word to refer to the previous sentence or stretch of speech. Listen again to the third part of the speaker's response. The final part of the long turn closes with: *These changes are important to maintain social cohesion and improve people's quality of life.* What does *these changes* refer to?

Part 3: Improving coherence (Part 2)

10 Practise giving a Part 2 long-turn answer.

- Look again at the Part 2 long-turn prompt in exercise 2.
- Give yourself a few minutes to prepare notes about a work-related problem faced by young people in your country.
- Record yourself speaking for at least 90 seconds.
- Listen to your recording and evaluate it against the criteria for coherence: logical sequencing of information, use of signposting expressions and cohesive devices.
- Repeat to practise giving a more coherent response.

4 Lexical resource 1: range

Aims | Understanding lexical resource; **Focusing on lexical range** (register, connotation and collocation); **Improving lexical range** (Part 2 long-turn answer and Part 3 questions)

Part 1: Understanding lexical resource
Lexical resource refers to the accurate and appropriate use of words and phrases.

1 Study the key components of the lexical resource descriptors for bands 5–7 below. Put each component in the correct column.

Band 5	Band 6	Band 7

1 has a wide enough vocabulary to discuss topics at length and make meaning clear in spite of inappropriacies
2 uses some less common and idiomatic vocabulary and shows some awareness of style and collocation, with some inappropriate choices
3 uses vocabulary resource flexibly to discuss a variety of topics
4 manages to talk about familiar and unfamiliar topics but uses vocabulary with limited flexibility
5 generally paraphrases successfully
6 attempts to use paraphrase but with mixed success
7 uses paraphrase effectively

ℹ Exam information: scoring well on lexical resource
For all three bands, you need a wide vocabulary to cover a range of topics and to paraphrase (i.e. refer to test questions in your own words). To score well, you also need an in-depth understanding of how to use each word or phrase accurately and appropriately.

Part 2: Focusing on lexical range

2 To make appropriate word choices, study the definitions of register, connotation and collocation 1–3 below. Then complete the examples with word pairs a–c.

a thrifty; stingy   b make; money   c conversation; chat

1 **Register** refers to language associated with a particular subject and to degrees of formality. For example, words or expressions may be old-fashioned, technical, formal, neutral, informal, slang, etc. For example, _____ is more formal than _____.
2 **Connotation** refers to the feeling or idea suggested by a word or phrase. For example, _____ has a positive connotation, whereas _____ has a negative connotation.
3 **Collocation** refers to the way that some words occur regularly whenever another word is used. For example, the word _____ collocates with _____.

Register

Which register you use depends on the type of question and the topic.

 Exam information: formal and informal language in IELTS speaking

When answering personal questions, for example in Part 1, you will sound more natural if you use neutral and occasionally less formal language. For more abstract or serious topics, for example in Parts 2 and 3, more formal language is often more appropriate.

3 For each exchange below, choose the expressions in italics that are most appropriate for the context. Then listen to check your answers.

🔊 39

1 Examiner: What did you like about your school?

  Test taker: Pupils who had *sufficient funds / pocket money* were allowed to *purchase / buy* cold *drinks / beverages* from the machines in the canteen.

2 Examiner: What do you think encourages young people to try their hardest academically?

  Test taker: Students need to feel that their efforts will be judged fairly. If they are confronted with a really challenging exam when they don't expect it, they can *freak out / panic*. That's what happened to one of *the guys in my class / my classmates*. When he failed, he was *gutted / devastated* and couldn't *carry on / be bothered* studying after that.

> 💡 **Exam tip**
>
> If you are unsure of the register of a word, a good learner's dictionary will indicate whether a word is old-fashioned, formal, informal, or is used only in a specialized context.

4 Identify the problems with register in the two responses below. Replace inappropriate words or expressions with suitable alternatives.

1 Examiner: What sort of practical skill would you most like to acquire?

  Test taker: I'm rubbish at culinary skills, so I'd be really pleased with myself if I could learn to cook. I'd make a nice meal for my mates, nothing too posh, just tasty.

2 Examiner: What makes a good boss?

  Test taker: An effective employer is someone who cares about their employees and takes the time to explain how to do stuff right. Furthermore, your boss should give you a second chance if you do something stupid.

Connotation

To communicate effectively, you should also be aware of the connotation of words and phrases, that is whether they convey a negative or positive message.

 Exam tip

Connotation can often be expressed by tone of voice. Higher tones often indicate positive feelings, lower tones are often used to convey negative feelings.

5 Pair the words with similar meanings but different connotations and place them in the correct column. Then check your answers by listening to the recording of the words used in context.

~~timid~~ unique youthful lazy aggressive nosy ~~reserved~~
strange assertive immature inquisitive easy-going

	positive connotation	negative connotation
1	*reserved*	*timid*
2		
3		
4		
5		
6		

Collocation

ℹ️ Exam information: collocation

To score well for lexical resource, you need to show an awareness of collocation, that is a knowledge of which words typically go together.

6 There are many types of lexical collocations in English, for example adverb + adjective *absolutely necessary*. Match the example collocations a–e with the common type of collocations 1–5.

a make progress
b rich history
c completely understandable
d apologize profusely
e highly recommend

1 Adverb + adjective
2 Adverb + verb
3 Adjective + noun
4 Verb + adverb
5 Verb + noun

🔆 Exam tip

There are thousands of collocations in English. Focus on learning those that relate to language functions commonly found in the Speaking exam, e.g. collocations that express feelings, thoughts and opinions: e.g. *truly believe, quite sure.*

7 Listen to the sentences on the recording and identify the common adjective + noun collocations. Complete the expressions below. The first letter of each adjective and noun in the collocation has been given for you.

1 c_____ k_____
2 h_____ o_____
3 i_____ f_____
4 i_____ a_____

5 m_____ p_____
6 p_____ a_____
7 s_____ p_____
8 v_____ r_____

8 Using the collocations from exercise 7, make sentences of your own expressing your thoughts, feelings and opinions about topics that matter to you. Practise saying them aloud.

Part 3 Improving lexical range (Parts 2 and 3)

9 Prepare for practising a long turn on the topic of a difficult decision. Match the words and expressions 1–6 to their meanings a–f.

1	opt (+ verb)	a	to choose *not* to do or accept something
2	compromise (noun)	b	a difficult choice
3	settle for	c	a middle position between two extremes
4	refuse (verb)	d	to choose to do something in preference to something else
5	decisive	e	to accept something that is less than what you want
6	dilemma	f	able to make quick decisions in difficult circumstances

10 Now practise giving a long turn using the prompt below.

- First, give yourself a few minutes to prepare notes and identify words from exercise 9 that would be appropriate for your response.
- Identify any additional key words you will need. Look them up in a learner's dictionary to check whether the register and connotation are appropriate and whether any useful collocations are given in the example sentences.
- Record yourself speaking for at least 90 seconds.
- Listen to your recording and evaluate your use of vocabulary.

> **Task 2**
> Describe a time when you needed to make an important decision.
> You should say:
> > what the circumstances were
> > what your options were
> > what decision you made
> and explain whether this was the right or wrong decision.

11 Practise answering the four Part 3 questions asked by the examiners in exercises 3 and 4.

- Identify key words you would like to use.
- Look them up in a learner's dictionary to check whether the register and connotation are appropriate.
- Record yourself and listen to identify any improvements you could make.

1 What did you like about your school?
2 What do you think encourages young people to try their hardest academically?
3 What sort of practical skill would you most like to acquire?
4 What makes a good boss?

5 Lexical resource 2: accuracy

Aims | Understanding lexical accuracy; **Focusing on lexical accuracy** (mistranslation, word class, prefixes, countable and uncountable nouns, collocation, dependent prepositions); **Improving lexical accuracy** (Part 1 and Part 3 questions)

Part 1: Understanding lexical accuracy

Look again at the band 5 to 7 descriptors for lexical resource in Unit 4 page 132. Notice that to score better than a band 5 you must have a broad vocabulary and be able to paraphrase successfully – that is, to restate information using different words. To score higher than a band 6, you need to show not only wider range but also greater accuracy and precision in your use of vocabulary.

1   Read the two responses to the question *What leisure activities are popular in your country?* and answer questions 1–4.

   1   Which speaker paraphrases the question most successfully?
   2   Which speaker makes fewer lexical errors?
   3   What type of errors does the first speaker make?
   4   Which speaker has better lexical range?

Speaker 1

"People where I come from spend their free time in different ways. It depends of their age. There is a big different between old and young people. Older people like taking time together for picnics or eating in a restaurant if it's raining. Some teenagers like sports, but most teenagers prefer doing things by their own, like computer games, but parents think that is a very waste of time."

Speaker 2

"The most popular activities for leisure in my country are watching films and TV, also browsing the Internet. Popular outdoor activities would be going to local parks or to the beach to surf or play volleyball. A lot of people enjoy socializing with friends, cooking barbecues in the summer or going out to eat if it's wet."

Part 2: Focusing on lexical accuracy

These exercises focus on some common types of lexical errors. They are designed to help you identify areas that you should continue to develop using paper-based and online learning resources as well as through extensive reading and listening practice.

 **Exam tip**

When you use a bilingual dictionary to find the English translation of a word, check the entry in an English learner's dictionary and study the example sentences along with any additional information about word class, collocations, grammatical patterns and common errors.

Mistranslation

One of the most common sources of error is translating directly from your own language.

2 Identify the lexical errors in sentences 1–6 below. Then check your answers by listening to the speaker saying each sentence with the correct words.

42

1 I will back to my hometown when I finish my studies.
2 We are waiting for the newest travel information before booking our flights.
3 Every time I open the TV, I see so many advertisements.
4 My sister borrowed me her textbooks, so I didn't need to buy new ones.
5 For lunch I usually drink some soup.
6 When my brother went to Australia to study, I decided I wanted to study outside as well, so I came to the UK.

Word class

Another common lexical error is to use the wrong word class. Many root words exist in a variety of forms, eg *difference* (noun), *differ* (verb), *different* (adjective).

3 Listen carefully to each sentence 1–7. When the speaker pauses, circle the word that you think comes next. Listen to the end to check your answer.

43

1	confidence	confident
2	success	succeed
3	choice	choose
4	exciting	excited

5	convenience	convenient
6	life	live
7	benefit	beneficial

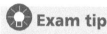 **Exam tip**

Different forms of a word can be difficult to distinguish because they often sound similar. When reading and listening, pay attention the endings of key words and their context of use.

Prefixes

Words which begin with prefixes *un-*, *in-* or *im-* can also cause problems when speaking, for example, **un**important, **in**complete, **im**personal. These prefixes are all used to create a word that has the opposite meaning of the root word.

4 Write the correct prefix un-, in- or im- for each word.

1 _____accurate
2 _____comfortable
3 _____convenient
4 _____direct

5 _____expensive
6 _____interesting
7 _____married
8 _____polite

9 _____practical
10 _____precise
11 _____true
12 _____usable

5 Circle the words in exercise 4 that have a negative connotation. Practise using them to talk about experiences that are or have been difficult for you, for example:

*I missed the deadline because the information given to me was **inaccurate**.*
*I feel **uncomfortable** sitting next to strangers on a bus.*
*Commuting to work is **inconvenient**, but I have no choice.*

Countable and uncountable nouns

Another source of difficulty is recognizing uncountable nouns. Words which are uncountable in English such as *advice* and *money* are often countable in other languages. Some nouns can be countable in some contexts and uncountable in others.

 **Exam tip**

Take care when using uncountable nouns. Uncountable nouns require singular verb forms and quantifiers e.g. *His advice was valuable. I didn't have ~~many~~ much money.*

6 Fill the gaps with the correct form of one of the words from the box and indicate whether it is being used countably (C) or uncountably (U).

> time   work   experience

1 The National Museum contains some wonderful _____ of art.
2 I was told I didn't get the job because I didn't have enough _____.
3 In my final year at school I had so much _____ to do I didn't have _____ for hobbies.
4 Travelling across the desert was such a memorable _____, we've done it several _____ since.

7 Read the audio script below of the speaker's first attempt to respond to the question: *How have leisure activities changed over time?* Underline and correct the five mistakes the speaker makes with nouns and associated modifiers. Then listen to the recording of the speaker using the correct noun forms and modifiers to check your answers.

 44

"Nowadays, in my country people – especially young people – don't have many free time. In the past, they used to be more active than now; they did sports or went out with friends. Nowadays, they prefer to stay indoors, play computer game and surf the Internet, use social medias, things like that. But not everyone has the equipments or softwares for that."

Collocation

Collocations are common word combinations. The speaker in the previous exercise uses several collocations related to computers: *computer games* (noun + noun), *surf the Internet* (verb + noun), *social media* (adjective + noun).

ℹ️ Exam information: collocation in IELTS speaking

Forming good collocations is an advantage in the IELTS Speaking test because it helps to make your language sound natural and idiomatic. These features of language are highlighted in the lexical range descriptors at Band 7 and above.

8 Read the audio script of the speaker practising her response to the question: Tell me about the last time you visited a friend or family member. Tick the phrases in bold that form good collocations. Rewrite the phrases that are faulty.

*"Last time I tried to **make a visit** to my sister, it was a **complete disaster**. I got to the **bus stop**, which is **a far way** from my house, and waited **a long time**. When the bus arrived, I realized I didn't have any money, so I ran to the bank to **take some money**. But there was no money in my account because my mother was supposed to **transport money** to my account the **before day**, but she didn't do that. So I had to call my father to **give me a drive** to my sister's flat. He was not happy about that."*

Dependent propositions

Notice that the final sentence in the sample response above contains the expression *happy about*. This is an example of a phrase which includes a *dependent preposition*. There are many such phrases in both written and spoken registers of English.

9 Sentences 1–8 contain phrases with either an incorrect or an unnecessary preposition. **Make the necessary corrections. Then practise saying each correct sentence aloud.**

Exam tip

Many phrases do not translate easily from one language to another. Try to avoid translating expressions word-for-word from your language into English. Use a dictionary to find equivalent English expressions.

1 I was very interested about art and design.
2 It took me a long time to get a job because I lacked of work experience.
3 I was very shy as a teenager, so I didn't go out from my house very often.
4 My best friend is going to marry with an engineer and move to Germany.
5 Not everyone is aware about the true cost of a university education.
6 Little children are not always capable for understanding the difference between right and wrong.
7 I thanked to my biology teacher for encouraging me to consider a career in science.
8 There's no point for studying something that you don't care about.

Part 3: Improving lexical accuracy (Parts 1 and 3)

10 Spend ten minutes preparing to answer the questions below: think about the key words and expressions you will need in your response. Look them up in a dictionary and study the example sentences, paying particular attention to the aspects of language covered in Part 2.

Speak for the recommended length of time, recording your responses.
- Part 1: *Tell me about the last time you visited a friend or family member.* (20–30 seconds)
- Part 3: *What leisure activities are popular in your country?* (1 minute)
  How have leisure activities changed over time? (1 minute)

11 **Listen to your recording and evaluate your use of vocabulary.**

- Have you paraphrased the question?
- Have you selected appropriate vocabulary?
- Have you used the right word class?
- Have you made appropriate collocations?
- Have you included dependent prepositions where required?
- Have you used countable and uncountable nouns correctly?

12 **Note any errors. Then repeat the exercise.**

6 Grammatical range

Part 1: Understanding how grammatical range is assessed

1 Read the extracts from band descriptors 5–7 for grammatical range and accuracy listed below. Highlight the elements that refer specifically to grammatical range.

Band descriptors

Band 7: The test taker uses a range of complex structures with some flexibility; frequently produces error-free sentences, though some grammatical mistakes persist.

Band 6: The test taker uses a mix of simple and complex structures, but with limited flexibility; may make frequent mistakes with complex structures, though these rarely cause comprehension problems.

Band 5: The test taker produces basic sentence forms with reasonable accuracy; uses a limited range of more complex structures, but these usually contain errors and may cause some comprehension problems.

2 For each question 1–3 indicate whether the statement is TRUE or FALSE and give a reason for your answer.

1 To achieve a score of 7 in the grammar descriptor, all of your sentences must be complex. TRUE / FALSE
2 To score a band 6 for grammar, you should use a lot of complex sentences, even if your exact meaning is unclear. TRUE / FALSE
3 You are likely to score no better than band 5 for grammar if all of your sentences are grammatically correct but simple. TRUE / FALSE

3 Listen to the three speakers responding to two questions about pet ownership. All three responses are grammatically correct, and the content and vocabulary are very similar. Decide which band, 5, 6, or 7+, each speaker would merit for grammatical range.

Part 2: Focusing on grammatical range

Types of sentences

Before doing this section, you may find it useful to revise the material on complex sentences on page 109 of Writing Unit 8.

Exam information: using different sentence types

The ability to use a range of sentence types is one of the most important aspects of grammatical range. A typical IELTS speaking response will contain a mix of simple, compound and complex sentences.

4 Match the type of sentence 1–3 with the explanations a–c and the examples i–iii.

Sentence type	Explanation	Example
1 A simple sentence has …		
2 A compound sentence has …		
3 A complex sentence has …		

Explanations

a   one clause consisting of a subject and a predicate (a verb plus additional words)

b   a main clause and one or more dependent clauses introduced by a subordinating conjunction *as, as if, although, because,* etc.

c   two clauses joined by a coordinating conjunction *and, but, or, nor, yet, so*

Examples

i   *I enjoy scuba diving,* but *it's an expensive hobby.*

ii   *I enjoy scuba diving.*

iii   *I enjoy scuba diving* even though *I'm not very good at it.*

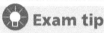 **Exam tip**

Both compound and complex sentences connect information and ideas, but complex sentences have two advantages: the main clause serves to highlight the key point, and a wider range of subordinating conjunctions can be used to express more precise relationships between ideas.

5 The sentences below all relate to the speaker's relationship with a childhood friend. Use the subordinating conjunctions in the box to join each pair of simple sentences. Make sure that you put the key information in the main clause. Then listen to the recording to check your answers.

as	because	even though	when (x2)	whereas (x2)	until

1   I met my best friend Samira. My family moved to a new village.

2   I liked her immediately. She was really fun to play with.

3   We got along well. We were very different.

4   I was a quiet, shy girl. She was outgoing and adventurous.

5   After school, we used to play in an abandoned hut in the outskirts of our village. My mother found us and made us play in our garden instead.

6   We got into trouble again. We made a fire at the bottom of the garden to roast apples.

7   We grew older. Our relationship changed.

8   I became more confident and outgoing. Samira became quieter and more serious.

Tense and aspect

 Exam information: tenses in IELTS Speaking

In the IELTS Speaking test, you will need to speak about present and past experiences. Correct use of the simple present (*I study*) and simple past (*I studied*) is essential for conveying basic meaning. To demonstrate good range, you should also make appropriate use of continuous and perfect aspect.

Revise the information about tense and aspect on page 113 in Writing Unit 9 and study the table below for examples of how these tenses would be used in speech.

Tense/aspect:	Typically used for:	Example:
Present continuous	current ongoing action	*I am studying now.*
Past continuous	action as context for a past event	*I was studying when he called.*
Present perfect	prior experience or action to the present	*I have studied abroad before.*
Present perfect continuous	action continuing to the present	*I have been studying for weeks.*
Past perfect	action completed prior to a point in the past	*I had studied for weeks before the exam last December.*
Past perfect continuous	action continuing to a point in the past	*I had been studying hard right up until the exam.*

 Exam tip

Some of the example sentences give the full forms of the auxiliary verbs *am* and *have*. For a more natural sound you should use the contracted forms, eg **I'm** *(I am)* **I've** *(I have)* **I'd** *(I had)* **she's** *(she is, she has)* **they're** *(they are)* **they've** *(they have).*

6 The speaker goes on to describe her current relationship with her childhood friend. Re-write the verbs in brackets in the correct tense. Listen to the recording to check your answers.
47

I **1** (**live**) _____ here in the UK for the last ten months, so I **2** (**not see**) _____ my friend Samira for a long time. We didn't really have a chance to say goodbye, because when I left for the UK she **3** (**visit**) _____ her brother and his new wife in Tunisia. At the moment, I **4** (**study**) _____ hard to improve my English, and she **5** (**work**) _____ long hours in her uncle's pharmacy. Even though we are both very busy, we try to speak on the phone or text each other every few days. But that's not always possible. When I phoned her last night I **6** (**not speak**) _____ to her for a week because I **7** (**prepare**) _____ for my exam.

7 Practise talking about a childhood friend using questions 1–5 to structure your speech. Pay attention to your use of tense and aspect.

1 How and when did you meet?
2 What were you doing at the time?
3 How has your relationship developed since you met?
4 What are you doing and what is your friend doing now?
5 How often do you see or speak to each other now?

The conditional mood

ⓘ Exam information: conditionals in Part 3 answers

The ability to use the conditional mood is important for Part 3 questions that require you to:
Speculate about future. e.g. *What will you do if the weather is stormy tomorrow?*
Talk about an imagined situation, e.g. *What would you do if you had unlimited funds?*
Imagine the result of an event that didn't happen, e.g. *What would you have done if you had failed?*

The three questions in the Exam information box are examples of the **first, second and third conditional**. Notice that each conditional consists of two clauses joined by the conjunction *if* and that each has a distinctive pattern of verb forms.

8 Underline the verb forms in each of the questions in the Exam information box above and identify the pattern of verb forms. The first one has been done as an example.

First conditional: <u>*will + infinitive*</u> *if* <u>*present tense*</u>
Second conditional: _____ *if* _____
Third conditional: _____ *if* _____

9 Listen to the speaker complete her long turn on the topic of her best friend and identify the conditional forms used.

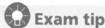 **Exam tip**

These responses demonstrate good accuracy by using the same conditional forms as in the questions. They show good range and flexibility by changing the order of the clauses and paraphrasing e.g. *unlimited funds = all the money in the world.*

Part 3: Improving grammatical range (Parts 1 and 2)

10 Record yourself giving short answers to the two Part 1 questions in exercise 2. Listen to your recording and evaluate your responses for grammatical range. Identify any improvements you could make and re-record your response.

- Have you ever kept a pet?
- Is it common in your country for people to own pets?

11 Practise giving a Part 2 long-turn answer using the prompt below:

Task 2
Describe a close friend
You should say:
   - what that person is like
   - how you met
   - how your relationship has developed
and explain why this person is important to you.

- Spend one minute to think about what you're going to say and make some notes.
- Record yourself speaking for 90 seconds if possible.
- Listen to your recording and evaluate your response for grammatical range.
- Identify any improvements you could make and re-record your response.

7 Grammatical accuracy

Aims | Understanding key components of grammatical accuracy; **Focusing on grammatical accuracy** (tense and aspect, verb patterns, nouns, articles and subject-verb agreement); **Improving grammatical accuracy** (Part 1 and Part 3 questions)

Part 1: Understanding key components of grammatical accuracy

1 Read the extracts from band descriptors 5–7 for grammatical range and accuracy listed below. Highlight the elements that refer specifically to grammatical accuracy.

Band descriptors

Band 7: uses a range of complex structures with some flexibility; frequently produces error-free sentences, though some grammatical mistakes persist.

Band 6: uses a mix of simple and complex structures, but with limited flexibility; may make frequent mistakes with complex structures, though these rarely cause comprehension problems.

Band 5: produces basic sentence forms with reasonable accuracy; uses a limited range of more complex structures, but these usually contain errors and may cause some comprehension problems.

ℹ️ Exam information: mistakes in IELTS Speaking

Even at band 7 some mistakes can still be considered acceptable as long as they occur infrequently within the context of complex speech and do not result in confusion.

2 Listen to the speaker responding to the question: *Tell me about a practical skill you learned at home.* Answer the questions 1–3 below.
🔊 49

1 Has the speaker attempted complex structures?

2 How frequent are the speaker's errors: **a** very frequent **b** frequent **c** somewhat frequent or **d** rare?

3 Do the speaker's errors cause significant misunderstanding?

3 Five common types of error are listed in the table below and examples underlined in the audio script. Correct the errors indicating in brackets the type of error 1–5. The first one is done as an example.

Error type	Typical error	Correct form
1 tense / aspect / verb form	~~They going away.~~	They**'re** going away. ✓
2 incorrect verb pattern	~~She made me to do it.~~	She made me do it. ✓
3 singular and plural nouns	~~I have six brother~~	I have six brother**s**. ✓
4 missing or incorrect articles	~~I have good idea.~~	I have **a** good idea. ✓
5 subject-verb agreement	~~Each candidate have a number.~~	Each candidate **has** a number. ✓

When I was **(a)** __twelve years old__ [3] my mother gave me a sewing machine and showed me

(b) _how can I make_ [_____] my own clothes. So **(c)** __I been sewing__ [_____] my own clothes

(d) __for long time__ [_____]. It's something **(e)** _I'm really enjoy_ [_____]. When **(f)** ___you making___

[_____] something new and beautiful, you feel satisfied because **(g)** _no one else have_ [_____] that outfit.

I feel grateful to my mother. She didn't have **(h)** same opportunities [_____] as me. When she was a child,

she **(i)** ___must sew___ [_____] her own clothes, but I can choose to do it. **(j)** _After graduated_ [_____]

from school, I decided to study costume design. I'm very excited about my future.

Part 2: Focusing on grammatical accuracy

Tense and aspect

Review the sections on tense and aspect on page 141 in Speaking Unit 6 and page 113 in Writing Unit 9, then do exercises 4 and 5 below.

4 In sentences 1–6 the speaker responds to the question: *What traditional crafts are common in your country?* Choose the correct verb form for each sentence, then practise saying each sentence aloud.

1 In my country people **are making / have been making** many different kinds of crafts for centuries – rugs, embroidery, pottery.
2 Traditional handicrafts **weren't / haven't been** so popular ten or twenty years ago.
3 But these days, they **become / are becoming** more and more popular, especially textiles.
4 Last time I went home, I noticed that more people my age **wore / were wearing** clothes made of traditional fabrics.
5 I **didn't see / hadn't seen** so many people dressed like that before.
6 It will be interesting if this trend **continues / will continue**.

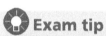

Exam tip

In speech, features of grammar such as auxiliary verbs and articles are usually unstressed and difficult to hear. It is therefore easy to forget to use them when speaking. Practise listening carefully for auxiliary verbs and articles so that they become a natural part of your speech.

5 Read the speaker's response to the question: *What is the best way to learn a craft?* below. There is a missing verb in each sentence 1–6. Correct the audio script by adding the missing verb. Then listen to check your answers, and practise saying each sentence aloud.

50

1 I think it easier and more enjoyable to learn in a class.
2 My sewing teacher been very good and kind to all the students.
3 He always says you shouldn't afraid of making a mistake because that's how you learn.
4 Some things are difficult to do, like when you making a pattern, you need to measure everything carefully.
5 So far everybody in my class been willing to help each other, so it's a good atmosphere.
6 The workshop just like my second home now.

Verb patterns

Another common source of error is difficulty with verb patterns, that is sentences in which one verb follows another, eg verb + infinite – *I learned to sew.* There are seven patterns, listed below. Which you must use depends on the first verb.

6 Match each pattern 1–7 with the examples a–g.

1 Verb + infinitive	a *They made me work.*
2 Verb + gerund	b *I want to work.*
3 Verb + preposition + gerund	c *They asked me to work.*
4 Verb + object + infinitive	d *I'm thinking about working.*
5 Verb + object + infinitive without *to*	e *They kept me from working.*
6 Verb + object + gerund	f *I enjoy working.*
7 Verb + object + preposition + gerund	g *They saw me working.*

7 For each sentence 1–6, write the verb in brackets in the correct form, using a preposition if required.

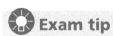

Exam tip

When you learn a new verb, you should check your dictionary and study the example sentences to see which pattern or patterns can be used.

1 My father suggested (**try**) _____ something new.

2 My mother encouraged me (**study**) _____ abroad.

3 I decided (**come**) _____ to the UK.

4 My sister insisted (**come**) _____ with me.

5 We persuaded her (**stay**) _____ at home.

6 My parents let me (**go**) _____ on my own.

7 I could hear my sister (**complain**) _____.

8 That didn't prevent me (**travel**) _____.

Nouns, articles and subject-verb agreement

Revise the section on countable and uncountable nouns on page 106 in Writing Unit 7 and the section on articles and subject-verb agreement on pages 112–113 in Writing Unit 9.

8 Match the rules 1–7 with the examples a–g, focusing on the words in bold.

Rules

1 Do not use **a or an** with uncountable nouns.

2 Use **the** with nouns that are specified.

3 Use **the** with nouns that are mentioned again.

4 Use **the** with nouns that are modified with superlatives.

5 Use **the** with nouns that are modified with ordinals.

6 Use **the** with nouns that are unique.

7 Do not use **the** when you are referring to people or things in general.

Examples

a ***Doctors*** *work **long hours**.*

b *This is the only building of its kind in **the world**.*

c ***The first time*** *I travelled abroad was when I was 16.*

d ***The person that I wanted to speak to*** *was not available.*

e *I signed up for a new course. I think **the course** covers everything I need.*

f ***The biggest mountains*** *are in the north.*

g *I need more specific **information and advice** about the programme.*

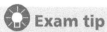 **Exam tip**

Singular and uncountable nouns take a singular verb form when they are the subject of the sentence. Do not be confused by modifiers placed between the subject and verb, e.g. *The **number** of students **is** rising.*

9 The student is practising her response to the question: *What is the value of traditional crafts in the modern world?* She has made the transcript below to help her identify her mistakes. There are ten mistakes: six involving articles and four involving subject-verb agreement. Correct the mistakes, then listen to the student's second recording to check your answers.

"There are many ways that crafts can improve our quality of life, but I think most important benefit is maintaining cultural traditions. Every country have its own crafting traditions. Crafts like weaving or wood carving is a part of people's identity. Objects that are made of natural materials like the wood or stone also helps us to connect with natural world. If everything you own have been made by a machinery, you lose the connection. Handmade objects are also more interesting because they are unique. I remember first time my grandmother gave me something she made – it was a basket she'd made when she was a little girl – I felt like I had a treasure. Whenever I hold basket, I remember her."

Part 3: Improving grammatical accuracy (Parts 1 and 3)

10 Practise giving your own responses to the sample exam questions in this unit. Speak for the recommended length of time, recording your responses.

- Part 1: *Tell me about a practical skill you learned at home.* (20–30 seconds)
- Part 3: *What traditional crafts are common in your country?* (1 minute)
  What is the best way to learn a craft? (1 minute)
  What is the value of traditional crafts in the modern world? (1 minute)

 **Exam tip**

When preparing for the IELTS exam, practise using correct grammatical forms in speech until they become automatic. During the IELTS Speaking test, focus on communicating the content of your message. Too much focus on accuracy during the exam could reduce your score for fluency and coherence.

11 Listen to your recording and evaluate your responses for grammatical accuracy.

- Have you used the right tenses and formed them correctly?
- Have you used singular, plural and uncountable nouns correctly?
- Have you used the correct articles?
- Do your subjects and verbs agree?
- Have you formed complex sentences correctly?

12 Note any errors. Then repeat the exercise.

8 Pronunciation 1: words and sounds

Part 1: Understanding how pronunciation is assessed

1 Read the band 6 descriptor for pronunciation below and answer questions 1 and 2. Check the key and commentary on page 203.

> ### Band descriptor
>
> **Band 6:** uses a range of pronunciation features with mixed control; shows some effective use of features but this is not sustained; can generally be understood throughout, though mispronunciation of individual words or sounds reduces clarity at times

1 Which aspect of pronunciation is most important for making your communication clear?
2 What pronunciation features do you think make spoken communication more effective?

ⓘ Exam information: speaking with an accent

It is perfectly acceptable to speak with a foreign accent in the IELTS Speaking test. There is, in fact, a wide variety of accents in English. As long as the examiner can understand your message without strain, you can achieve a high score for pronunciation.

Part 2: Focusing on pronunciation of words and sounds

The International Phonetic Alphabet (IPA)

English spelling and pronunciation can be confusing. Often the same letter can represent different sounds, e.g. the letter *a* in *back* and *bake*. To avoid confusion, IPA symbols are used to represent the exact pronunciation of words. In IPA, *back* = /bæk/ and *bake* = /beɪk/.

2 Use your dictionary to find the IPA symbols for each word in the sentence: *My favourite dessert is chocolate cake.*

💡 Exam tip

A good learners' dictionary will provide a full list of IPA symbols and use them to show the pronunciation of each word, including where the stress falls (indicated by the symbol /ˈ/) Learning IPA takes time, but it will help you achieve more accurate pronunciation and a better score on the IELTS test.

Voiced and unvoiced consonants

One difficulty learners often have is distinguishing between pairs of consonants such as /k/ and /g/. The sounds in each pair are similar because they are made in the same place in the mouth. However, one sound is *voiced*, e.g. /g/, and the other sound, e.g. /k/, is *unvoiced*.

3 Read the audio script of the student describing how to make her favourite dessert. Underline the most appropriate word in each highlighted pair and practise saying the word pairs aloud. Then listen to the recording and circle the word that you hear. Which type of consonant does the speaker have difficulty pronouncing – voiced or unvoiced?

To make this dessert you have to beat eggs and sugar together until you've **caught / got** the right consistency. Then, you need to **melt / meld** butter and chocolate and **bore / pour** it into the **pole / bowl** with the eggs and sugar. Add flour, then **dip / tip** the mixture into a **white / wide** tray and put it in a hot oven for about 30 minutes.

4 Now listen to the speaker's second attempt and notice the correct pronunciation of both voiced and unvoiced consonants. Record yourself reading the instructions and check your own pronunciation of these sounds.

5 Eight words beginning with an unvoiced consonant are paired with words beginning with their corresponding voiced consonant sounds. Listen and repeat each pair of words.

1	caught /kɔːt/	got /gɒt/		5	few /fjuː/	view /vjuː/
2	pole /pəʊl/	bowl /bəʊl/		6	thistle /θɪsl/	this'll /ðɪsl/
3	tip /tɪp/	dip /dɪp/		7	sip /sɪp/	zip /zɪp/
4	shun /ʃʌn/	vision /ˈvɪʒən/		8	cheer /tʃɪə/	jeer /dʒɪə/

Other problem pairs

Some consonant sounds may be difficult to distinguish and pronounce correctly if they do not exist in your language.

6 Listen to three test takers answering a question about foods they like and underline the words in the audio script that are pronounced incorrectly. Identify the two consonant sounds that each speaker has difficulty differentiating.

1 I eat chicken, but I don't eat red meat.

2 Something I really like to eat for breakfast is yogurt and fresh fruit.

3 Fish curry is very delicious in my opinion.

7 Record yourself saying the word pairs A–C below. If you have any difficulty differentiating the two initial sounds, do the corresponding practice exercise A–C on page 150.

A led /led/   red /red/
B sing /sɪŋ/   thing /θɪŋ/
C wary /weəri/   very /veri/

Exam tip
The vocal cords in your throat vibrate when you pronounce a voiced consonant but not when you produce an unvoiced consonant sound. You can monitor your use of voice by touching your hand to your throat when you pronounce a consonant.

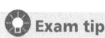
Exam tip
Study diagrams, photographs and video recordings of speakers articulating sounds that are difficult for you. Use a mirror when practising to help you position your mouth correctly.

🔊 **A** The sounds **/l/** and **/r/** are both made with your mouth slightly open. To pronounce /l/ move the tip
56 of your tongue to the roof of your mouth. For /r/ move your tongue to the middle of your mouth.

Listen and repeat: lid /lɪd/ – rid /rɪd/   late /leɪt/ – rate /reɪt/   alive /əˈlaɪv/ – arrive /əˈraɪv/ collect /kəˈlekt/ –
correct /kəˈrekt/   class /klɑːs/ – crass /kræs/

🔊 **B** The sounds **/s/ and /θ/** as in **s**ing and **th**ing are both pronounced with your lips slightly open. To
57 pronounce /s/ bring your teeth together and place your tongue immediately behind them. For /θ/ place
the tip of your tongue between your teeth.

Listen and repeat: seem /siːm/ – theme /θiːm/   sink /sɪŋk/ – think /θɪŋk/   mass /mæs/ – math /mæθ/
face /feɪs/ – faith /feɪθ/   tense /tens/ – tenth /tenθ/

🔊 **C** To pronounce **/w/** form a small circle with your lips. To pronounce **/v/** your lower lip should touch the
58 bottom of your top teeth.

Listen and repeat: why /waɪ/ – vie /vaɪ/   wane /weɪn/ – vein /veɪn/   wax /wæks/ – vax /vaks/
weird /wɪəd/ – veered /vɪəd/

8 Practise talking about a dish that you like and how to prepare it. Record yourself and listen carefully
to your pronunciation. Identify any consonant sounds that you need to pronounce more clearly.

Final -s and -ed

Voice also has an influence on how certain word endings are pronounced, in particular final -s and final -ed.
Depending on the preceding sound, -s ending can sound like /s/, /z/ or /ɪz/ and -ed can sound like /t/, /d/ or /ɪd/.

🔘 Exam tip

Clear pronunciation of final -s and -ed is important as they are very common. They are used to form plurals (cakes), the
possessive (Jane's cakes), third-person verb forms (Jane's baking cakes) and past tenses (Jane baked a cake).

9 Listen to the test taker answering the question: *What is your favourite restaurant?* In the audio script
🔊 below write the IPA symbol /s/, /z/ or /ɪz/ for the final -s sounds and /t/, /d/ or /ɪd/ for the final -ed
59 sounds that you hear (The first one has been done as an example).

When I **1** liv**ed** /d/ in Italy, I **2** lik**ed** / / going to a restaurant **3** call**ed** / / Il Pirata, which **4** mean**s** / / *The
Pirate* in English. The food was wonderful, especially the fish **5** dish**es** / /. I try making my favourite one at
home, but I've never **6** succeed**ed** / /. It never **7** taste**s** / / the same.

10 Listen again and read the passage aloud, paying attention to use of voice. Identify a pattern for the
🔊 pronunciation of -s and -ed endings. Then record yourself talking about a restaurant that you like.
60

Consonant clusters

It can be difficult to pronounce words containing several consonants together, particularly if these are
placed at the end of words, e.g. the sounds /sts/ in the word *tastes* /teɪsts/.

🔘 Exam tip

Practise clusters by slowing down and saying each sound separately, e.g. *tastes* /teɪ-s-t-s/. Then repeat until you can say
the word without gaps /teɪsts/.

11 Listen and repeat the word pairs below.

🔊 61 1 ask – asks   2 act – acts   3 text – texts   4 month – months   5 sixth – sixths

Short and long vowel sounds

There are seven short vowel sounds and five long vowel sounds in English. Depending on your first language, you may have difficulties distinguishing between short vowels such as *bad* /æ/ and *bed* /e/ or distinguishing between a short and long vowel, e.g. ship /ɪ/ and sheep /iː/.

12 Listen to three test takers talking about family mealtimes and underline the words in the audio
🔊 62 script that are pronounced incorrectly. Identify the two vowel sounds that each speaker has difficulty differentiating. Then listen to the correct versions.

1 My brother and I would set the table, then we would all sit down together to eat.

2 In my family we're all vegetarians; we don't eat meat of any kind.

3 My family loves strong flavours, so we had all sorts of sauces on the table.

Word stress

Another area of difficulty for many learners is word stress. Most multi-syllable words in English have one syllable that is emphasized or **stressed**. There are some common word stress patterns but many exceptions too.

13 Listen to the examples 1–5 and notice that the stress falls on the
🔊 63 first syllable. This is a common pattern for nouns and adjectives that are made up of two syllables.

1 **fla**vour   2 **ta**ble   3 **break**fast   4 **chi**cken   5 **tas**ty

14 Now listen to sentences 1–3 and underline the stressed syllable in
🔊 64 each word in bold. What is the pattern?

1 They decided to **present** me with a **present**.

2 I'm sure she will **object** to having that **object** in the house.

3 We had to **increase** our workload to achieve an **increase** in sales.

 **Exam tip**

Word stress is important in English. Incorrect word stress can cause greater misunderstanding than mispronouncing a vowel or consonant sound. Stressed sounds are normally clearer, longer, louder and higher in pitch than unstressed sounds.

Part 3: Improving pronunciation (Part 3)

15 Record yourself responding to the questions below.

Do people speak differently in different parts of your country?
Are some accents considered to be better than others?
Have people's accents changed over time?

16 Listen to your recording and evaluate your pronunciation.

- Is your speech easy to understand?
- Have you pronounced voiced and unvoiced consonants clearly?
- Are your short vowels, long vowels and diphthongs clearly differentiated?
- Have you stressed the correct syllable in multi-syllable words?
- Are your stressed syllables clearer, louder and longer than unstressed syllables?

17 Note any words or sounds that need improvement. Then repeat the exercise.

9 Pronunciation 2: rhythm and intonation

Aims | Understanding pronunciation features; Focusing on pronunciation features (sentence stress, strong and weak forms, varying stress for emphasis, linking and intonation); **Improving pronunciation** (Part 3 answers)

Part 1: Understanding pronunciation features

ℹ Exam information: effective communication

In the IELTS Speaking test, good pronunciation of individual words and sounds is essential to prevent misunderstandings. To communicate *effectively*, you need good control of pronunciation features including sentence stress, linking and intonation.

1 Highlight the words in the band 8 descriptor below that indicate the difference between good performance and very good performance.

> **Band descriptors**
>
> **Band 8:** uses a wide range of pronunciation features; sustains flexible use of features, with only occasional lapses
>
> **Band 6:** uses a range of pronunciation features with mixed control; shows some effective use of features but this is not sustained

Part 2: Focusing on pronunciation features

Sentence stress

One of the features of pronunciation that contributes most to effective communication is sentence stress. To understand why some words are stressed it is helpful to distinguish between **content words** (adverbs, adjectives, nouns, verbs) and **structure words** (articles, pronouns, auxiliary verbs, the verb *to be*, prepositions)

2 Listen and repeat the sentence below. Underline the words that 🔊 are stressed and answer the questions.
65

The most enjoyable holiday I've ever had was on the Greek island of Paxos.

1 Which type of words are stressed?

2 Which type of words are unstressed?

 **Exam tip**

Stressing content words aids communication because it ensures that the listener's attention is directed to the words that carry most meaning.

3 Underline the words that you would expect to be stressed in the passage below. Listen and read the 🔊 answer key to check your answers. Then answer questions 1–2.
66

I went there with my cousins last year. We flew to Corfu, then took a boat to Paxos. Paxos is a small island, so there isn't much to do. But it's a very beautiful and relaxing place to be. That's why I like it. You can have all your meals in a café on the beach and step into the water whenever you want.

1 In addition to articles, pronouns, auxiliary verbs, and prepositions, what other type of word in this passage is also unstressed?

2 What do you notice about stress and the verb *to be* in this passage?

4 Read the passage aloud putting the stress on the content words.

5 Underline the stressed words in the two sentences below. Then listen to the recording and answer
🔊 the questions.
67

Sentence A: We went to _____ shops, _____ a park, _____ a museum _____ and a castle.

Sentence B: We went to some shops, and a park, and a museum and then a castle.

1 How many words are in each sentence?

2 How long does it take to say each sentence?

Strong and weak forms

6 Listen to the two sentences and notice the pronunciation of the
🔊 preposition *for*.
68

Sentence A: Who did you do that for?

Sentence B: I did it for you.

1 In which sentence is *for* said more quickly?

2 What happens to the sound of the vowel /ɔː/ in *for* when it is said quickly?

> 💡 **Exam tip**
>
> For a more natural sound, aim to speak with a regular rhythm. English is a *stress-timed* language, which means the length of time between stressed syllables should be roughly the same, as in the example in exercise 5. To maintain a good rhythm, you need to be able to say unstressed syllables quickly.

> 💡 **Exam tip**
>
> The vowel sound of unstressed syllables and function words is often /ə/, referred to as the *schwa*. This is the most common sound in English. To pronounce the schwa you need to relax your mouth and drop your jaw slightly.

7 Listen and repeat the strong and weak forms of the words below along with the example
🔊 sentences.
69

Word	Strong	Example	Weak	Example
the	/ðiː/	We saw <u>the</u> castle, you know, the exact one that's in the film!	/ðə/	We liked the castle.
to	/tuː/	He insisted on going, but I didn't want <u>to</u>.	/tə/	He went to the beach.
of	/ɒv/	I didn't know what he was thinking <u>of</u>.	/əv/	I stayed in and had a cup of tea.
and	/ænd/	I said I wanted cake <u>and</u> ice cream, not cake or ice cream.	/ən/ /ənd/ + vowel	He had fish and chips. I had soup and a sandwich.
a	/eɪ/	I asked for <u>a</u> coffee, not three coffees!	/ə/	He asked for a cup of tea.
that	/ðæt/	I didn't say <u>that</u>!	/ðət/	I said that he would come.
have	/hæv/	You <u>have</u> to pay.	/əv/	I would have paid.

8 Decide whether the words in bold in sentences 1–5 should be strong or weak. Listen to the recording to check your answers. Then repeat each sentence.

1 They enjoyed going **to the** park **and** watching **the** children play.

2 He bought **a** pair **of** shoes **and a** new rucksack.

3 I wouldn't **have** paid **that** much **for** it.

4 They were **on** their way **to the** beach, not **from the** beach.

5 '**Have you** been **to** Athens?' 'Yes, I **have**.'

Varying stress for emphasis

Exam tip

You can vary the stress pattern in a sentence if you want to place special emphasis on a particular part of the message.

9 Listen to sentences 1–4 below and notice how the implied meaning changes when the stress moves to a different word. What do you think the implied meaning of sentences 3 and 4 might be?

Sentence	Implied meaning
1 I <u>think</u> my sister would like Paxos.	But I don't know for sure.
2 I think my <u>sister</u> would like Paxos.	But someone else, e.g. my brother, would not.
3 I think <u>my</u> sister would like Paxos.	But _____
4 I think my sister would like <u>Paxos</u>.	But _____

10 Indicate which word you would stress in the sentence below for the two implied meanings. Then listen and check your answers.

I thought the journey home would be fine.

Meaning A: Others didn't think the journey would be fine.

Meaning B: I believed the journey would be fine but in fact it was not.

Linking

11 Listen to the two versions of the sentence *I stayed in and had a cup of tea*. Then answer the questions:

1 Which version sounds more natural?

2 Why? What is the rule?

12 Now listen and practise phrases 1–3 linking the consonant and vowel sounds as shown.

1 Peter <u>ate a big ice</u> cream.

2 I wouldn<u>'t have done it</u>.

3 I'd prefe<u>r a flat in</u> the centre.

Intonation

13 Listen to the three versions of the first sentence and two versions of the question. What does the speaker's intonation convey?

🔊 75

1   We saw an interesting film.

2   Could you repeat that question?

> **💡 Exam tip**
>
> Intonation is important in speech because it helps to convey meaning in different ways, especially how the speaker feels about the message.

14 Now repeat sentences 1–4 using intonation to convey the intended meaning. Then listen and check your answers.

🔊 76

1   Would you mind saying that again? (politeness)

2   I really enjoyed my holiday last year! (enthusiasm)

3   The flight was long and dull. (boredom)

4   But the sun was shining when we arrived. (enthusiasm)

Part 3: Improving pronunciation (Part 3)

15 Read the script below written in response to the question *Tell me about an interesting holiday you have had*. Mark the pronunciation features:

- underline the stressed words, e.g. I'd <u>love</u> to <u>return</u>, and highlight the stressed syllables in multi-syllable words
- indicate the links between final consonants and initial vowels, e.g. she di<u>d it</u>
- use arrows to indicate where a particular intonation pattern would be appropriate

"The most interesting holiday I've ever had was when I went to Athens with my friend Mirna. It was a very educational holiday, but not a very relaxing one. Mirna was studying the history of ancient Greece and Rome at the time, so there was a lot she wanted to see. It was very hot, but that didn't stop us from visiting all of the most famous sites – several in one day usually. I remember spending an entire day in the Archaeological Museum looking at pots. I was exhausted at the end of it – but I learned a lot about ancient Greek pottery!"

16 Listen to the recording and compare your annotated script with the script in the answer key.

🔊 77

Record yourself repeating the script. Listen to your recording and evaluate your pronunciation.

- Are content words (and syllables) consistently stressed and function words unstressed?
- Does your speech have a stress-timed rhythm?
- Have you used strong and weak pronunciations of function words appropriately?
- Have you linked sounds together smoothly?
- Have you used intonation effectively?

17 Note any features that you could improve with practice.

18 Repeat the exercise, using your own holiday experiences to answer the question.

10 Review

Part 1: Reviewing the assessment criteria

1 Assess your understanding of IELTS assessment criteria. Decide if statements 1–8 are True or False.

1 It is importantly to speak as rapidly as you can to demonstrate fluency. TRUE / FALSE

2 Coherence refers not just to your use of linking words but also to the way you have sequenced your ideas. TRUE / FALSE

3 You don't have to use formal vocabulary to make a good impression. TRUE / FALSE

4 You will get a higher score for lexical resource if you use very unusual words. TRUE / FALSE

5 A set number of points is deducted for each grammatical error you make. TRUE / FALSE

6 You should demonstrate that you can use a variety of complex grammatical structures. TRUE / FALSE

7 To get a good score for pronunciation, you should pronounce each word slowly, carefully and clearly. TRUE / FALSE

8 For bands 8 and 9, you must be able to speak English without a foreign accent. TRUE / FALSE

Part 2: Reviewing key components of assessment

Fluency and coherence

🔅 Exam tip: length of answers in IELTS Speaking

It's important to give the right length of answer in each part of the exam. Avoid giving responses of a single word, phrase or sentence. In Part 1 each answer should be 20–30 seconds; in the Part 2 long turn you should speak for 1–2 minutes; in Part 3 each answer should be up to one minute long.

2 Read the audio script of two students role playing Part 1 questions and answers. Notice that the student with the examiner role has to ask multiple questions to get an extended response. What should the responding student do to show greater fluency and coherence?

Question 1: Describe a building that you really like.

Answer: I like modern buildings. Um, buildings that are different, um, how can I say? Like in a unique style.

Question 2: Can you give me an example of a building you particularly like?

Answer: The Guggenheim Museum. It's in Bilbao. In Spain. It's really famous.

Question 3: What's special about the building?

Answer: Um, it's very, it has a very unusual shape. And it's next to a river. From the outside, it looks like a big ship.

Question 4: Is there anything you don't like about the building?

Answer: Um, it's not perfect. Let me think … inside the rooms are very large. The paintings look very small. But the light inside is beautiful.

3 Read the Part 2 prompt below and the student's opening statement for each point. Then indicate briefly how the speaker could develop each main point 1–5.

Task 2

Describe a fictional character in a film that you have enjoyed.

You should say:

- who the character is

- what happens in the film
- what the character represents

- what you think about the character

Say whether you would recommend the film to others.

1 The character I'd like to describe is a ten-year-old girl called Chihiro.

2 The film has quite a complicated plot line.
3 Chihiro's story represents the transition from childhood into adulthood.

4 I find Chihiro an interesting character because of how she develops.

5 I think people of all ages could enjoy this film.

---

4 Now match the explanations a–e below to the opening statements 1–5 above. Underline the signposting expressions and linking words.

a At the beginning she's kind of spoiled and immature. But in the spirit world Chihiro has to learn who to trust and how to survive. She also develops compassion. At one point in the film, for example, she manages to make friends with a monster called No-face who terrorizes the other spirits.

b It deals with universal themes in a very imaginative way. Children would probably enjoy the characters and the action, whereas adults might appreciate the symbolic and psychological aspect.

c She's the main character in a film called *Spirited Away*, which is an animated Japanese fantasy from about 2000.

d Chihiro and her parents get lost in an abandoned theme park and enter a spirit world. Her parents are transformed into animals, and Chihiro has to try and rescue them and escape. In the spirit world, Chihiro meets a lot of strange spirits, like the witch Yubaba.

e The spirit world symbolizes the time between childhood and adulthood. The challenges that she has to overcome represent the qualities that you need to acquire in order to mature.

Lexical range and accuracy

5 Read the response to the Part 3 question below and underline the most appropriate word for each pair in bold. Use your dictionary if necessary and consider register, connotation and collocation. Check the key and then practise reading aloud the passage with the more appropriate vocabulary choices.

When a film is based on a book, how important is it to stay true to the original story?

That depends to some extent on the quality of the book and the quality of the film – and also the status of the book. If you make a film about a **1 famous / infamous** book, then people will sometimes **2 freak out / get upset** if you make changes. For example, when the film of the novel *The Great Gatsby* came out, the one with Leonardo Di Caprio, it was **3 bitterly / heavily** criticized. **4 Critics / Hypocrites** said the director's interpretation was **5 rubbish / inappropriate** because he used modern music. They also didn't like the way he **6 portrayed / glamourized** the lifestyle of **7 the rich / posh people**. But I think it's **8 perfectly / highly** reasonable to **9 modernize / renovate** a classic if you have a **10 valid / perfect** reason for the changes that you make.

6 Read the response to the Part 3 question below and identify the errors in word class, prefixes, countable and uncountable nouns and dependent prepositions. Then listen to the response to check your answers and practise reading the audio script aloud.

> *Have your viewing and/or reading habits changed over time?*

"I think they have changed a lot, special since I bought a tablet. It's so convenience, so I spend more time both reading and viewing than before, but I change from one thing to another more frequent. Before I would maybe read several chapters of a novel in a time. Now I read maybe one chapter, then I get distraction by some notification on my phone, so I watch a vlog or something like that. Nowadays, I read more non-fictions and I watch more rubbish online. I've become more unpatient."

Grammatical range and accuracy

7 Read the speaker's response to a question about a visit to a museum. Each line 1–9 contains an error in tense, verb pattern, use of article or subject-verb agreement. Correct the errors, then listen to check your answers.

1 About two years ago my sister taken me to an exhibition in London.
2 The exhibition was about Mexican painter Frida Kahlo.
3 It was such surprising experience.
4 I expected seeing her paintings,
5 but the exhibition was mainly of her possessions, including her clothings, jewelleries and make-up.
6 I seen some of these things in her paintings
7 but I really enjoyed to see the actual objects.
8 Everything in the cases were so colourful and unique.
9 I think the most interesting objects for me was her dresses.

Pronunciation

8 Read the passage from exercise 7 below.

- Circle and practise any words that contain sounds you find difficult to pronounce
- Underline the stressed words
- Highlight the main stressed syllable within each stressed word (check your dictionary)

"About two years ago my sister took me to an exhibition in London. The exhibition was about the Mexican painter Frida Kahlo. It was such a surprising experience. I expected to see her paintings, but the exhibition was mainly of her possessions, including her clothing, jewellery and make-up. I'd seen some of these things in her paintings, but I really enjoyed seeing the actual objects. Everything in the cases was so colourful and unique. I think the most interesting objects for me were her dresses."

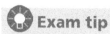

Part 3: Exam practice (Parts 1, 2 and 3)

9 Practise giving your own responses to the sample exam questions in this unit. Speak for the recommended length of time, recording your responses.

Exam tip

Throughout your study you should monitor how well you are developing in each aspect of the speaking skill. As you get closer to the exam, increase your focus on the points you most need to improve.

Part 1

Describe a building that you like. (20–30 seconds)

Tell me about a time when you visited a museum or art gallery? (20–30 seconds)

Task 2

Describe a fictional character in a book or film that you have enjoyed.
You should say:
- who the character is
- what happens in the book or film
- what the character represents
- what you think about the character
Say whether you would recommend the book or film to others.

You will have to talk about the topic for 1–2 minutes. You have one minute to think about what you're going to say. You can make some notes to help you if you wish.

Part 3

Have your viewing and/or reading habits changed over time? (60 seconds)

When a film is based on a book, how important is it to stay true to the original story? (60 seconds)

It is more effective to tell a story through words or through images? (60 seconds)

10 Listen to your recording and evaluate your responses against the four criteria:

- **Fluency and coherence** To what extent have you spoken with normal levels of continuity, rate and effort? How consistently have you linked ideas and language together to form coherent, connected speech?
- **Lexical resource** How broad is the range of vocabulary you have used? How precisely have you expressed meanings and attitudes?
- **Grammatical range and accuracy** How broad is the range of grammatical structures? How accurate and appropriate is your use of grammar?
- **Pronunciation** How comprehensible is your speech? How effective is your use of stress, linking and intonation?

11 Note any aspects that require improvement. Then repeat the exercise.

Audio scripts

Listening

Unit 1

Track 01

See audio script on page 10

Track 02

See audio script on page 11

Unit 2

Track 03

1 Hello. My name is Jake and I'm a biology student. I'm in the second year and I really enjoy my course.
2 I'm Vanessa and I live in an apartment in the city centre. It's on the tenth floor and has a great view.
3 My name's Elleanor and I work in a technology company. My job is really creative, and I enjoy it a lot.
4 Hi. I'm William. One of my hobbies is playing tennis. I play a couple of times a week with my sister.

Track 04

1 Take_it_all_out.
2 I went_out_at_eight_o'clock.
3 She's studying now.
4 I cannot tell you.
5 We must do it.
6 Pass me the salt and pepper.
7 <u>Do you</u> want to go? (jou)
8 I'll <u>meet you</u> later. (meechou)

Track 05

See audio script on page 13

Track 06

Kate:	I'm really <u>nervous</u> about my <u>presentation</u>.
Professor Watkins:	I **could** send you some <u>revision videos</u>. Last week I made a couple of videos, but I **haven't had** time to <u>upload</u> them to the <u>university online learning system</u>. I think **they'll be** <u>really useful</u> to help you feel <u>more prepared</u>.
Kate:	That **would be** <u>amazing</u> as I seem to learn much better with video. Maybe **if I'd** watched some more of your online <u>videos last semester</u>, **I might've got** <u>better grades</u> in my <u>final exam</u>. I **wasn't** <u>very happy</u> with my results.
Professor Watkins:	Well, after the presentation, let me know if the videos **were** useful.

Track 07

See information box on page 14

Track 08

See audio script on page 14

Track 09

See audio script on page 14

Annie: Hi guys. I just wanted to say that I haven't had time to work on our project this week.

Leon: Really, Annie? But you said you were going to finish it this week. I thought we could rely on you to do the research.

Annie: I know. I'm really sorry. The research is very time-consuming because there's so much to read.

Harry: Well, we're running out of time Annie, and if we rush it, we might not get a good grade. I really want to do well in this module.

Leon: I suggest we all work on the research together to save time. What do you think?

Harry: OK, let's do that.

Annie: Oh, that would be fantastic. I think it'll make a real difference.

Ben: What do you want to do on Friday evening?

Jessica: Oh, that's a good question. I've done so much studying this week so I should definitely get out of the flat. I think I should do some exercise. Um, you know, I think I'd like to go for a walk.

Ben: That sounds like a nice idea. We could go for a walk by the river.

Jessica: Yes, that would be lovely. Oh, wait a minute. I've just remembered that the weather report said that there's a high chance of rain on Friday night.

Ben: Oh no, that's a shame. Do you want to come over for pizza and we could watch a film?

Jessica: That's a nice idea, but then I wouldn't be going out anywhere. I think I'd prefer it if we went to the cinema.

Ben: OK, if you want.

Jessica: I know it's quite far for you to travel but I'd really appreciate it.

Ben: Yeah, I know!

Jessica: Remember that there's a new café in the cinema. My friend said that the cakes are amazing, and I can't wait to try them. So, shall we get tickets for that new horror film? I've read quite a few good reviews online and I'd love to see it.

Ben: No way! You know I hate horror films!

Jessica: Oh, of course, sorry I forgot! I'll have to see that with someone else who likes horror films like me – maybe my sister. Well, what about that documentary about the oceans?

Ben: Oh, yes, sure. That's a much better idea.

Jessica: Great, so let's meet (fade) …

Unit 3

Man: Hi … I want to book a holiday but I'm not sure where to. It's for me and my family – me, my wife and our kids – they're seven and four.

TA: I can help you with that. What type of holiday are you looking for?

Man: Just a beach holiday, somewhere hot!

TA: Well, we've got plenty of options. Greece is a good choice at this time of year, and really quiet and relaxing.

Man: Hmm … I need somewhere that will entertain the children, though.

TA: What about Mexico, or Egypt? There are great hotels in both places with kids' clubs, so the children will have something to do.

Man: I think Egypt is the best option – Mexico is a little far for us!

TA: And how long do you want to go for?

Man: Seven days.

TA: Well, the Seabreeze Hotel is a great option. Normally the cost would be £1,450 in total, but we can do a special rate for seven days there for £1,200.

Man: Hmm, it seems quite expensive.

TA: Well, that is the final cost with all the flights of course.

Man: And does it include meals and everything?

TA: Breakfast is in the cost, but it doesn't include other meals. This gives you the opportunity to get out from the resort and explore the area, though. You can try some of the local foods and restaurants and buy some souvenirs – they have great local products there. Oh, and the cost also includes two trips. You can choose where you'd like to go, but there are plenty of choices!

Man: Well, the pictures look nice … OK! I'll book it.

David: I don't know about you, Chloe, but I feel like we've done a good job on this research project. I think we've identified some clear areas that national parks need to deal with.

Chloe: Yes, I was surprised actually. The parks are really good in general at land conservation, but wildlife management is generally not very effective.

David: Although it's very hard to deal with. Animals just wander on and off national park lands, and they can't really put up barriers in such a large area.

Chloe: Yes, it's hard to protect animals while the animals don't stay in protected areas. But I think the biggest issue is development and modern society. The parks need to develop more pollution control. This might seem impossible, but unless they can preserve the natural environment as it is, then these lands are going to be devastated.

David: Yes, but there's very little the park management can do about that. It's a national and multinational issue.

Chloe: Well, let's start work on the recommendations for this project now. Hopefully, we will have some suggestions. We could look at parks that are the most successful and see what they do.

David: I think that's a good idea. Professor Davidson said that he wants us to make sure we have a list of sources. I've been doing that so far. Have you?

Chloe: Absolutely. I suppose we can just note down where we find examples of successful national parks too. Does he want us to add images to the report?

David: Not as far as I know, but he did say we need to do a short presentation on our findings, so we might want some images for that.

Chloe: OK … well, I suppose we'd better get working. We've only got a week left!

Unit 4

Good morning everyone and welcome on board the *Alexandra*. My name is Charlotte Perkins and I'd like to tell you about the ship and the services that we have available for all passengers. Can I just say that all the staff are here to make your trip as enjoyable as possible. If you have any questions, come to the information hub, which is located next to the gift shop. The hub is staffed all the time – in the afternoons and evenings by my colleagues Mark and Lorena, and I am there every morning, seven days a week. There is plenty of information aboard to tell you about the places that the ship is going to stop at. The gift shop has a range of interesting books for sale. Also, there are leaflets in your cabins and you can find maps of the cities in the gift shop and the library. You don't have to pay for the ones in the library, but can I ask that you return them at the end of the day.

The *Alexandra* has four restaurants, but you don't need to book a table in advance. This is a small ship, so we have enough seating capacity for all passengers. However, if you would like room service in the evening, please place your order by 4.00 p.m. so that our kitchen staff can make sure this is delivered to you on time.

Finally, we have lots of activities and entertainment options on the ship. There is a cinema, a small swimming pool on the upper deck and live music in the Marina restaurant every night. Places for the swimming pool are limited, so please make sure you sign up the night before if you'd like to use the pool. This can be done at the information hub or on the ship's app. Well, I hope you enjoy your stay … (fade)

Today I want to talk about the rise of social media platforms in business. When social media companies first started in the early 21st century, they were mostly used by people to connect with others. However, it wasn't long before businesses started to see the benefits of employing social media. Nowadays the majority of businesses use social media sites for a variety of reasons. A recent study showed that 73 per cent of marketers see social media as effective. The main aim, of course, is to influence our consumer behaviour and persuade us to buy more. For big corporations, social media is just another tool for brand development. But it is a powerful tool and not only for large corporations. Social media is seen as being particularly useful for small businesses because it is cost effective, and easy to set up and maintain. By increasing the number of their social media followers over time, their products and services can easily reach a wider audience. A few decades ago, marketing was far more difficult for smaller companies. Print advertising in the latter part of the 20th century was either in magazines or in the form of huge posters on roadside billboards. Understandably, the high costs of such advertising meant that it was beyond the budget of many small businesses. A similar situation existed with television, except that it was even more expensive. So, the rise of social media over the last 15 years has essentially made advertising for business more equal. Due to the fact that it is accessible to a wide range of organizations irrespective of their size, new companies, entrepreneurs and small businesses have a greater chance of being successful now than they did in the past. Although social media may have many negative aspects on a personal or societal level, it has contributed positively to business by allowing more people to start and sustain smaller companies.

Unit 5

Travel agent: OK, so are you interested in any destinations or types of holiday?
Customer: Well, beach holidays are usually my holiday of choice – I usually need to relax at this time of year rather than walking round all the museums and attractions in a city.
Travel agent: Of course! We have some excellent choices in the Caribbean.
Customer: Hmm. But actually, I've decided that it might be better to do something a bit more active.
Travel agent: Oh, I see. Well, how about a trekking holiday in the mountains? We have one which isn't too difficult. You don't have to do any climbing as the paths are mostly flat and the guide is excellent.
Customer: That sounds great. Can you reserve me a place?
Travel agent: Of course. The hotels on the trek are clean and comfortable and the food is included in the price. All the hotels have good restaurants too. The trek ends in a small town with amazing views over the mountains. There are plenty of places like little coffee shops to sit in and admire the scenery. There isn't a large choice of places for an evening meal, though.
Customer: That's no problem. Are there any supermarkets?
Travel agent: There's just a small one in the town.
Customer: OK, I'll have to mainly eat in the hotels then.

The technology sector has always had a bad reputation when it comes to the balance of male and female employees. For example, it is often said that large technology corporations do not have as many female employees as other industries and that the IT industry has few women working in important positions. In addition, it is easy to see that technology companies are usually led by inspirational men rather than women. Some of these points are obviously correct, but as with many areas of employment, the situation is complex. There are a range of professions that still suffer from a lack of female role models even in the 21st century, not just technology. Financial services and sport are still very much dominated by men.

So, let's look more closely at the IT industry. Although people think that technology firms would rather employ male engineers, that is not strictly true. More and more women are employed as engineers nowadays. The issue lies more in the type of work that women do. Many women engineers feel that their roles are limited and that finding a way to progress in the organization isn't easy.

Man: Excuse me. I'd like to reserve a hire car, please.
Assistant: Of course. When do you want to hire it from?
Man: I want to pick it up this Friday afternoon and return it on Sunday morning.
Assistant: We've got cars available to pick up on Friday, but I'm afraid we're closed at the weekends, so you'll need to hire it for the weekend and bring it back on the Monday. We're open from 9 o'clock in the morning.
Man: Hmm ... OK ... I could bring it back after work I suppose. Around 5 p.m.?
Assistant: Sure. We've got lots of options available. Our cheapest is the Fiat 500 ... that will cost £230.
Man: Hmm ... I might need something with more room.
Assistant: We've also got the Ford – it's our mid-range car and it's suitable for a family of four, that's £300 ... or if you want something more luxurious, then we've got a Porsche available.
Man: Mmm ... how much is the Porsche?
Assistant: It's a bit more ... it's £650.
Man: Hmm ... maybe not. I'll take the mid-range one then.
Assistant: Great. We can take a credit card reservation now, and then you can pay the rest when you pick it up. How will you pay?
Man: Can I pay in cash?
Assistant: Yes, but we'll still need a credit card for the insurance. Or you can do it all online and transfer it.
Man: No, that's fine. I'll put the insurance on my card and bring the rest in cash. What time do you close on Friday?
Assistant: Normally we shut at 4.30 p.m., but it's our busiest period, so we're open until eight this Friday.
Man: Great. I'll be here by seven.
Assistant: Great. Let me just take down your details ... (fade)

Gold is somewhat the pinnacle of metals. It is sought after around the world and is extremely valuable. However, this is surprising because it isn't the rarest of metals. Today we're going to explore why this is. Gold has been around for a long time, and ever since its discovery it has been prized. While many people thought this was because of its appearance – as we all know, the colour of gold can be very striking – actually, this was for a much more practical purpose. Gold was hard-wearing, much more than most other metals, and because of this it became used as a currency for trading. Obviously, these days there are more flexible and practical ways of paying, but gold hasn't lost its appeal. One key factor in its popularity today is the fact that it is very much seen as a status symbol, in the same league as diamonds. And this always means that it can command high prices.

The uses of gold are varied too. The most widely known uses are for either currency or decorative purposes, but there are plenty of other lesser-known uses. One is actually in airplane cockpits. This is because, as gold is a great conductor of electricity, it is used in a thin, semi-transparent form for de-icing windows. In fact, gold is used in many electronics, as well as in some medicines, and even in food ... (fade)

Unit 6

Now, I know some of you have asked about downloadable information instead of leaflets and I can tell you that all the museums have apps with maps and descriptions of the exhibitions. I'd recommend the app for the National Gallery of Landscapes because it's easy to use and provides a lot of detailed knowledge. There is a small charge for all these apps, but there's good news if you want to visit the Gallery of Textiles and you're enrolled on a university course. Just put in your identification number for your particular course and you won't have to pay for the app. Although do remember that there's an alternative to just staring at your phones as you walk around some places. The Ancient Arts Gallery trains all its employees in answering visitor questions and they really enjoy telling people everything they know about the artworks. And the National Gallery of Landscapes has an excellent introduction video in the reception area, as well as an audio guide, which I think is better value than the app. Right, there's just one more area I want to cover, which is entrance fees. Earlier some people asked me where they should go with young children. Even though parents probably think that The Ancient Arts Gallery would be most suitable because it's quite interactive, in my opinion The National Gallery of Landscapes is outstanding due to its wide range of activities and opportunities for learning in a fun way. Right, so does anyone have any questions? ... (fade)

Presenter: Today, we've got Sanjay Daily in to tell us about films out in the cinemas at the moment. Hi, Sanjay.
Sanjay: Hi, Belinda. Thanks for having me here.
Presenter: Our pleasure. I think you're going to start with *Keep on Running*, which I just saw yesterday and loved! Very moving.
Sanjay: Yes! It's about a teenager who breaks a world record while he's at school. Although it's about a young person, I'd say it isn't really suitable for the very young. It's about the ups and downs of life and is very inspiring, so it particularly appeals to families with older children as they can all appreciate the message.
Presenter: And what else is out at the moment?
Sanjay: There's a comedy called *My Best Life*. It follows the life of a woman who finds out she can remember anything she reads. Obviously, it's not real, but it has received really good reviews from male audiences as well as female.
Presenter: Ah, yes. I think my sister went to see it last week and enjoyed it a lot.
Sanjay: Next, we've got *Out in the Sun*. It's an animation that tells the story of a group of animals that get lost in the desert and how they get home. Many parents have said that they enjoyed it more than their children! The animation is beautiful, and it won best film in three categories at last month's Fine Films Festival.
Presenter: I just love animated films!
Sanjay: Me too! And the last option we have this week is called *Good Times in Bridgetown*. This is a great film for anyone who's ever worried about their parenting skills. It's about a couple who have two sets of twins and how they manage with life. It was actually inspired by the true story of an Australian couple back in the 1960s.
Presenter: Well, it sounds like a great week for cinemagoers! Which one would you ... (fade)

Nisha:	Hi, Oliver! Hi, Caroline!
Oliver:	Hello, Nisha!
Caroline:	Hi, Nisha. Hi, Oliver.
Oliver:	Hi, Caroline.
Nisha:	So, I was thinking. Shall we divide up the work for our presentation on disappearing languages?
Caroline:	That's a really good idea, Nisha, because we don't have a lot of time. I think the presentation should start with some images showing where most disappearing languages are in the world. Who do you think should do this part?
Nisha:	Actually Caroline, this kind of thing isn't my strong point. I'd rather focus on something that involves fewer design skills.
Oliver:	I wouldn't mind doing this. I work better with images than I do with numbers! How about I turn some of the statistics from Dr Mitchell's lecture into a colourful infographic.
Caroline:	Great. And I was thinking that I could put together some of the data about which languages are most endangered in the world. You know, collect some numbers and key information.
Nisha:	Um, would you mind if I did that part Caroline? I was reading a paper online last week with some statistics on the rate of language decline in different parts of the world, and I've already made quite a lot of notes about the many endangered languages in Oceania and North America, and the fact that there aren't many vulnerable languages in Europe.
Caroline:	OK, go ahead Nisha. Now, should we also add some specific case studies from each of the regions, you know, like one example from Africa, one from South America, and so on?
Oliver:	In my view, we're likely to find some good examples as we work through our different sections. Why don't we combine our ideas and do this together at the end? That way, we can choose the most interesting or common examples as evidence to support the first two sections. What do you think Caroline?
Caroline:	Yes, I see what you mean. Let's do that. In that case, if you both don't mind, I'd like to add in something about the effects of disappearing languages on society. There are actually quite a lot of negative effects in parts of the world where traditions are maintained through oral storytelling rather than written forms. In these cases, once a language has disappeared, ideas, values and folklore can all disappear with them.
Nisha:	Hmm. You know, this cultural perspective of endangered languages really interests me, especially how a lack of linguistic diversity impacts literature. Maybe I'll write about this for the essay we have to do later this semester.
Oliver:	OK, so I think we've all got enough work for this week. Why don't we meet up again on Friday … (fade)

Unit 7

Alison:	Hello. I've received your quotes online, and I'd like to book one of the flights, please.
Assistant:	Of course. Can I take your personal details down first, please? What's your first name?
Alison:	Alison, with one L.
Assistant:	And your surname?
Alison:	It's Russell, R-U-S-S-E-double L.
Assistant:	Great. And can I take a contact email address, please?
Alison:	Yes, it's ali dot 27@ example dot com.
Assistant:	Let me check that … A-L-Y twenty-seven at example dot com?
Alison:	No, A-L-*I*, like my name. A-L-I dot twenty-seven at example dot com.
Assistant:	Great. And your date of birth, please?
Alison:	The tenth of February nineteen eighty-eight.
Assistant:	That's great. Thank you. Now, what flight are you interested in booking?
Alison:	It's this one here. Leaving from Chicago and going to Singapore on the 20th of December.
Assistant:	We've got two on that day, one leaving at 10 a.m. and the other at twenty to eleven at night.
Alison:	I'd like the later one, please. I think the flight number is AM5-9-double 4-2.
Assistant:	Mmm … I've got here AM6-9-double 4-2. Let me just double check that … Yes, it's AM6-9-double 4-2.
Alison:	OK. And the price I've been quoted is $610. Is that still right?
Assistant:	That's right, but there is a telephone booking fee of $7 too. Is that OK?
Alison:	Yes, that's fine. I'd like to book two adult tickets, please.
Assistant:	Great. Let me take down the passenger details … (fade)

Student:	Thanks for seeing me, Professor Fernandez.
Professor:	No problem at all. I've had a look through your research project, and I think the topic looks very interesting, but I'm a little unclear about how you are actually going to carry out your research.
Student:	Well, I definitely want to do interviews with people, but I'm not really sure about how to do it.
Professor:	Hmm. Firstly, you need to identify potential participants and then email them to see if they will take part.
Student:	OK … how many should I email?
Professor:	Not many people usually say yes, so email as many as possible. You should try and get a representative sample, so don't just ask people you know. Then make sure you <u>set a date</u> for the interviews. This gives the participants lots of warning, and it gives you a time limit to design your questions.
Student:	Yes, when I design my questions, should I email them to participants in advance?
Professor:	They don't need to see the questions beforehand, but design them carefully, as you need to <u>get approval</u> for these, so make sure you leave yourself plenty of time.
Student:	How do I do that?
Professor:	Just give them to me and I can do it. It will take about four weeks. Once this is all done, you can go ahead and carry out the interviews. Now, a lot of people take notes in their sessions, but I wouldn't advise this as it can distract you from interviewing.
Student:	Yes, I was going to <u>record the sessions</u>.
Professor:	That's a much better idea, but ask your participants in the first email about this. Some people don't like it. The hard work starts when the interviews end, however. You need to try and find some <u>common themes</u> in the responses you get. This is harder than it sounds, so please read this article before you do it. It will help you a lot when you come to do this part.
Student:	Thank you so much. I've just got a couple more questions if I can …

Unit 8

Helicopters are much more versatile aircrafts than planes. They can move straight up and down and hover. They can also change direction from, say, east to west much more easily than a plane. The helicopter has a cockpit at the front where the pilot sits and controls the aircraft. Underneath the body of the helicopter are the landing skids. The main rotor blade is on the top and there is a smaller rotor on the tail. The rotor blades turn and as the speed increases the helicopter gradually lifts off the ground.

Good afternoon everyone. Welcome to the Museum of Nature. I'm Henry and I'd like to give you some information about our exhibitions and facilities. Before I start, I'd just like to remind you that we have plenty of maps here at the information desk, and if you would like to store any of your belongings, please use the lockers, which you can find over there between the main entrance and the toilets. We don't have a cloakroom, but the lockers are spacious.

Now, we're currently standing in the most beautiful part of the museum. As you can see if you look up, the ceiling is covered with amazing paintings of the natural world, including plants, fish and birds. This room used to be just called the reception area because it didn't have any special features, but when the artwork was discovered during some building works a few years ago, we renamed it the Great Hall. Now we do all of our introduction talks here so that we can draw everyone's attention to its beauty.

OK, so I'd like to give you an overview of the displays you can see throughout the different zones in the museum. One of the highlights is for anyone who is interested in the world's oceans. It's in the far-left corner, and there you'll find sea mammals, plants and all sorts of other creatures of the deep. Opposite is another really interesting zone, which is all about nature that can survive in extreme temperatures, such as the cold of the mountains or the heat of the desert. This is the Survival Zone.

The last and largest room is reserved for travelling exhibitions from other museums. At the moment it is empty, but in August it's going to have some fantastic displays of mountain animals for three weeks. I'd think about visiting again to see that if you can.

One final point I want to mention is about the library. The books here are not for sale. However, we do have a shop where you can buy a wide selection of books and other gifts. To get there walk towards the car park entrance – not the main entrance – and it's on the right.

OK, so does anyone have any questions?

Hello everyone. Today we're going to explore the research stations in Antarctica. Because travelling back and forth to this region of the world is costly, countries have constructed research stations for scientists so that they can spend long periods of time there in order to make their research more cost-effective. These stations are remarkable buildings. Here I have a diagram of the Halley VI station.

This station is the Halley VI and it's formed by a series of pods called modules, all of which perform different functions and are interlinked like the carriages of a train. Let's begin here in the middle with the largest. This is where the scientists live, so it contains fitness, entertainment and eating facilities. It is 120 tonnes and is twice as heavy as the other pods, which are about 60 tonnes.

Now let's move on to the other modules. To the right are the sleeping quarters, which include both a lounge area and the washing facilities for the scientists. The rest of the pods on the other side of the living module pod are dedicated to the actual research. At the far end is where the scientists do their work. Most of their work involves experiments, so this area is composed of lots of laboratories. It does also have a few offices.

Lastly, next to the labs are two key pods which power the station. They use an innovative range of methods for energy production and storage. One of these is the use of tanks that are positioned on the top of the modules to collect snow in order to meet the challenge of being able to provide a constant source of fresh water to the station.

The Halley VI station is located on the Brunt ice shelf, which is in the northeast. As with all research stations, the cost of both design and construction is huge, and the Halley VI is no exception as the total sum was over £25 million. However, it is important to bear in mind that these types of constructions are expected to last over 30 years, since they are built from extremely durable materials. Right, let's take a look at these materials in a bit more detail … (fade)

Speaking

Unit 1

Teacher:	I'm going to begin by asking you some questions about yourself. How did you spend your free time when you were a child?
Student:	When I was a child, I liked to play with my friends outside. In fact, I still like the outdoors, especially in the summertime because I love swimming and scuba diving. I go to a scuba diving club with my friends, and every year we like to go to a new place to explore. For example, last year we went to the Sipadan islands in Malaysia. It was really …
Teacher:	You mentioned playing outdoors with friends when you were a child. Can you tell me more about that?
Student:	OK … um … let me think. We went to … we used to fishing in a river. The river was near my house. It was outside our village. We didn't always caught any fish, but we had a good time.
Teacher:	OK, let's move on to the topic of health and fitness. If you could improve your health or fitness in one way, what would that be?
Student:	That is a good question. I am quite healthy, but I think I would like to improve my ah … sta … I would like to be able to exercise for long time and not, you know, become out of breath. Like run for a long way without stopping.

Someone who made big difference in my life is my Uncle Jae. I'm best friend with his middle son, Chul. We know each other since we were born, and we went to the same school. Chul is very good at school, but I was not such good student. Sometimes I don't understand what the teacher is explaining and I'm too shy to ask a question in the class. Sometimes I didn't do my homework. I preferred listen to music or watch films, stuff like that. The year before the college entrance exam, nobody expect me to do well. But I wanted to change. My Uncle Jae believed in me. He is a middle-school teacher. He taught me to study in a right way. He helped me make a plan and encourage me keep going, keep going. If I didn't understand something, he explained me how to find the answer. In the end, I got better result than I expected, and I got to university. I owe him a lot – he changed my life.

Teacher's feedback

Fluency was not bad – you spoke at a good steady rate, but you forgot to cover the second point on the task card: *what the person is like*. You told me a little bit about your cousin, but not about your Uncle Jae. Remember, you can check your notes to make sure that you cover all of the aspects of the task.

Coherence was OK in that I understood what you said, and you gave the information in a logical way. You used some introductory phrases, such as *the year before the college entrance exam* and *in the end*; however, you tend to overuse coordinating conjunctions *and* and *but*. Learn more linking techniques to express the relationship between points more precisely.

Your lexical range was adequate for the task and you showed some good collocations, for example, *believe **in** someone*. The vocabulary that you used was appropriate, but limited to high-frequency words. I would encourage you to expand your vocabulary so that you can express yourself more precisely. For example, rather than saying *study in the right way,* you could say *study in a more methodical way* or *study in a more efficient way.*

Grammatical range and accuracy could both be further improved. You included one or two complex sentences, for example, the conditional sentence *If I didn't understand something, he explained ....* However, the majority of your sentences are short and simple: *He is a middle-school teacher. He taught me to study in a right way.* Look for ways of combining sentences, for example, *because he's a middle-school teacher, he was able to teach me.* There were also some persistent errors, in tense, for example. When you are referring to events in the past, make sure you use the past tense consistently.

Your pronunciation was clear, and I was able to understand what you were saying throughout. However, make sure you pronounce word endings and consonant clusters clearly, for example, *di**dn't** understand.*

Unit 2

Examiner:	Good morning. My name is Paul Jones. Can I have your full name, please?
Test taker:	My name is Chen Jia.
Examiner:	And what can I call you?
Test taker:	Jia.
Examiner:	Where are you from Jia?
Test taker:	Tianjin, China.
Examiner:	Could I see your identification Jia? ... Thank you. OK, in this first part, I'd like to ask you a few questions about yourself. Let's start with your free time. What do you like to do in your free time?
Test taker:	Um, swimming ... and walking. I like swimming and walking.
Examiner:	Where do you like to go swimming?
Test taker:	The swimming ... ah ... pool. In my university, there is a swimming pool. I like to swim there.
Examiner:	What is it you like about swimming?
Test taker:	Um, calm ... um, it makes me feel calm. And ... ah ... it's good exercise. Good for your health.
Examiner:	And what about walking? Where do you like to go walking?
Test taker:	In the water park, near my university.
Examiner:	What is it you like about the park?
Test taker:	It's very large, and nice.
Examiner:	What is it that makes the park nice?
Test taker:	There are ... um ... ponds, some ponds. And it's very green.

See audio script on page 126

Good morning. My name is Karen Smith. Can I have your full name, please?

And what can I call you?

Where are you from?

Could I see your identification? Thank you. OK, in this first part, I'd like to ask you a few questions about yourself. Let's start with your experience of school. Can you describe your primary school for me?

What can you remember about your first day at school?

What was your favourite teacher like?
What was your least favourite subject?
Now let's turn to the subject of food. Do young people in your country have a healthy diet?
What is your favourite dish?
What is a common snack food in your country?
What sort of restaurants are popular in your country?

Unit 3

Track 34

One of the main difficulties facing young people in my country is lack of suitable work. If you graduate from a top university, you have a good chance of getting a well-paid job, and if you have only a high school education, you can easily find a low paying job, like working in a factory. But if you are a graduate of a low- or middle-ranking university, you will have difficulty because there are not enough professional jobs available. That is the main cause of the problem.

Track 35

The effects of this problem are complicated. When middle-ranking university students graduate, they can't find a graduate-level job, but they don't want to take low-paid work either. So they go back home and live with their parents. That means parents have to continue working hard in low-paid jobs to support their adult children at home. They keep working and encouraging their children to apply for good professional positions, because they don't want their university-educated children to do the kind of low-paid work they have always done. If their children still cannot find a good graduate-level job, families may go into debt to pay for their children to do further studies. But even after post-graduate studies, there is still no job for them in the end.

Track 36

This is a difficult problem to overcome, but I think there are two things that could be done. The government should make more effort to grow other industries like financial services or research and development. That would create more graduate jobs. Secondly, it should improve working conditions in factories. The pay gap between manual work and professional work should be narrower. If manual work were better paid, people who are not suited to higher education would not feel so pressurized to study for a university degree. They could still have a good life with an ordinary job. These changes are important to maintain social cohesion and improve people's quality of life.

Track 37

The effects of this problem are complicated. When middle-ranking university students graduate, they can't find a graduate-level job, but they don't want to take low-paid work either. So they go back home and live with their parents. That means parents have to continue working hard in low-paid jobs to support their adult children at home. They keep working and encouraging their children to apply for good professional positions, because they don't want their university-educated children to do the kind of low-paid work they have always done. If their children still cannot find a good graduate-level job, families may go into debt to pay for their children to do further studies. But even after post-graduate studies, there is still no job for them in the end.

Track 38

This is a difficult problem to overcome, but I think there are two things that could be done. The government should make more effort to grow other industries like financial services or research and development. That would create more graduate jobs. Secondly, it should improve working conditions in factories. The pay gap between manual work and professional work should be narrower. If manual work were better paid, people who are not suited to higher education would not feel so pressurized to study for a university degree. They could still have a good life with an ordinary job. These changes are important to maintain social cohesion and improve people's quality of life.

Unit 4

1
Examiner: What did you like about your school?
Test taker: Pupils who had pocket money were allowed to buy cold drinks from the machines in the canteen.
2
Examiner: What do you think encourages young people to try their hardest academically?
Test taker: Students need to feel that their efforts will be judged fairly. If they are confronted with a really challenging exam when they don't expect it, they can panic. That's what happened to one of my classmates. When he failed, he was devastated and couldn't carry on studying after that.

My classmates used to see me as a timid person who liked to read strange books and listen to strange music, but I see myself as a reserved person with unique interests.
People of my parents' generation tend to regard young people today as immature and lazy, but I would describe my generation as youthful and easy-going.
My neighbours complain that my dog Alfie is nosy and aggressive, but I think he's just inquisitive and a little bit assertive – but only when he's provoked!

1 It is common knowledge that spending too much time on screen is bad for you.
2 I have a high opinion of people who strive to overcome disadvantages in order to succeed.
3 I'm not sure what will happen in the immediate future, but I hope the job market will improve over time.
4 When I was growing up, my grandmother gave me a piece of invaluable advice: try to find something to laugh or smile about every day.
5 A major problem facing young people today is the lack of job security.
6 Skills are important, but a positive attitude will get you further.
7 If temperatures continue to rise, there is a strong possibility that some parts of the world will become uninhabitable.
8 Poverty has always existed, but that is not a valid reason for avoiding the issue.

Unit 5

1 I will go back to my hometown when I finish my studies.
2 We are waiting for the latest travel information before booking our flights.
3 Every time I turn on the TV, I see so many advertisements.
4 My sister lent me her textbooks, so I didn't need to buy new ones.
5 For lunch I usually have some soup.
6 When my brother went to Australia to study, I decided I wanted to study abroad as well, so I came to the UK.

1 I worked hard and became more and more confident.
2 Which school you go to can affect both your view of life and your chances of success.
3 Whether to go abroad or not is your own choice.
4 When I found out I was going to be acting in a play, I felt really excited.
5 Modern technology can bring comfort and convenience.
6 People are so busy these days, they hardly have time to enjoy life.
7 When learning a language, watching foreign language television can be very beneficial.

Nowadays, in my country people – especially young people – don't have much free time. In the past, they used to be more active than now; they did sports or went out with friends. Nowadays, they prefer to stay indoors, play computer games and surf the Internet, use social media, things like that. But not everyone has the equipment or software for that.

Unit 6

Speaker 1
Have you ever kept a pet?
No, unfortunately, I've never had a pet, but I would love to own a dog. It wasn't practical to have a pet when I was a child. We didn't have a very large house or garden.

Is it common in your country for people to own pets?
It's more common now than in the past. People used to think that certain animals like dogs were dirty. These days, it's fashionable to own a pet. People spend a lot of money on their pets, and they sometimes treat them like children.

Speaker 2
Have you ever kept a pet?
No, I like pets, but I never kept a pet. It wasn't practical. We lived in a small house, and we didn't have a garden.

Is it common in your country for people to own pets?
It's common now. In the past, people thought that animals like dogs were dirty. Now, it's fashionable to own a pet. People spend a lot of money on their pets. Their pets are sometimes like children for them.

Speaker 3
Have you ever kept a pet?
No, unfortunately, I've never had a pet, but I would have loved to own a dog. It wasn't practical to own a pet when I was growing up because our house wasn't large enough, and there was no garden.

Is it common in your country for people to own pets?
It's more common now than in the past, when certain animals, like dogs, used to be considered dirty. These days, it's becoming quite fashionable to own a pet. People spend a lot of money on their pets and sometimes treat them as if they were children.

1   I met my best friend Samira when my family moved to a new village.
2   I liked her immediately because she was really fun to play with.
3   We got along well even though we were very different.
4   Whereas I was a quiet, shy girl, she was outgoing and adventurous.
5   After school, we used to play in an abandoned hut in the outskirts of our village until my mother found us and made us play in our garden instead.
6   We got into trouble again when we made a fire at the bottom of the garden to roast apples.
7   As we grew older, our relationship changed.
8   Whereas I became more confident and outgoing, Samira became quieter and more serious.

I've been living here in the UK for the last ten months, so I haven't seen my friend Samira for a long time. We didn't really have a chance to say goodbye, because when I left for the UK she was visiting her brother and his new wife in Tunisia. At the moment, I'm studying hard to improve my English, and she's working long hours in her uncle's pharmacy. Even though we are both very busy, we try to speak on the phone or text each other every few days. But that's not always possible. When I phoned her last night, I hadn't spoken to her for a week because I'd been preparing for my exam.

I think I would be a very different person if I didn't have Samira in my life. She encouraged me to be more adventurous, to take risks. I wouldn't have had the courage to come to the UK if I hadn't met her. I would probably be a housewife like my mother and sister.

Unit 7

When I was twelve year old, my mother gave me a sewing machine and showed me how can I make my own clothes. So I been sewing my own clothes for long time. It's something I'm really enjoy. When you making something new and beautiful, you feel satisfied because no one else have that outfit. I feel grateful to my mother. She didn't have same opportunities as me. When she was a child, she must sew her own clothes, but I can choose to do it. After graduated from school, I decided to study costume design. I'm very excited about my future.

1   I think it's easier and more enjoyable to learn in a class.
2   My sewing teacher's been very good and kind to all the students in the class.
3   He always says you shouldn't be afraid of making a mistake because that's how you learn.
4   Some things are difficult to do, like when you're making a pattern, you need to measure everything carefully.
5   So far everybody in my class has been willing to help each other, so it's a good atmosphere.
6   The workshop's just like my second home now.

There are many ways that crafts can improve our quality of life, but I think the most important benefit is maintaining cultural traditions. Every country has its own crafting traditions. Crafts like weaving or wood carving are a part of people's identity. Objects that are made of natural materials like wood or stone also help us to connect with the natural world. If everything you own has been made by machinery, you lose the connection. Handmade objects are also more interesting because they are unique. I remember the first time my grandmother gave me something she made – it was a basket she'd made when she was a little girl – I felt like I had a treasure. Whenever I hold the basket, I remember her.

Unit 8

To make this dessert you have to beat eggs and sugar together until you've **caught** the right consistency. Then, you need to melt butter and chocolate and pour it into the **pole** with the eggs and sugar. Add flour, then tip the mixture into a **white** tray and put it in a hot oven for about thirty minutes.

To make this dessert you have to beat eggs and sugar together until you've **got** the right consistency. Then, you need to melt butter and chocolate and pour it into the **bowl** with the eggs and sugar. Add flour, then tip the mixture into a **wide** tray and put it in a hot oven for about thirty minutes.

1	**c**aught	**g**ot	5	**f**ew	**v**iew
2	**p**ole	**b**owl	6	**th**istle	**th**is'll
3	**t**ip	**d**ip	7	**s**ip	**z**ip
4	**sh**un	vi**si**on	8	**ch**eer	**j**eer

1 I eat chicken, but I don't eat **red** meat.
2 **Something** I really like to eat for breakfast is yogurt and fresh fruit.
3 Fish curry is **very** delicious in my opinion.

lid-rid   late – rate   alive – arrive   collect – correct   class -crass

seem – theme   sink – think   mass – math   face – faith   tense – tenth

why – vie   wane – vein   wax – vax   weird – veered

When I lived in Italy, I liked going to a restaurant called Il Pirata, which means *The Pirate* in English. The food was wonderful, especially the fish dishes. I try making my favourite one at home, but I've never succeeded. It never tastes the same.

When I lived in Italy, I liked going to a restaurant called Il Pirata, which means *The Pirate* in English. The food was wonderful, especially the fish dishes. I try making my favourite one at home, but I've never succeeded. It never tastes the same.

1 /ɑː/ /s/ /k/ - /ɑːsk/   /ɑː/ /s/ /k/ /s/ - /ɑːsks/
2 /æ/ /k/ /t/ - /ækt/   /æ/ /k/ /t/ /s/ - /ækts/
3 /t/ /e/ /k/ /s/ /t/ - /tekst/   /t/ /e/ /k/ /s/ /t/ /s/ - /teksts/
4 /m/ /ʌ/ /n/ /θ/ - /mʌnθ/   /m/ /ʌ/ /n/ /θ/ /s/ - /mʌnθs/
5 /s/ /ɪ/ /k/ /s/ /θ/ - /sɪksθ/   /s/ /ɪ/ /k/ /s/ /θ/ /s/ - /sɪksθs/

Incorrect versions:
1 My brother and I would set the table, then we would all **sit** down together to eat.
2 In my family we're all vegetarians; we don't **eat meat** of any kind.
3 My family loves strong flavours, so we had all **sorts** of **sauces** on the table.

Correct versions:
1 My brother and I would set the table, then we would all sit down together to eat.
2 In my family we're all vegetarians; we don't eat meat of any kind.
3 My family loves strong flavours, so we had all sorts of sauces on the table.

1 flavour   **2** table   **3** breakfast   **4** chicken   **5** tasty

1 They decided to **present** me with a **present.**
2 I'm sure she will **object** to having that **object** in the house.
3 We had to **increase** our workload to achieve an **increase** in sales.

Unit 9

The most enjoyable holiday I've ever had was on the Greek island of Paxos.

I went there with my cousins last year. We flew to Corfu, then took a boat to Paxos. Paxos is a small island, so there isn't much to do. But it's a very beautiful and relaxing place to be. That's why I like it. You can have all your meals in a café on the beach and step into the water whenever you want.

Sentence A: We went to shops, a park, a museum and a castle.
Sentence B: We went to some shops, and a park, and a museum and then a castle.

Sentence A: Who did you do that for?
Sentence B: I did it for you.

Word	Strong	Example	Weak	Example
the	/ðiː/	We saw the castle, you know, the exact one that's in the film!	/ðə/	We liked the castle.
to	/tuː/	He insisted on going, but I didn't want to.	/tə/	He went to the beach.
of	/ɒv/	I didn't know what he was thinking of.	/əv/	I stayed in and had a cup of tea.
and	/ænd/	I said I wanted cake and ice cream, not cake or ice cream.	/ən/ /ənd/ + vowel	He had fish and chips. I had soup and a sandwich.
a	/eɪ/	I asked for a coffee, not three coffees!	/ə/	He asked for a cup of tea.
that	/ðæt/	I didn't say that!	/ðət/	I said that he would come.
have	/hæv/	You have to pay.	/əv/	I would have paid.

1 They enjoyed going **to the** park **and** watching **the** children play.
2 He bought **a** pair **of** shoes **and a** new rucksack.
3 I wouldn't **have** paid **that** much **for** it.
4 They were **on** their way **to the** beach, not **from the** beach.
5 '**Have you** been **to** Athens?' 'Yes, I **have**.'

1 I think my sister would like Paxos.
2 I think my sister would like Paxos.
3 I think my sister would like Paxos.
4 I think my sister would like Paxos.

A: I thought the journey home would be fine.
B: I thought the journey home would be fine.

I stayed in and had a cup of tea.
I stayed in and had a cup of tea.

1   Peter ate a big ice cream.
2   I wouldn't have done it.
3   I'd prefer a flat in the centre.

1a We saw an interesting film.
1b We saw an interesting film!
1c We saw an interesting film.
2a Could you repeat the question?
2b Could you repeat the question?

1   Would you mind saying that again?
2   I really enjoyed my holiday last year!
3   The flight was long and dull.
4   But the sun was shining when we arrived.

The most interesting holiday I've ever had was when I went to Athens with my friend Mirna. It was a very educational holiday, but not a very relaxing one. Mirna was studying the history of ancient Greece and Rome at the time, so there was a lot she wanted to see. It was very hot, but that didn't stop us from visiting all of the most famous sites – several in one day usually. I remember spending an entire day in the Archaeological Museum looking at pots. I was exhausted at the end of it – but I learned a lot about ancient Greek pottery!

Unit 10

I think they have changed a lot, especially since I bought a tablet. It's so convenient, so I spend more time both reading and viewing than before, but I change from one thing to another more frequently. Before I would maybe read several chapters of a novel at a time. Now I read maybe one chapter, then I get distracted by some notification on my phone, so I watch a vlog or something like that. Nowadays, I read more non-fiction and I watch more rubbish online. I've become more impatient.

About two years ago my sister took me to an exhibition in London. The exhibition was about the Mexican painter Frida Kahlo. It was such a surprising experience. I expected to see her paintings, but the exhibition was mainly of her possessions, including her clothing, jewellery and make-up. I'd seen some of these things in her paintings, but I really enjoyed seeing the actual objects. Everything in the cases was so colourful and unique. I think the most interesting objects for me were her dresses.

Answer key

Listening

Unit 1

Exercise 1

1 False. You should answer all parts. 2 True 3 False. Part 1 and 2 are more general and parts 3 and 4 use more academic language. 4 False. You will hear each part ONCE only. 5 True.

Exercise 2

1 Part 4 2 Part 1 3 Part 2 4 Part 3 5 Part 2 6 Part 1 7 Part 4 8 Part 3

Exercise 3

1 General 2 Academic

Exercise 4

1 general 2 academic

Exercise 5

This cinema <u>has been open</u> since 1953 and has been <u>at the heart of (idiomatic expression)</u> the local community all this time. That's why we've decided to give it a <u>makeover (informal vocabulary)</u> and <u>open up (phrasal verb)</u> coffee shop in the ground floor area, as well as giving each of the screens an upgrade.
Function = informative
<u>The impact of cinema in modern society</u> (noun phrase) is vast. While films are <u>a reflection of society</u> (noun phrase), they also serve to shape opinions in general. This can be seen in many films that have a social or political <u>element</u> (academic vocabulary) to their themes.
Function = explanatory

Exercise 6

1   A Part 2   B Part 3   C Part 4   D Part 1
2   A informational monologue, with general English features, e.g. *show you around* (phrasal verb), *you can grab a bite to eat* (informal expression), *get back* (phrasal verb)
B A dialogue with explanatory and some academic features, e.g. *submit* (single-word verb – informally, *hand in* is the phrasal verb), *plenty of primary studies* (noun phrase), *reference* (single-word verb).
C An explanatory and evaluative lecture with academic features, e.g. *the rise of online learning* (noun phrase), *the advancement of technology* (noun phrase), *access* (single-word verb)
D Transactional dialogue with general English features, e.g. verb-based phrases (*we've got a city guide here*, rather than *there are city guides available*), *pick one up* (phrasal verb)

Unit 2

Exercise 1

1C 2B 3A 4D

Exercise 2

2 join   3 disappear   4 change

Exercise 3

Student's own answers

Exercise 5

Robert: Hi, Susanna. How are you? I'm making lunch for us. (types 1 and 2)
Susanna: Oh, thanks. Would you like any help? (types 4 and 1)
Robert: That would be great. (type 3)
Susanna: OK. Tell me what to do. (type 2)
Robert: Could you get a couple of glasses of water and cut up some bread. (types 4 and 1)

Exercise 6

1B   2 no

Exercise 7

1   The underlined are easier to hear because they are the content words.
2   The bold words help you to answer the questions because they tell you when something happened. For example, the professor says he could send Kate some videos which refers to the future so B is correct. He says he hasn't had time to upload them to the university online learning system so the answer cannot be A. Kate is talking about her last exam in the past so C is not the correct answer.

Exercise 8

The pronunciation is the same. The part of a word where the schwa sound appears can be written with different letters, but the pronunciation is the same.

Exercise 9

We are totally focused on helping you to get the best out of your time at the school. Now, you should've received a welcome pack when you came in. Inside you can see that there's a map of the campus and some general information.

Exercise 10

1 Leon 2 Harry 3 Annie

Exercise 11

1B 2A 3C 4A 5A 6C 7B 8B

Unit 3

Exercise 1

The first answer 'They are going to Australia ...' is wrong because there are more than three words.

Exercise 2

A = Part 2, B = Part 1

Exercise 3

1 when
2 where
3 Possible answers: 7.45 p.m., 12.30 a.m., twelve thirty. 'Monday morning' is not a time and 'half past eleven' has too many words.
4 Possible answers could be countries (e.g. France, Switzerland), continents (e.g. Africa, Asia), towns (e.g. Cambridge, Bury) or places (e.g. river, cave)

Exercise 4

1 blackbird and crow are types of birds; flock is a group of birds; chick is a young bird; squirrel, herd and puppy are not possible answers.
2 sighted = seen, observed, spotted

Exercise 5

Sentences 1, 3, 4

Exercise 6

1 The question is in the present continuous which indicates a future plan.
2 Locations mentioned in the audio: town hall, main square, community centre
3 *Main square* is the correct answer
4 Town hall is where it is usually held, but this year it is going to be held in a different location.
The community centre is mentioned to indicate the location of the main square, but the festival won't be held there.

Exercise 7

1 Possible answers:
D Russian / Polish / Japanese / French
E Earthquakes / Droughts / Wildfires / Volcanic Eruptions; Do the speech / Prepare the slides
F tell the time / planting crops / navigating

2

D: The correct answers are Polish and French. Russian was a course but is not now. Japanese has not started yet.
E: The answers are wildfires and (prepare) the slides. There are three more options given for the first question, but all are distracting from the answer. Peter is going to do the speech. Anna says *I'd prefer to leave the speech to you.*
F: The correct answers are planting crops and navigating. Note that you cannot write *navigating at sea* because this is too many words. There are some distracting parts of this text: *Stars now tell us about the history of the solar system.* The text does not mention the past, so it cannot be the answer. *Tell the time* cannot be the answer because that refers to the sun and the moon. These also do not fit the word count.

Exercise 8

Part 1
1 Egypt 2 £1,200 3 flights 4 breakfast 5 two trips
Part 3
6 wildlife management 7 pollution control 8 (the) recommendations 9 (list of) sources 10 (short) presentation

Unit 4

Exercise 1

1 sentence completion 2 summary completion

Exercise 2

1 A is a summary completion and B is a sentence completion.
2 A is probably from Part 4 and B is probably from Part 2.

Exercise 3

The answer to this question is **radio-controlled car** (remember a hyphenated word is one word). There is one distractor: *video games console.* This is not the answer, because it was a suggestion from the assistant, but also there are too many words.
Also, if one part is essential to the meaning of the answer or the sentence, then you cannot exclude it from the answer. You cannot write *radio-controlled* without *car* because the sentence would be incomplete. You also cannot write *car* without *radio-controlled* because the meaning is different (a real car is not the same as a radio-controlled car).

Exercise 4

The answer is *clock tower* (two words). You do not need to use all three words here. *Tower* or *clock* alone is incorrect as they are not the same things alone as a *clock tower*. *Monument* cannot be the answer because you would need to write *oldest monument in the town*, which is too many words.

Exercise 5

2 (The number of calories recommended for people depends on _____ .

3 (Students can _____ their tutors) at 6 p.m. onwards.

4 For teenagers, (texting apps are now the most common way to _____ .

Exercise 6

2 a noun is required for the object of the sentence
3 a verb is required 4 an infinitive verb goes here to describe the way (we know it is infinitive from the use of *to*, but there may be additional words after the infinitive).

Exercise 7

1 Things that fly take off. This is likely to be an early mechanical way of flying (e.g. airship / plane) because of the date. 2 The word *calories* tells us that the topic is about food and nutrition. Calorie intake can depend on many

factors including physical activity, age, body size, etc. These are all possible answers. 3 The words tell us that this topic is educational, possibly a talk about starting college or university. Students could meet / email / telephone / access / visit /arrange meetings with their tutors. 4 We can send messages /send photos / share images / chat to friends / make plans, etc. on texting apps. Teenagers might do any of these things.

Exercise 8

1 too many words. The answer would be just *first airship*. 2 incorrect spelling of *factors* 3 incorrect spelling of *email* 4 incomplete sentence – we need to write what they share, e.g. photos

Exercise 9

Part 2
1 morning 2 Maps 3 room service 4 sign up
Part 4
5 brand development 6 followers 7 in magazines 8 accessible

Unit 5

Exercise 1

1B   2A   3 a specific detail – when something will happen   4C   5 by predicting the content of the conversation and thinking of synonyms and paraphrases for the questions and options

Exercise 2

1 Part 1   2 Part 1   3 Part 4   4 Part 4   5 Yes

Exercise 3

2 price, fee, value 3 look, style, form 4 quantity, more/less, total 5 duration, extent, period 6 minutes, hours, days

Exercise 4

Task A: aspect = feature, form, element; modern = new, up-to-date, contemporary; people = consumers, buyers; suit = like, want, appeal to; innovative = creative, imaginative
Task C: pick up = collect, go and get; afternoon = after lunch; tomorrow morning = early the day after, the next day; Friday = the end of the week

Exercise 5

1   All the options are types of holiday. It's likely that all the holiday types will be mentioned but it might be difficult to hear which one the customer wants. For example, the customer may say that he or she does NOT want to book one or two of the options. Also, the holiday descriptions will use synonyms or paraphrases in the recording.
2   The options are all places connected with food. The recording will probably describe the selection of all the options in the town, but it is important to listen out for which one has a GOOD selection.

Exercise 6

1C 2C

Exercise 7

Question 1
1   I've decided that it might be better to do something a bit more active (customer)
Well, how about a trekking holiday in the mountains? (assistant)
That sounds great. Can you reserve me a place?'(customer)
2   synonyms: kind of holiday = holiday of choice; sightseeing = museums and attractions; walking holiday = something a bit more active, trekking holiday in the mountains
Question 2
1   There are plenty of places like little coffee shops to sit in and admire the scenery
There isn't a large choice of places for an evening meal There's just a small one in the town.
2   synonyms: good selection = plenty of, large choice; restaurants = places for an evening meal; cafes = coffee shops

Exercise 8

fewer = less, not as many; women = female; working = employed, engaged in; IT industry = technology field / companies / firms; because = due to, as a result of, as, since; lack of = none, no, not many, not enough; role models = inspirational figures; difficult = challenging, not easy, hard; promoted = get a better job / senior position; companies = corporations, organizations, firms; prefer = would rather, want to; hire = employ, engage, give jobs to; men = males

Exercise 9

B

Exercise 10

Part 1
1C 2A 3C 4B
Part 4
5D, F 6B

Unit 6

Exercise 1

1   Letters A, B or C
2   Question 1
3   Question 1 is likely to be in Part 2 and Question 2 in Part 3.

Exercise 2

1 costs 2 technology 3 employees 4 visitors
The speaker is likely to start by talking about the costs of different museums and then mention one which is good value. Then talk about apps and the cost of an app for one of the museums. Next the speaker will give a positive evaluation

about the staff in one of the places and finally talk about the cost of tickets with some information about families.

Exercise 3

Good morning everyone. My name is Georgia and I'd like to go give you some details about the city's museums as this afternoon you have tome to explore the city yourselves. There are lots of interesting places for families as well as adults. The National Gallery of Landscapes is free, but I don't think it's worth spending too much time there unless you want to learn about ancient geography. In my opinion there are better places. So, for example, even though you have to pay for The Ancient Arts Gallery, there is so much to see and there's something for everyone so in my view the price is completely justified.

Exercise 4

1 No, it is free 2 Not for everyone 3 Yes 4 Yes, the 'price is completely justified'.

Exercise 5

Question 4 – *worth paying for* / *value for money* / *price is justified* mean the same thing

Exercise 6

even though you have to pay for the Museum of Ancient Arts, there is so much to see and there's something for everyone so in my view the price is completely justified.

Exercise 7

Suggestions: 2 There is no charge for the app if you're studying at university. / Students don't have to pay for the app. 3 The people working there know a lot. / If you want to know more, ask the employees to give you more details. 4 People with children are likely to enjoy it. / Young people always have a great time there.

Exercise 8

2B 3C 4A

Exercise 9

Part 2
1B 2D 3E 4C
Part 3
5A 6C 7D 8B

Unit 7

Exercise 1

1C Forms are used for things like job applications, and bookings. In a form completion question, you have to complete some specific information like names, addresses, times or dates.

2A A table categorizes information. They have rows and columns and can be used to list features of different things. In a table completion question, you have to complete some parts of the table.

3B A flow chart shows the order of a process. The process starts from the first action and continues until the final action. In these questions, you have to complete some steps in the process.

4D Notes show key information written in a shorter form. They usually contain only important points and no details. In these questions, you have to complete some of the information in the notes.

Exercise 2

1 The information will be heard from left to right (the arrows indicate this)

2 'Problem identified' is the first thing to happen.

3 You might attempt to fix it yourself, find your own solutions, etc. This gives you an idea of what kind of content might go in the space.

4 The two arrows mean that there might be two results from the action in the second box.

5 If the problem continues, you might contact support, email support, use the intranet, look at the FAQs, etc. Predicting this can help you think of what content you might hear.

Exercise 3

1 The average wind speed for a category 6 wind. 2 Some form of damaged caused by a category 7 wind. 3 The description of a category 8 wind.

Exercise 4

1 We should write numbers in the table. This is because there are numbers in the boxes below for the other wind speeds. We should not use decimal spaces but copy the format of two numbers. 42 is more likely the answer because the wind speeds are getting stronger. This tells us we are looking for a lower number. **2** They use note form. We can see this by *Umbrellas difficult to use*, which misses the *are*. This tells us we should write our answers in note form (as long as it is the same as in the audio). **3** The descriptions are an adjective + noun (*strong breeze, moderate gale*). We should try and follow the format, so the answer is probably an adjective + noun combination.

Exercise 5

Yes, the questions in exercise 5 still apply to the note format. We can see that the format of notes is similar throughout the categories, and from the other bullet points we can see that the sentences are in note form.

Exercise 6

1 Assistant: There's two that day, which one are do you want to book? The one at 4.30 or the one at 8.15?
   John: I'll go for the 4.30 one.
   Assistant: Ooh, I'm afraid the last space has been taken.
   John: OK. 8.15 then.

2 Assistant: OK … I just need a few details. What's your name?
 John: John Hayden.
 Assistant: How do you spell your surname?
 John: (H–A–Y–D–E–N.)
 Assistant: That's H–E–Y …
 John: No, H–A–Y …
3 Assistant: Great and what's your contact number?
 John: (0–5–double 6–4–3–double 1–2–8)
 Assistant: 0–5–double 6–4–3–double 1–8
 John: No, double 1–2–8.

Exercise 7
Part 1 1 ali.27@example.com 2 Chicago 3 AM69442
Part 3 4 set a date 5 get approval 6 record the sessions
7 common themes

Unit 8

Exercise 1
Plan = A, Map = C, Diagram = B

Exercise 2
1 You must write letters 2 You would get 0 marks 3 No, you need to write five letters 4 Write words or numbers 5 Yes Questions 1 and 2 could have numbers in them because the nouns are plural. 6 Write words only.

Exercise 3
A (plan)1 It will probably start at the entrance. 2 The speaker will probably follow the numbers. 3 The rooms already labelled, the furniture and the images of the gym equipment.
B (diagram) 1 It will probably start at the top of the diagram. 2 The speaker will probably move down and round the diagram in an anti-clockwise motion. 3 The arrows
C (map) 1 It will probably start in the top left by number 1. 2 The speaker is likely to follow the numbers across the top of the plan and then down the right side and along the bottom. 3 The trees, the other labels, the roads.

Exercise 4
1 straight up 2 down 3 east 4 west 5 at the front 6 Underneath 7 on the top 8 on 9 turn 10 lifts

Exercise 5
cockpit, landing, main, tail

Exercise 6
1 cockpit 2 landing 3 main 4 tail
The first answer was on the right of the diagram and the answers moved from right to left across the diagram.

Exercise 7
Location: at the front, underneath, on the top, on; Phrases for direction; straight up, down; Geographical position: east, west; Verbs of movement: turn, lift

Exercise 8
Suggested answers:
Location: opposite, near, just beyond, by the side of, above, central; Phrases for direction: head towards, go backwards, on the left, pass through, turn right; Geographical position: south, north, southeast, on the west side, to the north; Verbs of movement: spin, rotate, cut, twist, circle, drive, flow

Exercise 9
Part 2
1H 2A 3C 4G 5B
Part 4
6 120 tonnes 7 washing facilities 8 laboratories 9 fresh water 10 over 30 years

Reading

Unit 1

Exercise 1
1 scan 2 skim 3 skim 4 scan 5 skim

Exercise 2
1 B 2 D 3 C 4 A

Exercise 3
1 Saturn, Jupiter 2 1847 3 Nantucket 4 Amy Brill, Renee Bergland, Maria Mitchell 5 Dolland telescope

Exercise 4
Summary A

Exercise 5
1 teacher 2 astronomy PhDs 3 women 4 conduct surveys 5 19th 6 UNESCO Institute for Statistics 7 paid jobs 8 30%

Exercise 6
1 b 2 a 3 False – it is bad for consumers 4 False – it is becoming less popular

Exercise 7
1 60,000 (sixty thousand) 2 18 (eighteen) months 3 Amsterdam 4 350,000 tonnes 5 library of things 6 20th 7 short time 8 1950s

Unit 2

Exercise 1
2 Paragraph B – In the workplace, Paragraph A – In business
 = a, words with similar meanings
3 Paragraph B – businesspeople often make bad financial decisions due to overconfidence, which is something that happens more often than people think Paragraph A – it can be disastrous when people invest money in badly performing stocks or support new business ideas which have little chance of success. These kinds of poor choices happen more frequently than many people realize
 = f, meaning over more than one sentence is reduced.

4 Paragraph B – <u>can be confused with</u> Paragraph A – can easily mistake
= d, active and passive forms (note that synonyms are also used)

5 Paragraph B – <u>in order to completely understand</u> Paragraph A – has not been fully understood yet
= e, positive and negative structures

6 Paragraph B – <u>the origins of overconfidence even though some theories do exist.</u> Paragraph A – Despite the fact that there are several theories on where overconfidence comes from, this characteristic has not been fully understood yet.
= c, changing the order of information

Exercise 2

The preposition 'of' indicates that a noun is required. Answer = 'confidence'

Exercise 3

1 is regularly cited … as being highest on their list / would like to 2 increase our ability / improve 3 employees / workers

Exercise 4

4 Missing word is 'vague'.
Explanation: The gap requires an adjective describing types of answers. It is best here to look for words which are similar to 'practical' or 'useful' (as the whole paragraph is about the workplace). Here the similar words are 'less reliable' and 'more helpful … than saying that it depends on a range of unknown factors'. The first sentence with 'less reliable' has an adjective to describe the type of answers, whereas the second sentence has a description of the type of answers. Therefore, we need to use the adjective from the first sentence (vague). Pay attention to the change from positive to negative in the text and question sentence.

Exercise 5

1 The text describes people as cautious, not the answers they give.
2 This is the opposite of what the question is asking. Clear answers are seen as more helpful.
3 Tough answers might not be popular but this is not the same as practical or useful.

Exercise 6

1 popular culture 2 unreliable 3 changes 4 commercially attractive 5 (the) American government 6 rate of success 7 psychological effect

Exercise 7

1 <u>The polygraph machine or lie detector as it is more commonly known is a universally recognized object. In general, this is due to its constant use in popular culture, especially American movies and television shows.</u>
The question has put the information from the text in a different order. It uses three synonyms: as a result = due to; long history = constant use; widely = universally. There is also a change in word form: recognized – recognizable.

2 <u>From increased heart rates to muscle twitches and tiny facial expressions, everyone is different. As a result, it is difficult to be sure when a person is being deceptive. Many studies have highlighted the fact that humans can distinguish between truth and lies in only 54 per cent of cases, which makes us extremely unreliable.</u>
The question has put the information from the text in a different order. Also, the question covers information across three sentences in the text. The first sentence = 'body language' in the question. The second sentence = 'they notice … deception'. The third sentence =' only half the time'. There is a synonym: very = extremely.

3 <u>The machine was connected to a person and it measured their blood pressure, breathing and sweat. Any changes in these measurements as suspects were answering questions were considered by the machine to be signs that they were not telling the truth.</u>
The question has changed the passive structure in the text to an active structure: 'Any changes … were considered by the machine' = Lie detectors changed …' It has also changed a negative phrase to a positive one: 'they were not telling the truth' = 'who were telling lies'. There are also two synonyms: 'signals' = 'signs'; 'physical' = 'blood pressure, breathing and sweat'.

4 <u>John Larson worked with Leonarde Keeler, who made the device more commercially attractive by making it smaller and putting it inside a box so that it was portable. In the late 1920s, after the Wall Street crash, the polygraph became popular with financial organizations who wanted to interview employees that they suspected of theft.</u>
The question has changed the passive structure in the text to an active structure: 'Leonarde Keeler who made the device …' = 'The polygraph machine was redesigned … by Leonarde Keeler'. There are two synonyms: 'redesigned' = 'made'; 'companies' = 'financial organizations'. Note: the answer cannot be 'smaller' or 'portable' because of the preposition 'to'. The phrase is 'to be attractive to something or someone'.

5 <u>Then the lie detector was commissioned by the American government, and by the 1950s thousands of government employees had taken lie detector tests to assess their suitability for certain kinds of work.</u>
The question has changed the passive structure in the text to an active structure: 'The lie detector was commissioned by' = which organization began using the lie detector. There are two synonyms: 'began using' = 'was commissioned'; 'mid-20th century' = '1950s'. Note: the answer cannot be 'financial organizations' because it is plural.

6 <u>A surprising point about the lie detector is that it continues to be used today, despite the fact experts have long questioned its rate of success over time. Even today, over 2.5 million tests are conducted annually in the USA,</u>

yet there is little evidence from over 50 studies to suggest that the polygraph actually works.

The question mostly uses synonyms: 'aspect' = 'point'; 'academics' = 'experts'; 'have repeatedly challenged' = 'have long questioned'. There is also a synonym of the answer: 'there is little evidence from over 50 studies' = 'lack of success'.

7 As Dr Andy Balmer from the University of Manchester notes, the popularity of the machine was based on the fact that people thought it was effective, not that it *was* effective. In other words, its psychological effect is the key to the endurance of the lie detector.

The question uses various synonyms in the phrase: 'the popularity of the machine was based on' = 'the reason for the success of the polygraph' ('popularity' = 'success'; 'machine' = 'polygraph'; 'based on' = 'reason for'). This is reinforced in the next sentence: 'key' = 'reason', 'endurance' = 'success', 'lie detector' = 'polygraph'. The direct question is a reporting phrase in the text: 'What does Dr Balmer say ...' = 'As Dr Andy Balmer ... notes'.

Unit 3

Exercise 1
1 False. These are complete sentences. **2** True. A summary is usually a short paragraph. **3** True. Notes contain important information on the topic. **4** False. You might be able to, but you should follow the style used in the task.

Exercise 2
A Table completion – Not grammatically complete sentences (missing articles, the verb 'to be', and subjects in places, so answers should follow this format) B Summary completion – Grammatically complete sentences (answers should follow this format) C Sentence completion – Grammatically complete sentences (answers should follow this format) D Note completion – Not grammatically complete sentences (note that in this case, only the omission of the subject stops these notes being complete sentences).

Exercise 3
1   **2** intensive courses (spelling) **3** delete 'to' (no more than two words) **7** letter, not written word **8** different colours (spelling) **10** delete 'all' or 'the' (no more than three words).
2   The students hasn't checked their spellings and hasn't taken notice of the instructions.
3   Try to check your answers against the instructions and check any spellings carefully.

Exercise 4
1 adjective 2 phrase 3 noun 4 verb

Exercise 5
The answer is located in section C. 'Well-respected' is a synonym of 'valued' and 'interacted' is a synonym of 'socialised'.

Exercise 6
1 Noun 2 The question sentence is a passive sentence (were well-respected), with the active subject removed (captain), while in the text the sentence is in the active (valued). 3 Crew members are paraphrased as 'seamen' and 'able seamen' in the text. 4 The possessive forms take the form of a pronoun in the question sentence (their) and 'of' in the text, meaning 'belonging to'. 5 expertize

Exercise 7
1 miserable 2 hands-on experience 3 expertize 4 becoming captain

Exercise 8
1 energy   2 farmers 3   small   4 built structures
5 (logically) fit   6 (scientific) research   7 biology   8 damage

Unit 4

Exercise 1
1 B   2 D   3 A   4 C

Exercise 2
1   warn, threats, scare, competition and mating chances are easier to find synonyms for
2   cuttlefish, colour and sex are more difficult to find synonyms for. Note: while there are synonyms for colour they are not near enough without further context.

Exercise 3
1 A   2 C   3 D   4 B

Exercise 4
1   Cuttlefish can change their colour to indicate potential hazards.
2   Cuttlefish often change their colour to indicate potential hazards.
3   Cuttlefish often change their colour to indicate possible mates.
4   Male cuttlefish often change their colour to indicate possible mates.
5   Male cuttlefish often change their colour to attract possible mates.
    The first and last sentence have completely different meanings. Every sentence has a slightly different meaning.

Exercise 5
1   A   to transmit basic emotions, warnings or attraction
    B   to trick other potential male rivals
    C   a male pattern when facing a female to try and attract her, and a female pattern on the other side to trick other potential male rivals
    D   a male pattern when facing a female to try and attract her, and a female pattern on the other
2   A   cannot be the answer. This part of the text talks about many animals, and not specifically the male cuttlefish, and does not indicate that it is colour-based communication.

B cannot be the answer. While males use colour to keep away competition, 'trick' and 'scare' do not have the same meaning.

C is the answer. One colour pattern attracts females, while the other side keeps away other males. This happens to help them try and mate with females, so the colour improves their chances.

D cannot be the answer. They display male and female colour patterns, but the text does not mention that they actually change their sex.

Exercise 6

B 'The most obvious example is perhaps its use in challenge and submission in a fight. (confrontation, challenge, fight)'

D 'is often used to reaffirm bonds and hierarchies amongst groups' (integration, reaffirm bonds and hierarchies, group not paraphrased)

E 'Many insects also use touch to round up a group' (round up a group, locating others)

Exercise 7

1 B   2 C   3 D   4 A,C

Unit 5

Exercise 1

1 True 2 False 3 Not Given (although the look like a family, we have no proof) 4 False (the woman is holding a plate) 5 Not Given (although it looks like orange juice, we don't know. Mango juice for example is the same colour).

Exercise 2

2 No, all of the parts of each sentence do not correspond : 'when they think about', and 'who have the ability to think of', do not mean the same. The first sentence means people choose the stairs when they think of benefits. The second sentence means only those people who are able to think of benefits choose the stairs.

Exercise 3

1 False. The writer says that people are 'less inclined' to do things that seem like hard work. This is not the same as 'do not do'.

2 True. The sentences mean the same thing.

3 Not Given. We know the stairs became more popular, but we have no information on this in comparison to the escalator.

Exercise 4

1 Of course, this kind of experiment needs to be replicated a great many time before it can be definitively stated that fun makes us change, but the results are encouraging. (view)

2 Injecting fun into daily habits, especially when it is organized at a governmental level, can have great benefits on the overall health of the population. (view)

3 Obesity levels are rising in most countries around the world, especially in young people according to recent data, and it is common knowledge that this is largely due to a lack of nutritional foods and exercise. (fact)

4 Therefore, initiatives like this could be the perfect way to turn the tide around. (view)

Exercise 5

1 YES. The writer says the study would need to be replicated to before we can state that. **2** NO. The writer says that governmental-level initiatives regarding daily habits 'can have great benefits'. **3** NOT GIVEN. We know that data shows they have high obesity levels and that there could be solutions to this, but we don't know that the writer thinks they need to urgently change their habits.

Exercise 6

1 YES (it's far more advanced than most people would expect) **2** NOT GIVEN (there is no mention of danger or violence) **3** NO (Around 4,000 years ago cities with distinct characteristics emerged) **4** TRUE (Most academics and governments debate what the oldest city might be) **5** NOT GIVEN (although two Middle Eastern and Asian cities are mentioned from 10,000 years ago, the text does not state that ALL the oldest cities are in those regions) **6** FALSE (They had none, not few) **7** NOT GIVEN (we do not know if the public used it). 8 TRUE (no city so far back could offer such exceptional examples of engineering)

Unit 6

Exercise 1

1 Matching features 2 Matching information

Exercise 2

2 a Factors which contribute to foods becoming 'super foods'. B The response to recommendations from doctors. C Explanations for the increase in coconut oil consumption.

Exercise 3

1 B 'guidance', 'solid evidence' = recommendations; 'This information tends to be well received' = response

2 C 'main reasons' = explanations; 'rise', 'going up' = increase

3 A 'several things in common' = factors; 'Firstly', 'They are also likely to be', 'and' = factors; 'they usually contain a lot of' = contribute

Exercise 4

B The answer is in the sentence: 'Many people follow suggestions about diet online from non-experts and tend to ignore (this is a type of response) the advice (recommendations are a form of advice) that they receive from medical professionals (this is a synonym for doctors).'

Exercise 5

Even though many of these claims have been challenged by scientists, people still believe in these so-called miracle foods.

This problem has many causes but is mostly due to the way in which society processes information nowadays.
A is incorrect because the text does not give any reasons or factors that make people call certain foods 'miracle foods'. The text has the phrase 'This problem has many causes', but the causes are related to why people believe in miracle foods and not reasons why foods are miracle foods.
An example of this can be seen with coconut oil. The American Health Association has specifically advised people not to eat coconut oil in large amounts due to its high fat content, yet people continue to consume it, believing that it protects the human body from a range of diseases.
C is incorrect because although the text does talk about coconut oil, it states that despite advice people still eat it, but the text does not say anything about an *increase* in people eating coconut oil.

Exercise 6
The statements will be paraphrased.

Exercise 7
1   specific behaviour (d, f)
2   unexpected results (b, e)
3   not universal (a, c)

Exercise 8
1 B (people must only eat chocolate in small quantities = specific behaviour) 2 C (unexpected results = was surprised to find) 3 A (not universal = do not apply to everyone)

Exercise 9
1 B   2 A   3 C   4 G   5 B   6 A   7 A   8 C   9 D

Unit 7

Exercise 1
1 False 2 True – in numbers ii and iii 'young children' and 'children under five' are similar, and 'how … make friends' and 'social skills development' are similar 3 True 4 True 5 False. There will be more headings than you need.

Exercise 2
2 1 iv 2 i 3 iii

Exercise 3
A
Research has shown that removing road signs and markings can significantly reduce accidents. Although it sounds like a strange idea, towns and cities that have introduced these measures have far fewer accidents than before. The idea came from a Dutch engineer called Hans Monderman during the 1980s who noticed that when roads had fewer markings and signs, drivers reduced their speed and drove more carefully. More recently a study in Wiltshire in the UK found that removing road markings reduced accidents by 35 per cent. This approach appears to be much more effective than increasing the amount of traffic calming ideas.

B
However, these traffic measures can give us many insights. Psychologists are interested in the effectiveness of these different measures because they help to understand people's relationship with authority. Road markings display driving laws which people know that they should follow. However, removing road markings and traffic signals means that people have to take responsibility for their own decision making rather than just following these laws. Studies have shown that that people respond differently to these changes in how roads look. Many people begin to drive more responsibly when there are fewer signs to follow but for others not having official rules to follow makes them more nervous drivers. This gives psychologists an insight into which people value authority and independence.

Exercise 4
1 and 3 have the same meaning. best = most effective, safer = less dangerous

Exercise 5
1 No   2 Yes   3 No   4 No

Exercise 6
ii *Research has shown that removing road signs and markings can significantly reduce accidents. This approach appears to be much more effective than increasing the amount of traffic calming measures.* These sentences say that road safety has improved as a result of removing signs not adding new signs, which means doing less not more.

Exercise 7
The idea came from a Dutch engineer called Hans Monderman during the 1980s, who noticed that when roads had fewer markings and signs, drivers reduced their speed and drove more carefully. = a change – the clue is in the result of the situation
More recently a study in Wiltshire in the UK found that removing road markings reduced accidents by 35 percent. = an example – the clue is in the study in a specific place.

Exercise 8
i is the correct heading. It focuses on the main idea. ii is incorrect as it just focuses on removal of road signs which is a supporting example.

Exercise 9
A iv   B vii   C i   D ii   E v   F viii

Unit 8

Exercise 1
1 B became founded is grammatically incorrect. 2 All of them are possible – 'was' can be followed by a comparison (A), a past participle to form the passive (B), a noun (C) and an adjective (D).

Exercise 2

1 modal verb 2 plural noun 3 present simple *to be*
4 preposition 5 conjunction 6 past simple *to be* 7 present
simple *to be* negative   8 Future form
The following could grammatically follow the bold words:
1 infinitive verb without *to* 2 verb, adverb 3 a noun or noun
phrase, a that clause 4 a noun, *the fact that* + clause 5
subject + verb clause, *of* + noun 6 past participle, adjective
7 adjective, adverb, verb, noun 8 Verb in the infinitive
without *to*

Exercise 3

3 1 c 2 c and g 3 b, e and h 4 e and h 5 f 6 a and d 7 a and
d 8 c

Exercise 4

a work on average 3 hours per night. b received a grant of
$500. c are the main focus of the Ministry of Education.
d in Bangladesh work very hard.

Exercise 5

1   sentence 1 = C, E sentence 2 = D, E sentence 3 = F, G
2   Ending A can be discounted because it is a past form
    and singular, so it does not match any of the sentence
    beginnings. Ending B can be discounted because it is a
    present simple singular verb so it does not match any of
    the sentence beginnings.

Exercise 6

1   Question 2 can be matched to paragraph 2 by scanning
    for the name Sempegua. This means that question 1
    must be before, probably in paragraph 1. It also means
    that question 3 must come after the section of the text
    which mentions Sempegua.
2   If you scan paragraph 3 looking for two schools, you can
    see both Nigeria and Bangladesh are mentioned. It is
    likely that there is an example of a floating school in each
    country mentioned in this paragraph.

Exercise 7

1E   2C   3G   4H

Unit 9

Exercise 1

1 True 2 False. They help you understand the order. 3 True
4 False. Flow charts are usually boxes and arrows, while
diagrams have more specific images.
A flow chart shows a series of steps in a process or the
order of events. The steps in a flow chart are often presented
in boxes with arrows showing the order of the steps. The
information in the flow chart may be in a line from top to
bottom or left to right, or it may be circular.
A diagram explains how something works or shows the
parts of something. These use specific images. It could be
a machine like an engine, an image of a natural process

like a volcano erupting with steps to explain each part, or a
mind-map with information grouped into categories such as
different food groups.

Exercise 2

The correct order of the process is: C, F, A, D, B, G, E

Exercise 3

1 customer 2 in stock 3 shipping

Exercise 4

A is static, and B is a process

Exercise 5

1 adjoining S   2 either side of S   3 after that P
4 dissolves P   5 in the far corner S
6 The final step P   7 prior to this P   8 cleans P
9 at this point P   10 on the outer edges S

Exercise 6

1 collected   2 join   3 filtered   4 remove   5 disinfected
6 deposited

Exercise 7

1 open ocean 2 ripples 3 slow down 4 lip 5 observe 6 (the)
same speed 7 wave location 8 more stable

Unit 10

Exercise 1

1 The question asks for two factors not three. The candidate
may have misread the question or perhaps other problems
were mentioned in the text, but about a different topic.
2 The question asks for one group not two. The candidate
may have read the question too quickly and focused on
people in the plural rather than group of people which is
singular. **3** The answer should be Romania. The candidate has
not noticed that the instructions say write TWO words. **4** The
answer is 1953 only. The candidate has probably forgotten to
double check the answer and not noticed that only the year
is required. **5** The answer is incomplete. The candidate may
have struggled to find two changes in the text because there
aren't any words or numbers in the question that are easy to
scan for. **6** The answer should be a name of a company not
a description. The candidate may have misunderstood that
'name in' this question actually means 'write the name of',
whereas in question 5 it means 'describe'.

Exercise 2

1 records, cassettes, CDs 2 $0.007 3 2017 4 95% 5 Beyoncé
Heat 6 advertising (on video sites) / crowdfunding

Exercise 3

1 What three musical formats were used in the past? 2 How
much money is paid out to stream a song? 3 In what year
did U2 earn $55 million? 4 What percentage of earnings did
U2 make from concerts? 5 What is the name of Beyoncé's
fragrance? 6 How can less-known artists make money?

Exercise 4
1 traditional album sales 2 sum 3 made 4 of their income came from touring 5 perfume 6 an increase in revenue

Exercise 5
$550,000; $150,000; $1 million; $1 billion

Exercise 6
1 B   2 C, E   3 A   4 D

Exercise 7
The correct answer to the question is $150,000 ('an amount which he now makes every 24 hours')

Exercise 8
1 bravery   2 scurvy   3 1768   4 omnibus, train
5 four / 4 years   6 *Time* (magazine)

Writing

Unit 1

Exercise 1
1 FALSE Task 1 requires you to summarise the data, that is, to describe the key features. You are not required to express your opinion about it.
2 FALSE You should focus on key details.
3 TRUE
4 FALSE You can agree or disagree strongly, or to some extent. In IELTS terms, a strong argument is not one that expresses an extreme opinion, but one that is well supported with reasons and examples.
5 TRUE Your Task 2 response should be longer, and it carries more weight in your final mark.

Exercise 2
1c   2e   3a   4d   5b

Exercise 3
1 No, not fully; the answer is too short and contains the writer's speculation.
2 Grammatical range and accuracy; there are some good complex sentences and relatively few errors.
3 Range and appropriacy of vocabulary; logical development of ideas and linking

Exercise 4

The teacher's assessment:	excellent	good	needs work	poor
Task achievement			x	
Coherence and cohesion			x	
Lexical resource			x	
Grammatical range and accuracy		x		

Exercise 5
Not a bad first attempt. You have a rough structure with a brief introduction and conclusion and two body paragraphs. You have linked some of the information and used some complex grammatical structures (e.g. the paragraph beginning 'According to the chart' contains two well-formed complex sentences). There are relatively few grammatical or lexical errors, but your style is a little too informal. You should focus on task achievement and following instructions carefully. Your response is too short (add 20+ words). Use your own words in the introduction. You have also speculated about the reasons for the trend in your conclusion and made a recommendation – remember, you should only summarize and describe.
The other areas to develop are coherence and lexical range. To improve the coherence, focus on one key trend in each body paragraph and include more details from the graph. To improve your lexical range, look for more formal synonyms for words that you repeat, e.g. get better.

Exercise 6
Sample response:
The bar chart provides information about how students have performed on average in their final examinations for four different academic subjects in three consecutive years. According to the chart, exam results for history and English both fell in the second year and recovered strongly in the third year. This trend was particularly strong for history results, which dropped by more than one mark (middle C to low D) in year two and rose sharply to high B in year three, the highest average mark for all four subjects.
The science subjects, biology and chemistry followed a different trend. Both subjects rose in year two and year three. The rise was steeper for chemistry. In the first year, chemistry results were about half a band lower than biology results. In year three they were nearly even at high B.
In conclusion, the chart shows that average exam results in year 3 had improved in all subjects. For English and history this improvement followed a fall in performance in the previous year, whereas for the science subjects, the rise was steady. (180 words)

Exercise 7
Student's response:
1 The safety and well-being of children is very important. No reasonable person would want a child to be seriously hurt just to learn a lesson. But it is also true that avoiding all risk is not good for children. There are three reasons.
5 The first reason is that children can become too scared. They will think everything is dangerous. They will learn to avoid new experiences. Maybe they will doubt themself, lose their confidence. For example, in my city some young people never take a bus or train by themself, even when
10 they are 15 or 16 years old. They learn to expect the world is a dangerous place.
The second reason is that some children may learn to

be sly if they are not allowed to take risks. Maybe they would like to have an adventure. So, they do something
15 dangerous secretly. They go to some dangerous place, like a fast river, to go swimming by themself. They want to prove they are strong and brave. If nobody is with them, they will maybe have a serious accident.

The third reason is that children could become bored and
20 lazy. Challenge is exciting. When you face a challenge by yourself, you have to think quickly, maybe try different solution. Some solutions may be wrong, so you try different ones. You can be creative. And maybe in the end, even you fail, you maybe have a funny story to tell
25 someone. These experiences build character.

In conclusion, I can understand why people want to protect children from danger. But, children need to face some risk to become brave, open, and good in solving problems in life. (274 words)

Exercise 8

Assessment criteria	good aspects	aspects requiring improvement
Task response	The test taker answers the question, has a clear position, gives relevant reasons and some examples, and meets the word count at 274 words.	no significant changes to content required
Coherence and cohesion	Ideas and examples are logically developed; paragraphs are well-structured and clearly signposted.	There could be clearer signposting of examples and more linking within paragraphs, e.g. at lines 5–6.
Lexical resource	The vocabulary is generally clear and appropriate; there are some good phrases, e.g. *seriously hurt* (line 2), *face a challenge* (line 20), *build character* (line 25).	There is some unnecessary repetition, e.g. *maybe* (lines 7, 13, 18 & 23). There are some problems with accuracy, e.g. *themselves* (lines 7, 9 & 16) and use of informal language, e.g. *you* in the third body paragraph and *I* in the conclusion.

Assessment criteria	good aspects	aspects requiring improvement
Grammatical range and accuracy	Many sentences are error free and word order is good.	There is a lack of range, e.g. few complex sentence structures linking ideas and information (lines 5–6, 6–7, 13–14, 15–16 & 17–18)

Exercise 9
Writing Task 2, Revised draft

The safety and well-being of children is very important. No reasonable person would want a child to be seriously hurt just to learn a lesson. But it is also true that avoiding all risk is not good for children. There are three main reasons.

The first reason is that without the opportunity to learn from experience, children can become too scared. If they think everything is dangerous, they will learn to avoid new experiences. Maybe they will doubt themselves and lose their confidence. For example, in my city some young people never take a bus or train by themselves, even when they are 15 or 16 years old. They learn to expect that the world is a dangerous place.

The second reason is that some children may learn to be sly if they are not allowed to take risks. Perhaps they would like to have an adventure, so they do something dangerous secretly. They go to a dangerous place, like a fast river, to go swimming by themselves to prove they are strong and brave. If nobody is with them, they could have a serious accident.

The third argument in favour of risk-taking concerns boredom; without the opportunity to take risks children could become bored and lazy. On the other hand, children can find challenges exciting. When young people face a challenge by themselves, they have to think quickly and come up with a way to solve the problem. Some solutions may not work, so then they have to be creative and try something else. Perhaps in the end, even if they fail, they could have a funny story to tell people. These experiences are character-building.

In conclusion, it is understandable that people want to protect children from danger. However, young people need to face some risks to become brave, open and good at solving problems in life.

Exercise 1

1 Numbers of bird sightings in the first week of May.
2 3
3 Farmland species and woodland species show a similar falling trend.
4 The particularly dramatic fall in numbers of woodland species from 1975 to 2000, and low numbers from 2000 to 2020; the slightly higher figure for farmland species at the end.
5 The pattern for coastal species is the opposite of the pattern for the other two species.
6 The rise in sightings of coastal species; the higher number of sightings in 2020 compared to the other species.

Exercise 2

1 highlights key features
2 presents a clear overview of a main difference
3 could be more fully extended (for example, with clearer references to the timeline. *Figures nearly doubled between 1975 and 2000, and then fluctuated around 100 for the next 20 years.*)

Exercise 3

Band 6: d, b, a
Band 5: f, c, e

Exercise 4

1 The first three subjects were significantly more popular than the last two subjects
2 Modern languages (the highest number of enrolments) and philosophy (the lowest number of enrolments)
3 Students enrolling for all five courses preferred face-to-face instruction
4 Students enrolling for the three most popular courses had the strongest preference for face-to-face instruction
5 Philosophy students

Exercise 5
Sample answer:

The table shows the number of people who enrolled on five different types of courses. The courses were taught in three different ways. There was considerable variation in the enrolment figures by course and by mode of instruction. The most popular type of course was modern languages, chosen by 130 people. Also popular were courses involving creativity: Art and Art History, with 92 enrolments, and Creative Writing with 86. People who selected these subjects had a strong preference for face-to-face teaching. This was especially true for Art and Art History and Modern Languages, with over two thirds of students choosing the face-to-face option.
The more serious academic subjects – Literature and Philosophy – were less popular, with 54 and 45 enrolments respectively. However, there was not such a big difference in the numbers of people who chose the face-to-face, online and blended options, especially for Philosophy where 17 chose face-to-face teaching and 14 each of the other modes.
Overall, the table shows that Modern Languages and courses involving creative expression were particularly popular, especially when taught face-to-face. (175 words)

- presents a clear overview of main trends
- presents a clear overview of main trends
- clearly presents and highlights key features
- presents a clear overview of main trends
- clearly presents and highlights key features
- presents a clear overview of main trends
- clearly presents and highlights key features
- presents a clear overview of main differences
- clearly presents and highlights key features
- presents a clear overview of main differences
- clearly presents and highlights key features
- presents a clear overview of main trends
- covers the requirements of the task

Exercise 6

The graph represents the various stages involved in building a new house. There are twelve stages altogether and it takes sixteen weeks.
The process can be divided into the preparation and the building stages and the longest process is drawing up the plans which takes three weeks.
Hiring builders, and purchasing insurance; Installing plumbing and electricity, and painting the exterior and the interior can be done at the same time.

Exercise 7
Sample answer:
The diagram lists the steps involved in building a new house and the time required for each step in weeks.

There are 12 steps in total and the process is scheduled to take 16 weeks. The process can be divided into two phases: preparation and building.

The first phase, preparation, involves six steps over an eight-week period beginning with site assessment and ending with site preparation. The four stages in between concern paperwork: drafting plans, securing permission to build, employing a building firm, and obtaining insurance for the project. The most time-consuming step is the drafting, which requires three weeks.

The second phase, building, is scheduled to take eight weeks and involves six steps, each requiring one or two weeks to complete. The main structure is built from the bottom up over five weeks. First the concrete foundation is laid, then the frame of the house is erected and the roof and walls built. The final stages concern finishing: installing the windows, pipes and electric cables and, finally, painting outside and inside.

Overall, the diagram shows that there are many stages involved in building a house and that preparation takes as long as construction.

Unit 3

Exercise 1
1 d 2 a 3 c 4 b

Exercise 2
1 Many educational systems have become increasingly focused on training young people for successful careers and neglected subjects that are considered non-essential, such as music and art. In my view, this approach can be very limiting. Exploring the arts can have many benefits for pupils, no matter what their intended career.

2 Low educational achievement can be the result of many factors, not all of which are directly related to schools. However, schools can undoubtedly do a great deal to raise educational attainment. There are three main initiatives that I believe could be effective.

3 The causes of low motivation for learning may be diverse and complex. Giving young learners more responsibility for choosing what they learn could certainly increase their motivation, but only up to a point.

4 There have been many attempts to find evidence in favour of both a co-educational and single-sex education. I believe that both that both types of schools can be effective and it is up to parents to decide which would be most suitable for their child.

Exercise 3
1 Makes a general statement about the nature of the issue.
2 Introduction 2: *undoubtedly*; Introduction 3: *certainly*

3 Introduction 3: *could, up to a point*; Introduction 4: *would*

Exercise 4

Band	Meets requirements	Presents a position	Develops the position
7	addresses all parts of the task	presents a clear position throughout the response	**d** presents, extends and supports main ideas, but there may be a tendency to over-generalize and /or supporting ideas may lack focus
6	addresses all parts of the task although some parts may be more fully covered than others	**b** presents a relevant position although the conclusions may become unclear or repetitive	**c** presents relevant main ideas but some may be inadequately developed / unclear
5	addresses the task only partially; the format may be inappropriate in places	**a** expresses a position but the development is not always clear and there may be no conclusions drawn	presents some main ideas but these are limited and not sufficiently developed; there may be irrelevant detail

Exercise 5
The first body paragraph makes a clear main point (identify problems early) and is better developed because it:
- clearly links to the introduction (*the first initiative*) showing the writer sustaining the position
- gives two examples of problems (reading and numeracy)
- explains why and how tackling these problems can be effective

The second body paragraph also makes a main point (teachers could improve their skills) but is less effectively developed because it:
- makes a general claim about teachers (some teachers are not as effective as they could be) without sufficient explanation
- simply restates the first and second sentence in a different way (teachers will be better if they improve their skills)

This paragraph could be improved with a specific example of which skill or skills could be improved and an explanation of why or how this would raise attainment.

Exercise 6
Body paragraph 2 redrafted:
Another effective measure could be to help teachers develop additional teaching skills. Not all teachers have the opportunity to acquire the specialized skills needed to teach learners with specific difficulties, for example second language learners, or learners with dyslexia. Providing additional specialized training would help teachers quickly recognize and assist pupils with specific needs.

Body paragraph 3 sample answer:
A third strategy would involve developing a strong relationship and regular communication between teachers and parents. Most parents know their children well and could explain their children's needs and difficulties to teachers. Teachers would also be able to explain to parents how they can best support their children with learning at home, for example when doing homework. This partnership could help children feel more secure and confident in their learning.

Exercise 7
Introduction
Low educational achievement can be the result of many factors, not all of which are directly related to schools. However, schools can undoubtedly do a great deal to raise educational attainment. There are three main initiatives that I believe could be effective.

Conclusion
These three measures may not be necessary for every child, but they could help children who would have particular needs. Although schools may not be able to directly address all of the causes of low attainment, it is important that schools are given the support they need to educate all children, not just those who find learning easy.

> the first sentence in the conclusion paraphrases and extends the last sentence in the introduction

> the second sentence paraphrases and extends the first and second sentences in the introduction

Exercise 8
Many educational systems have become increasingly focused on training young people for successful careers and neglected subjects that are considered non-essential, such as music and art. In my view, this approach can be very limiting. Exploring the arts can have many benefits for pupils, no matter what their intended career.

When young people do something like painting a picture, they need to consider many aspects. First, they need to plan the design. If the

> there are examples of how the study of art and music can develop problem-solving skills, but there could be a clearer link between the idea of problem-solving and the key term *benefit* in the introduction

painting is not looking good, they have to think about what the problem is and decide how to change it. If they play a musical instrument, for example in an orchestra, they may have problems playing together with the other players. They need to work out how to solve those conflicts.

Art and music are aspects of culture and take many different forms in different parts of the world. Maths and science are the same everywhere. If you want to understand people from different parts of the world, you should study their culture, including their art and music. This will give you broader understanding and help you connect with diverse people. This is one of the reasons travelling is so valuable.

> presents some relevant ideas but they could be more clearly developed and linked to the introduction to show how the position is sustained; the point about travelling is not relevant to the topic

Another advantage of education in art and music is that it instils discipline and can

> presents relevant ideas adequately developed

lead to increased self-confidence. Becoming better at these skills requires a great deal of practice and repetition. The individual can develop the ability to receive criticism and try harder next time. Overcoming these difficulties repeatedly over time can help the person to develop genuine self-confidence.

These points show that exploring the arts can have many benefits for pupils, no matter what their intended career.

> the conclusion could be developed, e.g. by summarizing the key points made in the body paragraphs; should be rephrased so to avoid repeating the exact words of the introduction

Exercise 9
Many educational systems have become increasingly focused on training young people for successful careers and neglected subjects that are considered non-essential, such as music and art. In my view, this approach can be very limiting. Exploring the arts can have many benefits for pupils, no matter what their intended career.

One such benefit is the development of problem-solving skills. When young people do something creative like painting a picture, they need to consider many aspects.

> the link to the introduction helps to present a clear position throughout the response

First, they need to plan the design. If the painting is not looking good, they have to think about what the problem is and decide how to change it. If they play a musical instrument, for example in an orchestra, they may have problems playing together with the other players. They need to work out how to solve those conflicts.

Another benefit of studying the arts is that, like travel, it provides an opportunity to gain a broader understanding and ability to connect with diverse people. Art and music are aspects of culture and take many different forms in different parts of the world,

> the link to the introduction helps to present a clear position throughout the response
> the relevance of travel is clarified and now supports the main idea

whereas maths and science are the same everywhere. If you want to understand people from different parts of the world, you should study their culture, including their art and music.

Another advantage of education in art and music is that it instils discipline and can

> presents relevant ideas adequately developed

lead to increased self-confidence. Becoming better at these skills requires a great deal of practice and repetition. The individual can develop the ability to receive criticism and try harder next time. Overcoming these difficulties repeatedly over time can help the person to develop genuine self-confidence.

Developing problem-solving skills, an appreciation of diverse cultures and self-discipline are three of the main benefits of studying art and music. While the ability to produce beautiful

> the conclusion is more fully developed and does not repeat the exact wording of the introduction

works of art or music may not be directly related to a young person's intended career, they can develop skills and attitudes that are useful for any career.

Unit 4

Exercise 1
Band 7: b The response logically organizes information and ideas; there is clear progression throughout
Band 6: a The response arranges information and ideas coherently and there is a clear overall progression
Band 5: c The response presents information with some organization but there may be a lack of overall progression

Exercise 2
1c   2d   3b   4a

Exercise 3
1d   2c   3a   4b

Exercise 4
5, 1, 4, 3, 2

Exercise 5
1   present and justify an opinion; rhetorical pattern b
2   evaluate an argument; rhetorical pattern c
3   propose a solution to a problem; rhetorical pattern d
4   compare and contrast opinions or arguments; rhetorical pattern a

Exercise 6
Pattern: Classification / compare and contrast
Problem: There is no indication of a general pattern and an inconsistent point-by-point comparison
Redraft: The pie charts show the average household expenditure of families living in urban areas and families in rural areas. Rural households tend to spend more of their income on essentials, whereas urban households spend a higher percentage of their money on non-essential items. Rural households spend 18 per cent of their income on transport in comparison to 14 per cent for urban households. They also spend more on housing and fuel (32 per cent of income vs 27 per cent). People living in the countryside allocate 12 per cent of their income to groceries and people in the city only 10 per cent. Urban families, on the other hand, spend more of their income on restaurants and recreation than rural families (9 per cent vs 7 per cent on eating out and 13 per cent vs 8 per cent on recreation).

Exercise 7
Question type: Evaluate an argument
Body paragraph 1: Main point: it is reasonable to associate sustainability with rural life
Reason 1: close contact with nature = valuing nature
Reason 2: opportunity to take action, e.g. grow food

> begin by demonstrating understanding of the position stated in the question

Body paragraph 2: Main point: rural living is not actually more sustainable
Reason 1: more fuel needed for transport
Reason 2: more fuel needed for heating

> refute the position stated in the question

Body paragraph 3: Main point: city living is more sustainable
Reason 1: less travel, more access to public transport
Reason 2: flats more efficient to heat
Reason 3: better access to sustainably produced goods

> state the main point first; position this paragraph at the end so that there is clear progression to your conclusion

Exercise 8

Sample answer:

It is understandable that people associate an interest in the environment with rural life. Regular contact with nature could help people value the environment and take action to protect it. People who live in the countryside can grow their own food.

However, living in the countryside is not necessarily more sustainable. People who live remotely tend to use more fuel for transport because they often have to travel greater distances to access goods and services. More fuel is also required to have goods delivered to rural locations. People are also more likely to live in detached houses, which require more energy to heat.

City dwellers may have less contact with nature, but they tend to have a lower average carbon footprint. They are more likely to live near their workplace and have access to good public transport. They also commonly live in flats, surrounded by other flats, which can help to retain heat and reduce fuel consumption. City dwellers have easier access to services and often have more choice as consumers, so it is often easier for them to buy sustainably grown food and products that have been made in a sustainable way.

Unit 5

Exercise 1
cohesive devices: c referencing: a paragraphing: b

Exercise 2
1 CD   2 RW   3 CD   4 CD   5 RW   6 CD

Exercise 3
1   in addition, also
2   whereas, but, in contrast
3   therefore, as a consequence, so
4   secondly, next, finally
5   for instance

Exercise 4
The two youngest age groups (aged 3–4 and 5–6) rated cartoons as their favorite, ranked drama as their least favorite, _and_ (1) gave comedy and music middle rankings. The older children (7–8 and 9–10) _also_ (1) identified the same category, factual programmes, as their top choice; _however_ (2), their other preferences were ranked quite differently. _For example_ (5), children aged 7 to 8 chose music programmes as their least favourite, _while_ (2) those in the older age bracket liked cartoons least.

Exercise 5
1 c, in contrast to   2 a, while   3 b, However

Exercise 6
1 whereas   2 in comparison to   3 also   4 on the other hand

Exercise 7
1 whereas   2 also, on the other hand   3 in comparison to
4 also 5 whereas, on the other hand, in comparison

Exercise 8
1 she, he, her, them, him   2 that, which   3 his, their, her

Exercise 9
City dwellers may have less contact with nature, but (1) they tend to have a lower average carbon footprint. (2) They are more likely to live near (3) their workplace and have access to good public transport. (4) They also commonly live in flats, surrounded by other flats, (5) which can help to retain heat and reduce fuel consumption. City dwellers have easier access to services and often have more choice as consumers, so it is often easier for (6) them to buy sustainably grown food and products (7) that have been made in a sustainable way.

Exercise 10
Exercise 6: Rural households tend to spend more of their income on essentials, whereas urban households spend a higher percentage of their money on non-essential items. Exercise 9: City dwellers may have less contact with nature, but they tend to have a lower average carbon footprint.

Exercise 11
Healthcare is essential for well-being but expensive to provide. While some people would argue that individuals should pay for their own healthcare in order to incentivize healthier lifestyle choices, I believe that the state should bear this responsibility.

The first argument in favour of this approach is that it would reduce health inequality among the population. All people would have access to the same level of care regardless of income. Equal access to health care is particularly important for children in lower income families, whose well-being should not be compromised because of their parents' lack of income.

Universal government funded healthcare would also help to protect all people from certain harms, even those who can easily afford to pay for care themselves. Many infectious diseases, such as flu, can easily pass from one person to another. Vaccination programmes paid for by the government can help to protect the whole population, rich and poor alike.

Exercise 12
Rising living standards in many countries around the world have been accompanied by an increase in health problems associated with more affluent lifestyles, **in particular** the consumption of tobacco and high-calorie processed foods. In this environment, people need help to look after themselves more responsibly. There are three main ways this can be achieved.

Firstly, public health campaigns could be used to educate the population about the dangers of smoking and excessive consumption of unhealthy foods. **They** should point out the long-term consequences, **which** are not always obvious in the short-term. If possible, real people should be invited to talk about their experiences, **so** the public can relate personally to the message.

Public health messages could be reinforced by legislation. **For example,** a higher rate of sales tax could be imposed on products that are unhealthy to discourage consumers from buying them.   Supermarkets and shops could **also** be required to limit the quantity of certain products that can be purchased at one time to discourage excessive consumption. On a more positive note, parents should be encouraged to model healthy lifestyles for their children, **for example** by cooking and eating together. Schools could **also** be involved in helping children to develop the necessary knowledge and skills by providing practical lessons in an interesting and fun way. **If** children learn about healthy food choices and develop cooking skills from an early age, **they** are more likely to maintain these habits as adults.

There is no simple or easy way to address the problem of unhealthy lifestyle choices and their consequences. **However,** together, these three approaches could help to reduce unhealthy behaviours and encourage healthier alternatives.

Unit 6

Exercise 1
Band 7: uses a sufficient range of vocabulary to allow some flexibility and precision; uses less common lexical items with some awareness of style and collocation; may produce occasional errors in word choice, spelling and/or word formation

Exercise 2
The second extract shows better lexical range because the writer uses less common lexical items such as *enabled*, *expand* and *thrive*. The writer shows greater flexibility by not repeating words in the question, e.g. *wild animals*, and using a synonym instead, e.g. *wildlife*. The choice of *thrive* (to live well or flourish) as opposed to *live* expresses a more precise meaning. The phrase *exploited natural resources* shows an understanding of collocation (= words which commonly go together). These word choices help to convey a more academic style.

Exercise 3
1b   2d   3c   4a

Exercise 4
1 supply   2 donate   3 award   4 provide

Exercise 5
1 c e f h j l
2 a b d g i k

Exercise 6
1 savour   2 cherish   3 enjoy, appreciate   4 argue
5 confirm   6 claim   7 state

Exercise 7
1 b   2 d   3 a, e   4 c

Exercise 8
1   Consumer confidence fell sharply from January to March.
2   There was then a marginal increase in consumer confidence over the next three months.
3   Confidence dipped slightly in July.
4   After that, there was a rapid rise in confidence until December.

Exercise 9
1 c   2 a   3 d   4 e   5 f   6 b   7 h   8 g

Exercise 10
Sample answer:
The graph shows how the population density of the capital city and the next-largest city changed over a 100-year period. There were significant differences between the two cities, especially from 1970 onwards.

Between 1940 and 1970, the pattern of change was very similar. Population density in both cities grew rapidly between 1940 and 1950 then fell sharply over the next ten years. There was then a steep rise in population density within the capital city and a dramatic fall in the second city. Between 1980 and 2000 population density in the capital city fluctuated widely, between approximately 45,000 and 55,000 inhabitants per square kilometre. Over the same period, density in the second city rose slightly, dipped marginally, then levelled off.

In the future, however, the trend is predicted to go into reverse, with some growth in the second largest city and a fairly significant drop in population density in the capital.

Unit 7

Exercise 1
1 word choice 2 spelling 3 word formation

Exercise 2
1   spelling error – exaggerate requires a double 'g'
2   word formation – the adjective form is required, i.e. beneficial
3   word choice – the word *principal* means *governing officer* (n) or *primary* (adj); this sentence requires the word *principle* (n) that looks and sounds similar but which means *fundamental truth or law*.

Exercise 3
1   replace the cliché *dip your toe in the water* with *try new experiences*
2   replace the informal term *rubbish* with *absurd*

3 replace the old-fashioned term *schoolmistress* with *teacher*

4 replace the literary term *wondrous* with *impressive* or *unusual*

5 replace *assure* (meaning: *to remove someone's doubts*) with *ensure* (meaning: *to make certain or guarantee*) e.g. They *assured* him it was safe. They *ensured* it was safe.

Exercise 4

1 with   2 to   3 of   4 about   5 in

Exercise 5

There has been a significant increase ~~of~~ **in** social media platforms designed to appeal ~~for~~ **to** young people. This can pose a risk to children. Parents often disapprove ~~against~~ **of** their children's online viewing habits, but they are not always as familiar ~~about~~ **with** new platforms as the younger generation. There is a need ~~of~~ **for** more regulation of social networking sites. These measures could prevent young people ~~against~~ **from** accessing unsuitable online content. As a society, we are all responsible ~~with~~ **for** protecting children from harm.

Exercise 6

several (contains unstressed vowels -*e* and -*a*; unstressed vowels sound very similar and can be difficult to distinguish in speech and easily confused when writing)

excellent (contains a silent -*c*; it is common to forget silent letters when writing)

suggestions (contains a double letter *gg*; in English double consonants are pronounced the same as single consonants so are often incorrectly spelled)

Exercise 7

1 dou**b**t   2 condem**n**   3 recei**p**t   4 i**s**land   5 rei**g**n 6 g**u**ess
7 govern**m**ent   8 **p**sychology   9 debri**s**   10 g**u**ilty
11 de**b**t   12 ex**c**ellent

Exercise 8

1 importance, appearance   2 access, opportunity
3 aggressive, afford   4 common, separately
5 categorized, environmental

Exercise 9

Nouns	Verbs	Adjectives
democra<u>cy</u>	demonstr<u>ate</u>	avail<u>able</u>
confid<u>ence</u>	streng<u>then</u>	grate<u>ful</u>
teach<u>er</u>	class<u>ify</u>	differ<u>ent</u>
likeli<u>hood</u>	organ<u>ize</u>	benefic<u>ial</u>
clar<u>ity</u>	abol<u>ish</u>	neg<u>ative</u>
relation<u>ship</u>		fear<u>less</u>
constru<u>ction</u>		stat<u>ic</u>
govern<u>ment</u>		spontan<u>eous</u>
bus<u>iness</u>		

Exercise 10

1 de- 2 un- 3 ir- 4 in- 5 un- 6 de- 7 dis- 8 un-

Exercise 11

1 a, c   2 d, e, g   3 b, f, h

Exercise 12

In many parts of the world, big corporations have caused smaller companies to go out of business. ~~To be honest,~~ The big brands can be seen everywhere, and they have been successful **at** capturing the market for many products. They may be more **efficient** at selling products, but they do not **necessarily** improve living standards.

In some countries, independent shops have almost **disappeared**, and shopping districts are becoming the same everywhere. Consumers can buy products more cheaply, but they often have less choice. When small traders close down, a town can **lose**, its **character** and possibly part of its history. People may feel sad and empty because ~~money doesn't buy happiness.~~ **money does not satisfy all of their needs.**

- cliché omitted
- dependant preposition *at* required
- adjective required to modify the pronoun *they*
- incorrect spelling – necessarily
- double *p* required
- incorrect spelling – double *o* creates a different word meaning *slack* or *not tight*
- silent *h* required after *c*
- cliché replaced

Unit 8

Exercise 1

1 FALSE You must also use a variety of complex grammatical structures.

2 TRUE The grammar score is based on both complexity and accuracy.

3 FALSE You should always try to ensure that your meaning is clear.

Exercise 2

1 A simple sentence has one clause consisting of a subject, e.g. *Good learning skills* and a predicate (a verb plus additional words) *make it possible to learn other school subjects.*

2 A complex sentence has one main clause, e.g. *The first years of schooling are particularly important*, and one or more dependent clause, e.g. *because this is when children learn to read and do arithmetic.*

3 Sentence 3 is simple because it has one clause consisting of the subject (*Basic numeracy*) and a predicate (*is essential for …*)

4   Sentence 4 is complex because it has a main clause (*they should be given extra individual help immediately*) and a subordinate clause (*If pupils have any problems with reading and maths at this stage*). This type of complex sentence is referred to as a conditional sentence because the subordinate clause contains the conjunction *if*.

Exercise 3
1c   2d   3a   4b

Exercise 4

comparison	concession	cause and effect	condition
whereas *while*	*although* *even though*	*because* *as* *since*	*as long as* *if* *provided (that)* *unless*

Exercise 5
1 Unless   2 even though, although   3 because, as, since
4 Whereas, While   5 provided, if, as long as   6 Because, Since, As

Exercise 6
1   *regions*
2   the relative adverb *where*
3   *in the southern coastal regions*; there is a comma between the main clause and the relative clause because the relative clause now gives 'extra' information rather than 'defining' information about the noun *regions*.
4   *who* (when a person or people is/are the subject of the relative clause), *whom* (when a person or people is/are the object of a preposition), *that* (when a person or people is/are the object in the relative clause); *that, which* for things; *when* for time; *why* for reason

Exercise 7
1   The chart shows there was a significant difference between the male respondents, who preferred full-time courses, and female respondents, who expressed a preference for part-time study.
2   Electric vehicle sales rose significantly unlike conventional car sales, which increased only slightly.
3   Young children benefit a great deal from playing in the countryside, where they can learn about wildlife and develop an appreciation for nature.
4   According to the chart, the youngest athletes, most of whom were between 16 and 18, ran the fastest times in the trial races.
5   Countries that plan to be carbon neutral by 2040 will have to work hard to achieve this target.

Exercise 8
1   sentence b
2   The object of the action (*high-density housing*) is made the subject of the sentence; the action is expressed with the verb *to be* in the appropriate tense and form (*was*) + the past participle of the action verb (*built*).
3   it does not convey any necessary information because the reader can assume the housing was built by people.
4   The passive sentence because it foregrounds the essential information.

Exercise 9
1   Promises are often broken.
2   The production of single-use plastic items should be banned.
3   Children can be taught to read before they start school.
4   Ancient forests have been cut down and cash crops (have been) planted instead.
5   People were encouraged to move out of crowded cities and into the countryside.

Exercise 10
The table displays data in relation to beaches around Seal Island. Beaches in the north, east, south and west **were rated** against five criteria relating to cleanliness, safety, and the provision of facilities. There were significant differences among the four areas.
Beaches in the north, **which received excellent scores in three categories,** were most highly rated overall. Beaches in this area were particularly strong in terms of water quality, absence of litter and facilities for changing. **Although** they did not score well in the lifeguard category, their provision in this area was still regarded as sufficient.
Beaches in the east and west of the island had similar overall ratings but had different strengths and weaknesses. **Eastern beaches scored well in terms of cleanliness but poorly in terms of safety whereas western beaches had good safety provision but were not very clean.**
The beaches with the lowest ratings were those in the south. The poor ratings in safety related categories – water quality, the presence of lifeguards, and signage – is the most worrying thing about these beaches.
The beaches on Seal island all have some room for improvement. However, the beaches in the south require urgent attention.

Unit 9

Exercise 1
1   FALSE Your writing must show both grammatical range and accuracy; if you write only simple sentences, you are likely to score a Band 5, even if your sentences are error free.

2   FALSE Some errors in both grammar and punctuation are permissible at Band 7 as long as your writing shows good range, errors are infrequent and any errors that do occur do not cause confusion.

3   FALSE If an error causes confusion, it is more likely to be considered problematic

Exercise 2

1   You should not use the indefinite article *a* or *an* with an uncountable noun (e.g. *evidence*) – delete *an*.

2   You should not use articles when referring to people or things in general rather than a specific group – delete *the* before *politicians* because it refers to politicians generally; retain *the* before *people* because it refers specifically to those represented by politicians

Exercise 3

1   *The* table shows *the* number … (*The* is required because both nouns refer to specific things in the visual prompt)

2   *The* two youngest age groups … (*The* is required with the superlative *youngest*)

3   ⊖ Rising living standards … around *the* world (⊖ because *rising living standards* is presented as a general trend; *the* is required because the world is unique and therefore specific)

4   *the* problem of ⊖ unhealthy lifestyle choices (*the* is required because the problem is specified by the prepositional phrase that follows; ⊖ because *unhealthy lifestyle choices* are not specified)

Exercise 4

1 & 2 The writer has missed the connection between the subject and the verb because they are separated by modifiers, e.g. *International* **cooperation**, *even among countries with different priorities,* **is** *essential.* **People** *who live in overcrowded accommodation* **are** *often disadvantaged.*

singular subject	
modifier	
singular verb form	
plural subject	
modifier	
plural verb form	

3 & 4 The writer has not recognized that indefinite pronouns *any, some, more, most, all* and percentages can be singular or plural depending on whether the noun they refer to is singular, uncountable or plural, e.g. **Most** *of the* **respondents were** *employed, and* **most** *of the* **money was** *spent.* **Six per cent** *of the* **items were** *never returned, and* **six per cent** *of the* **food was** *wasted.*

plural noun
plural verb form
uncountable noun
singular verb form
plural noun and plural verb form
uncountable noun and singular verb form

Exercise 5

1 will   2 have not been   3 shows   4 speak

Exercise 6

In sentence 1, the subordinate clause is placed first and a comma is required between the subordinate and the main clause. Note that you cannot use a full stop in this circumstance because that would create a sentence fragment: *Unless the government does more to alleviate poverty.* Sentence fragments don't make a complete sentence

Exercise 7

1e   2d   3a   4c   5b

Exercise 8

Increased awareness of **the** environmental issues has led some people to look for opportunities to travel to places, where they can engage with nature. This is understandable, particularly when it involves conservation work. However, ecotourism may have undesirable consequences. Many of **the** most exotic natural landscapes can be found in parts of the world where there **has** been little development. People who **live** in these places, **they** may be relatively poor. They might welcome tourists who bring income; however, the difference in wealth between the local people and visitors could make it difficult for locals to defend their interests.

The issue of power can be a particular problem when, tourism is controlled by large companies **that** are not local. Tourism **requires** infrastructure: hotels, transport and other facilities. To attract visitors, developers may build these in the most desirable locations. Local people may be cut off from their own environment, even forced to leave their homes.

no article required because *environmental issues* is general
no comma because the relative clause is defining
definite article required because of the superlative *most exotic*
a singular verb form is required with *little development*
present tense needed because the essay discusses a current situation
no comma or pronoun needed as this is a defining relative clause
semi-colon or full stop needed before the conjunctive adverb
no comma required as the subordinate clause comes after the main clause
use the relative pronouns *that* or *which* for things, and *who* for people
a singular verb form is required with the uncountable noun *tourism*

Natural environments can be fragile, and may be damaged by visitors who do not understand how to behave with unfamiliar plants and animals. A Wildlife may be harmed if it is handled or fed unsuitable food. Too much interaction with wild animals may cause them to change their behaviour, so they could become domesticated. Visitors could also damage the environment by taking things they have found and keeping them as mementos, pieces of coral, for example.

For all of these reasons, we should discourage mass ecotourism. There are many ways that people can interact with natural environments closer to home. There is no need to travel. If people wish to know more about exotic locations, they can learn about them through books and films.

no comma required as what follows does not have a subject and is not an independent clause	
no article *a* required as wildlife is uncountable and referred to in general	
the conjunction *so* is used to connect clauses	
a comma is required because the subordinate clause comes first	

Unit 10

Exercise 1

1 FALSE The four assessment criteria are each worth 25 per cent of your mark
2 FALSE The whole of your response should be closely related to the question
3 TRUE
4 FALSE You should show that you can use cohesive devices appropriately. If your response is logically organized, you may not need cohesive devices in every sentence.
5 TRUE
6 TRUE
7 TRUE
8 FALSE The examiner will judge not just the number of mistakes but the extent to which they interfere with the clarity of your message.

Exercise 2
Sample answer:
The chart shows people's preferred means of accessing news by age group. All five age groups accessed the same amount of news, but they preferred to access the news in different ways: online, print and television. There is a big difference between the top age group and the bottom age group.

Exercise 3
d, g, c

Exercise 4
Paragraph 2: e, i, b
Paragraph 3: h, a, j, f

Exercise 5
Sample answer:
The most striking finding is that people under 35 years old have a preference for online news sources. Eighty per cent of 18- to 24-year-olds **chose the Internet as their preferred means of accessing news**. Over 60 per cent of 25- to 34-year-olds **also favoured online news. However,** fewer than 20 per cent of the oldest respondents **selected web-based news as their first choice.**

Exercise 6
1 statement of the writer's position on the question
2 sentence a, because it states a position that is relevant to the topic

Exercise 7
Local sports clubs can provide a focus for their communities **because** they can help to bring people together. They can promote inclusivity and people's sense of belonging. Team sports**, which** require cooperation and respect for rules, can model **good values and behaviours** to people in the community. **Although** not all sports men and women always behave appropriately, most of the time they do. This is important particularly for young people, **who** often choose sporting figures as role models.

Exercise 8
Another way local sports clubs contribute to their communities is by providing training facilities and **opportunities** to aspiring sports women and men. Sports **programmes** encourage young people to maintain healthy and **active** lifestyles and can help to divert them **from anti-social** behaviour. **Participants** can learn not only sporting skills but also skills such as refereeing and coaching.

Exercise 9
Sample answer:
The chart shows how people in low-, middle- and high-income groups engage with social media. Each bar shows the proportion of time respondents within the specified income group spend on five activities.

One of the most striking findings is the proportion of time respondents in the lower income group spend sharing visual content and buying and selling online (25 per cent of time online for each activity). The proportion of time spent by middle-income respondents on those activities is roughly half that figure and even lower for upper-income people (10 per cent).

Another obvious feature is the differences in the use of social media for professional networking. Upper-income respondents spend the highest proportion of their time online this way (over 40 per cent) whereas the corresponding figure for those on lower incomes is only 15 per cent.

The middle-income group is distinctive for their relatively high interest in reviewing products and services (25 per cent of time spent online) and discussing common interests (30 per cent), an activity also popular among the higher income group.

Overall, the chart shows that income is a significant factor in how people choose to use social media. (183 words)

Exercise 10
Sample answer:

The Internet has undoubtedly transformed the relationship between many businesses and their customers. Online review sites are one aspect of this change. Over time, it has become clear that the popularity of these sites has brought with it some benefits but also some significant harms.

Online reviews, whether positive or negative, can benefit consumers, enabling them to make a more informed choice. Without this type of information, consumers would normally have to rely on the information businesses provide through their advertisements, the recommendations of friends and family, or reviews available in paid-for published guides. Free direct access to consumer reviews online overcomes these limitations. Businesses also benefit from the increased free publicity that positive online reviews can bring.

However, the system can be abused if consumers and businesses post reviews that are not genuine. Businesses can, for example, solicit others to post fabricated favourable reviews, creating the impression that the product or service is more popular than it is. Rival businesses could also impersonate disgruntled customers and post reviews that are damaging to their rivals.

Harm can also come from genuine customers who behave unreasonably. Customers who have had unrealistic expectations may post reviews that are unfairly negative. Although business usually have a right to reply, the damage to their brand can be difficult to repair. Sometimes the threat of a negative review can pressurize a business to provide refunds that are not really due.

Given these pitfalls, it is important that consumers use online review sites with caution and seek objective sources of information wherever possible. Business should also advertise their products and services through a variety of channels and be prepared to rebut false reviews when necessary. (278 words)

Speaking

Unit 1

Exercise 1
Part 1 b   Part 2 c   Part 3 a

Exercise 2
1   b fluency, d coherence
2   a lexical resource
3   c grammatical range, f grammatical accuracy
4   e pronunciation

Exercise 3
1   F You will be given one minute to prepare for the long turn in Part 2 only.
2   F You are required to speak for 1–2 minutes in the long turn.
3   T The questions will relate to the topic but require you to elaborate on it in a more abstract way.
4   F The IELTS speaking test is a test of communicative ability not a memory test. If you produce speech that has been clearly memorized, the examiner is likely to discount it and/or use questions to prompt you to produce unrehearsed speech.
5   F Rate of speech is only one aspect of the fluency and coherence criterion. It is equally important to speak with a natural rhythm and in a joined-up way.
6   T Showing that you can use a good circumlocution (an alternative way of saying something) will count in your favour.
7   F It is not just the number of mistakes you make that is important, but the type of mistake and its impact on the listener's comprehension. It is also important to demonstrate that you can use a variety of complex sentence structures. A better strategy is to focus on both range and accuracy in grammar.
8   T It is good to be able to use sentence structures flexibly to enhance the meaning of your message.

Exercise 4
1   How did you spend your free time when you were a child? If you could improve your health or fitness in one way, what would that be?
2   The speaker is not answering the question and is producing speech that appears to be memorized. In an exam situation, this would not contribute to the assessment.
3   Circumlocution for the word 'stamina': *exercise for long time and not […] become out of breath […] run for a long way without stopping.*

Exercise 5
1   but, and
2   Incorrect verb form after *used to* (correct form is *used to **go** fishing* or *used to **fish***); incorrect verb form after *didn't* (correct form: *didn't always **catch***); missing article in the phrase *for long time* (correct form: *for **a** long time*)

Exercise 6
1   No, the speaker hasn't covered the second point 'say what that person is like'.
2   Fluency, coherence, punctuation, and some aspects of vocabulary were generally good.

3 Lexical range, grammatical range, grammatical accuracy and some aspects of pronunciation could be improved.

Exercise 7

1 Check your notes to make sure that you cover all of the aspects of the task. Learn more linking techniques to express the relationship between points more precisely.

2 Expand your vocabulary so that you can express yourself more precisely. For example, rather than saying *study in a right way,* you could say *study in a more methodical way* or *study in a more efficient way.*

3 Look for ways of combining sentences, for example, *because he's a middle-school teacher, he was able to teach me.*

4 Make sure you pronounce word endings and consonant clusters clearly, for example *didn't understand.*

Exercise 8

Ex 8 Tick 1, 2, 4, 5

Exercise 9

1b   2c   3a

Exercises 10–12

Students' own answers

Unit 2

Exercise 1

1 F While it is important to speak at length, even at band 7 it is acceptable to make occasional errors, especially if you are able to self-correct.

2 T It is normal to pause from time to time when speaking to reflect and organize your thoughts. The examiner will be noting the frequency and timing of hesitations and making a judgement about whether these are reasonable pauses for reflection or due to difficulty with language.

3 F The ability to give extended responses and to maintain a flow of speech is more important than speed.

Exercise 2

The test taker merits no more than a band 5 for fluency. Her responses are short, and she pauses at key points to recall vocabulary.

Exercise 3

Topic 1 Hobbies/leisure time – a, k, m, p
Topic 2 School – b, g, h, j
Topic 3 Food – c, e, l, n
Topic 4 Neighborhood/home – d, f, i, o

Exercise 4

Subjects: visual arts – enjoyable, esp. painting; chemistry – tiresome

People: janitor – always helpful, e.g. for lost & found; head teacher – distant & strict

Places: gym – too small; library – peaceful; playing fields – dusty

Exercise 5

OPINION (languages are OK) **+ REASON** (necessary) **+ EXAMPLES** (job & travel) **+ COUNTER OPINION** (languages are sometimes boring) **+ REASON/EXAMPLE** (vocabulary learning)

Exercise 6

Students' own answers

Exercise 7

Students' own answers

Suggested topics: snacks, restaurants, healthy foods, dishes + food preparation, your favourite dish, food for celebrations, food production

Exercise 8

Gaps: I liked the most; Another thing I liked about

Examiner: Who was your favourite teacher?

Test taker: The teacher **I liked the most** was my history teacher [opinion] in secondary school, Miss Yao. She was very creative, and her lessons were fun. [reasons] At the end of term, she used to make the classroom into a cinema so we could watch a film. We could bring snacks to eat, like in a real cinema. [example]
Another thing I liked about her was the way she used games to make lessons more enjoyable. [example]

Exercise 9

1 The restaurant I like the most is …   Another thing I like about it is …

2 The television programmes I liked the most when I was a child were …   Another thing I liked about it was …

3 The writer I like the most is …   Another thing I like about him/her is …

4 The films I like the most are …   Another thing I like about them are …

5 The subject I liked the least was …   Another thing I disliked about it was …

Exercise 10

Sample answer

Examiner: Good morning. My name's Karen Smith. Can I have your full name, please?

Test taker: Good morning. My name's Samira Ismat.

Examiner: And what can I call you?

Test taker: Samira is fine.

Examiner: Where are you from?

Test taker: I'm from Muscat, Oman.

Examiner: Could I see your identification? Thank you. OK, in this first part, I'd like to ask you a few questions about yourself. Let's start with your experience of school. Can you describe your primary school for me?

Test taker: I went to a large primary school, with about, let me think, maybe three or four hundred pupils. There were about 25 or 30 girls in my class. The building was new, modern. I remember we had a beautiful library and that the classrooms were very bright. We each had a box with our names on to put our things in, like our pencils and crayons.

Examiner: What can you remember about your first day at school?

Test taker: I don't remember very much, to be honest. I know I walked there with my mother and my big sister. There were crowds of children and their parents in front of the school. I was very excited, but also nervous and a little shy. Then we went in and I met my teacher. She was tall and slim, with a long nose. I didn't like her at first. I don't think I spoke at all that day, except to say my name.

Examiner: What was your favourite teacher like?

Test taker: The teacher I liked the most was my history teacher in secondary school, Miss Yao. She was very creative, and her lessons were fun. At the end of term she used to make the classroom into a cinema so we could watch a film. We could bring snacks to eat, like in a real cinema. Another thing I liked about her was the way she used games to make lessons more enjoyable.

Examiner: What was your least favourite subject?

Test taker: The subject I liked the least was chemistry. It was very difficult. We had to learn all the elements in the periodic table. I didn't find that very interesting. We also had to do experiments, which involved measuring everything very exactly. If you made a mistake, you had to repeat everything. I hated that.

Unit 3

Exercise 1
1c   2a   3b

Exercise 2
One of the main difficulties facing young people in my country is lack of suitable work. **If** you graduate from a top university, you have a good chance of getting a well-paid job, **and if** you have only a high school education you can easily find a low paying job, **like** working in a factory. **But if** you are a graduate of a low or middle-ranking university, you will have difficulty **because** there are not enough professional jobs available. **That** is the main cause of the problem.

introductory phrase linking to the question

main point

reasons

summary

1   explains the causes of the problem
2   *One of the main difficulties facing young people in my country is …*
3   a like b but if c because d that

Exercise 3
4, 6, 2, 3, 5, 7, 1
After the opening general statement, much of the information is sequenced as a chain of CAUSE + EFFECT, with each effect serving as a cause for the next effect: CAUSE + EFFECT/CAUSE + EFECT/CAUSE …

Exercise 4
1   Large to small description: large to small features of a place (building – classroom – personal storage box)
2   Chronological: narration (journey – arrival – entering)

Exercise 5
1   Proposing solutions
2   GENERAL COMMENT + SOLUTION 1 + OUTCOME 1 + SOLUTION 2 + OUTCOME 2 + CONCLUDING COMMENT
3   *I think there are two things that could be done*; *Secondly*

Exercise 6
Describing a person place or thing: 2, 3   Narrating: 5, 7, 11   Explaining cause and effect: 6, 9, 15   Describing problems and solutions: 1, 13   Expressing an opinion: 4, 10, 12   Making a prediction: 8, 14

Exercise 7
1 *so, and*   2 *because, if, who, when, although, unless, as soon as*

Exercise 8
1 When   2 but   3 so   4 because   5 If   6 But

Exercise 9
These changes refers to the two recommendations made by the speaker:
1   creation of more graduate jobs through investment in certain industries
2   improvement in wages and working conditions among manual workers

Exercise 10
Students' own answers

Unit 4

Exercise 1
Band 5	Band 6	Band 7
4, 6	1, 5	2, 3, 7

Exercise 2
1c   2a   3b

Exercise 3
1   For this response to a personal question, the terms *sufficient funds, purchase* and *beverages* sound too

formal. The more neutral terms *pocket money, buy* and *drinks* are more appropriate for the context.

2   For this question about a general topic, the terms *freak out, guys, gutted* and *be bothered* are slang and too informal for the context. The more formal or neutral terms *panic, my classmates, devastated* and *carry on* are more appropriate.

Exercise 4

1   This response has a mix of formal expressions (*culinary skills*) and informal expressions (*I'm rubbish at, mates, posh*). To make the register more consistent, replace the informal expressions with neutral alternatives.
I *don't have good* culinary skills, so I'd be really pleased with myself if I could learn to cook. I'd make a nice meal for my *friends*, nothing too *sophisticated,* just tasty.

2   This response also has a mix of formal expressions (*effective employer, furthermore*) and informal register (*how to do stuff right, you* (meaning an employee), *do something stupid*). To make the register more consistent, remove the expression *furthermore*, which is more typically used in writing, and replace the informal expressions with more formal or neutral alternatives:
An effective employer is someone who cares about their employees and takes the time to explain *the correct procedures. An employer* should *also* give *workers* a second chance if *they make a careless error.*

Exercise 5

	positive connotation	negative connotation
1	*reserved*	*timid*
2	unique	strange
3	youthful	immature
4	easy-going	lazy
5	assertive	aggressive
6	inquisitive	nosy

Exercise 6
1c   2e   3b   4d   5a

Exercise 7
1 common knowledge 2 high opinion 3 immediate future
4 invaluable advice 5 major problem
6 positive attitude 7 strong possibility 8 valid reason

Exercise 8
Students' own answers

Exercise 9
1d   2c   3e   4a   5f   6b

Exercise 10
Sample answer
One of the most important decisions I've ever had to make was choosing which university to go to for my undergraduate studies. I was 18 years old and still living with my family.

I received offers from two universities. One from a very prestigious institution in another city quite far away from my hometown. My second offer was from a good university in my hometown which I knew several of my friends were hoping to attend. I'm not a very decisive person, so I find it very hard to come to a decision. I had a binary choice: I wanted to follow my dreams and ambitions and at the same time I wanted to be near my family and friends. It was a real dilemma and no real compromise was possible. In the end I opted for the more prestigious university. I don't regret my decision. It was a difficult adjustment at first, but I think this was the right choice for me. I learned to be more independent and took a step closer to achieving my life goals. I also found ways of staying connected to family and friends. It was the right thing for me to do.

Exercise 11
Students' own answers

Unit 5

Exercise 1
1   The first speaker. The paraphrase is clear and natural and does not repeat any of the words in the question.
2   The second speaker makes only two errors: *activities for leisure* and *cooking barbecues*. These are both awkward collocations, that is, word combinations that do not sound natural. The appropriate collocations are *leisure activities* and *having barbecues*.
3   The first speaker makes three types of lexical error:
   • Dependent prepositions: *depends **of*** should be *depends **on***; doing things **by** *their own* should be **on** *their own*
   • Word class: *a big **different*** (adjective) *between* should be *a big **difference*** (noun) *between*
   • Collocation: ***taking time*** *together* should be ***spending time*** *together; a **very waste*** of time should be *a **real waste*** of time
4   The second speaker has better lexical range. There are some good collocations, e.g. *browsing the Internet, socializing with friends.* The language is more idiomatic, e.g. *going out to eat* (= eat in a restaurant), *if it's wet* (= if it's raining), and more precise, e.g. *surf or play volleyball* (vs the more general term *sports* in the first speaker's response)

Exercise 2
1 I will **go back**   2 the **latest** travel information   3 I **turn on** the TV   4 **lent** me her books
5 **have** some soup   6 study **abroad**

Exercise 3
1 confident 2 success 3 choice 4 excited 5 convenience 6 life
7 beneficial

Exercise 4

1 inaccurate	5 inexpensive	9 impractical
2 uncomfortable	6 uninteresting	10 imprecise
3 inconvenient	7 unmarried	11 untrue
4 indirect	8 impolite	12 unusable

Exercise 5

Circle all words except: 4 indirect (neutral) 5 inexpensive (positive) 7 unmarried (neutral)

Exercise 6

1 works (C) 2 experience (U) 3 work (U), time (U)
4 experience (C), times (C)

Exercise 7

Nowadays, in my country people – especially young people – don't have **much** free time. In the past, they used to be more active than now; they did sports or went out with friends. Nowadays, they prefer to stay indoors, play computer **games** and surf the Internet, use social **media,** things like that. But not everyone has the **equipment** or **software** for that.

Exercise 8

Last time I tried to **pay a visit** to my sister, it was a **complete disaster √.** I got to the **bus stop √,** which is **far away** from my house, and waited **a long time √.** When the bus arrived, I realized I didn't have any money, so I ran to the bank to **withdraw some money.** But there was no money in my account because my mother was supposed to **transfer money into** my account the **day before**, but she didn't do that. So I had to call my father to **give me a lift** to my sister's flat. He was not happy about that.

Exercise 9

1 interested **in** 2 I lacked ~~of~~ work experience 3 go out **of** my house 4 marry ~~with~~ an engineer
5 aware **of** 6 capable **of** 7 thanked ~~to~~ my biology teacher
8 no point **in** studying

Exercises 10–12

Students' own answers

Unit 6

Exercise 1

Band 7: uses a range of complex structures with some flexibility
Band 6: uses a mix of simple and complex structures, but with limited flexibility
Band 5: uses a limited range of more complex structures

Exercise 2

1 F You need to show that you can use a range of complex structures, but that does not mean that you will be marked down for using simple structures, especially if a simple structure conveys your message more effectively. Grammatical range also refers to the ability to use a range of tenses and other grammatical forms, such as passive structures and conditionals.

2 F At band 6, any loss of clarity should be rare; a better strategy is to use complex sentences when they help to convey your message effectively.

3 T To score band 5 or higher, you should try to use some complex structures and advanced features of grammar.

Exercise 3

1 Band 6 2 Band 5 3 Band 7+

Exercise 4

1 a ii 2 c i 3 b iii

Exercise 5

1 I met my best friend Samira **when** my family moved to a new village.
2 I liked her immediately **because** she was really fun to play with.
3 We got along well **even though** we were very different.
4 **Whereas** I was a quiet, shy girl, she was outgoing and adventurous.
5 After school, we used to play in an abandoned hut in the outskirts of our village **until** my mother found us and made us play in our garden instead.
6 We got into trouble again **when** we made a fire at the bottom of the garden to roast apples.
7 **As** we grew older, our relationship changed.
8 **Whereas** I became more confident and outgoing, Samira became quieter and more serious.

Exercise 6

1 I've been living 2 I haven't seen 3 she was visiting 4 I'm studying 5 she's working 6 I hadn't spoken 7 I'd been preparing

Exercise 7

Students' own answers

Exercise 8

What will you do if the weather is stormy tomorrow?
What would you do if you had unlimited funds?
What would you have done if you had failed?
Second conditional: would + infinitive *if* past tense
Third conditional: would + perfect infinitive *if* past perfect tense

Exercise 9

I think I would be a very different person if I didn't have Samira in my life. She encouraged me to be more adventurous, to take risks. I wouldn't have had the courage to come to the UK if I hadn't met her. I would probably be a housewife like my mother and sister.

> second conditional

> third conditional

> Notice that the final sentence does not include the subordinate *if* clause

Exercises 10–11
Students' own answers

Unit 7

Exercise 1
Band 7: frequently produces error-free sentences, though some grammatical mistakes persist.
Band 6: may make frequent mistakes with complex structures, though these rarely cause comprehension problems.
Band 5: produces basic sentence forms with reasonable accuracy; uses a limited range of more complex structures, but these usually contain errors and may cause some comprehension problems.

Exercise 2
1 Yes, four of the nine sentences are complex.
2 b) frequent – there are ten errors
3 The errors do not cause significant misunderstanding as they are relatively minor, and the overall message is clear.

Exercise 3
(a) twelve year**s** old [3]
(b) how to make [2]
(c) I've been sewing [1]
(d) for a long time [4]
(e) I really enjoy [1]
(f) you make/are making [1]
(g) no one else has [5]
(h) the same opportunities [4]
(i) had to sew [1]
(j) After graduating [1]

Exercise 4
1 have been making   2 weren't   3 are becoming
4 were wearing   5 hadn't seen   6 continues

Exercise 5
1 I think **it's** easier …
2 My sewing teacher**'s** been very good …
3 He always says you shouldn't **be** afraid …
4 Some things are difficult to do, like when **you're** making a pattern …
5 So far everybody in my class **has** been willing …
6 The workshop**'s** just like my second home now.

Exercise 6
1b   2f   3d   4c   5a   6g   7e

Exercise 7
1 trying   2 to study   3 to come   4 on coming
5 to stay   6 go   7 complaining   8 from travelling

Exercise 8
1g   2d   3e   4f   5c   6b   7a

Exercise 9
There are many ways that crafts can improve our quality of life, but I think **the** most important benefit is maintaining cultural traditions. Every county **has** its own crafting traditions. Crafts like weaving or wood carving **are** a part of people's identity. Objects that are made of natural materials like ~~the~~ wood or stone also **help** us to connect with **the** natural world. If everything you own **has** been made by ~~a~~ machinery, you lose the connection. Handmade objects are also more interesting because they are unique. I remember **the** first time my grandmother gave me something she made – it was a basket she'd made when she was a little girl – I felt like I had a treasure. Whenever I hold **the** basket, I remember her.

Exercises 10–12
Students' own answers

Unit 8

Exercise 1
1 Good articulation of **individual words and sounds** are often essential for the clarity of your message. Frequent mispronunciation can reduce the intelligibility of your speech and have a disproportionate effect on your overall score. Unit 8 focuses on this aspect of pronunciation.
2 Good **sentence stress, rhythm, and intonation** contribute to effective communication because they allow you to emphasize key information and engage the listener's interest. Unit 9 will focus on these features of pronunciation.

Exercise 2
maɪ ˈfeɪvərɪt dɪˈzɜːt ɪz ˈtʃɒkəlɪt keɪk

Exercise 3
To make this dessert you have to beat eggs and sugar together until you've (caught) / got the right consistency. Then, you need to (melt) / meld butter and chocolate and bore / (pour) it into the (pole) / bowl with the eggs and sugar. Add flour, then dip / (tip) the mixture into a (white) / wide tray and put it in a hot oven for about thirty minutes.
The speaker has difficulty pronouncing voiced consonants /g/ /b/ /d/.

Exercises 4–5
Students' own answers

Exercise 6
1 red, the speaker says /led/ instead of /red/ so has difficulty differentiating /l/ and /r/
2 Something, the speaker says /sʌmsɪŋ/ instead of /sʌmθɪŋ/ so has difficulty differentiating /s/ and /θ/
3 very, the speaker says /weri/ instead of /veri/ so has difficulty differentiating /w/ and /v/

Exercises 7–8
Students' own answers

Exercise 9
1 lived /d/   2 liked /t/   3 called /d/   4 means /z/
5 dishes /ɪz/   6 succeeded /ɪd/   7 tastes /s/

Exercise 10

-s sounds like /s/ when it follows an unvoiced consonant and like /z/ when it follows a voiced consonant

-ed sounds like /t/ when it follows an unvoiced consonant;

-ed sounds like /d/ when it follows a voiced consonant

-s sounds like /ɪz/ when it follows the sounds /s/, /ʃ/, /z/, /tʃ/ and /dʒ/

-ed sounds like /ɪd/ when it follows the sounds /t/ and /d/

Exercise 11

Students' own answers

Exercise 12

1 sit, the speaker says /set/ instead of /sɪt/ so has difficulty differentiating the two short vowel sounds /e/ and /ɪ/

2 eat and meat, the speaker says /ɪt/ and /mɪt/] instead of /iːt/ and /miːt/ so has difficulty differentiating the short vowel sound /ɪ/ and the long vowel sound /iː/

3 sorts and sauces, the speaker says /sɒts/ and /sɒsɪz/ instead of /sɔːts/ and /sɔːsɪz/ so has difficulty differentiating the short vowel sound /ɒ/ and the long vowel sounds /ɔː/

Exercise 14

1 They decided to **present** me with a **present**.
2 I'm sure she will **object** to that **object** in the house.
3 We had to **increase** our workload to achieve an **increase** in sales.

The words in bold can be either a verb or a noun. The stress commonly falls on the second syllable of the word when it is used as a verb and on the first syllable when it is used as a noun.

Exercise 15

Sample answer

Examiner: Do people speak differently in different parts of your country?

Test taker: Yes, I would say the way people speak in different regions varies quite a lot. In the capital, which is in the east, most people speak in a way that is considered standard. It's the accent that you most often hear on the television or radio. In the west, people's way of speaking is considered rougher and more difficult to understand. The vowels are shorter, and consonants like /r/, /tʃ/ and /dʒ/ are pronounced more strongly. In the north, especially in rural areas, the accent is softer, and people speak more slowly. The vowels are longer, and the sound is more melodic.

Examiner: Are some accents considered to be better than others?

Test taker: I think the answer to that depends on where you come from and what accent you are used to. People who live in the capital tend to see their own accent as the standard one – the one that is most correct and the easiest to understand. But not everyone agrees. Many people prefer the way people in the north speak, because of the sound of their speech, but also because they associate positive qualities with northerners. Northerners are considered easy-going, friendly and gentle. People tend to strongly like or dislike the accents of people who come from the west. Western people are associated with honesty and humour, so some people have positive associations with that accent. Other people think it is a little impolite or too rough.

Examiner: Have people's accents changed over time?

Test taker: That is difficult to say. I know accents have changed because when I watch old films or listen to old radio programmes, I notice the difference. I think change happens very slowly. People in my country spend longer in education than they used to, so I think their accents have become more similar, more standard. People tend to associate strong regional accents with a lack of education, which is unfortunate because I like to hear different accents. The mass media and social media has also had an influence on how people speak. I think young people especially imitate the accents of people they admire and hear a lot in the media or online.

Exercises 16–17

Students' own answers

Unit 9

Exercise 1

Band 8: uses a wide range of pronunciation features; sustains flexible use of features, with only occasional lapses

Exercise 2

The most enjoyable holiday I've ever had was on the Greek island of Paxos.

1 content words: adverbs (most, ever), adjectives (enjoyable, Greek), nouns (holiday, island, Paxos), verbs (had), but not the verb to be when it is used as a main verb

2 structure words: articles (the), pronouns (I), auxiliary verbs (have – 've), the verb to be (was), prepositions (on, of)

Exercise 3

I went there with my cousins last year. We flew to Corfu, then took a boat to Paxos. Paxos is a small island, so there isn't much to do. But it's a very beautiful and relaxing place to be. That's why I like it. You can have all your meals in a café on the beach and step into the water whenever you want.

1 conjunctions (*so, but*), demonstratives (*this, that, these, those*), wh- words (*what, which, who, where, why*)
2 the verb *to be* is stressed when it is negative (*isn't*) or in the infinitive (*be*)

Exercise 5
Sentence A: We <u>went</u> to <u>shops</u>, a <u>park</u>, a <u>museum</u> and a <u>castle</u>.
Sentence B: We <u>went</u> to some <u>shops</u>, and a <u>park</u>, and a <u>museum</u> and then a <u>castle</u>.
1 A 11 words; B 15 words
2 five seconds each

Exercise 6
1 Sentence B   2 /ɔː/ becomes /ə/

Exercise 7
Students' own answers

Exercise 8
1 all words in bold are weak
2 all words in bold are weak
3 **have** & **for** are weak, **that** is strong
4 **to** & **from** are strong, **on** & **the** are weak
5 in the question, **have, you** and **to** are weak; in the answer, **have** is strong

Exercise 9
3 But someone else's sister would not.
4 But there is another place she would not like, e.g. Corfu.

Exercise 10
A I   B thought

Exercise 11
1 version 2
2 words that end in a consonant link with the next word if it begins with a vowel

Exercise 12
Students' own answers

Exercise 13
1a gently falling intonation indicates a neutral, factual tone
1b sharply rising and falling intonation conveys enthusiasm
1c the low pitch and slow tempo indicates irony or boredom; the speaker feels the film was not interesting
2a the falling intonation conveys rudeness
2b the rising intonation conveys politeness

Exercise 14
Students' own answers

Exercises 15–16

The <u>most</u> <u>interesting</u> <u>holiday</u> I've <u>ever</u> <u>had</u> was <u>when</u> I <u>went</u> to
<u>Athens</u> with my <u>friend</u> <u>Mirna</u>. It was a <u>very</u> <u>educational</u> <u>holiday</u>,
but <u>not</u> a <u>very</u> <u>relaxing</u> one. <u>Mirna</u> was <u>studying</u> the <u>history</u> of <u>ancient</u>
<u>Greece</u> and <u>Rome</u> at the <u>time</u>, so <u>there</u> was a <u>lot</u> she <u>wanted</u> to <u>see</u>.
It was <u>very</u> <u>hot</u>, but <u>that</u> <u>didn't</u> <u>stop</u> us from <u>visiting</u> <u>all</u> of the <u>most</u>
<u>famous</u> <u>sites</u> – <u>several</u> in one <u>day</u> <u>usually</u>. I <u>remember</u> <u>spending</u>
an <u>entire</u> <u>day</u> in the <u>Archaeological</u> <u>Museum</u> <u>looking</u> at <u>pots</u>.
I was <u>exhausted</u> at the <u>end</u> of it – <u>but</u> I <u>learned</u> a <u>lot</u> about <u>ancient</u>
<u>Greek</u> <u>pottery</u>!

Exercises 17–18
Students' own answers

Unit 10

Exercise 1
1 F Fluency means speaking at an appropriate length at a pace that is easily comprehensible without distracting hesitations.
2 T It is important to be able to develop your response in a way that is easy for the examiner to follow.
3 T However, you should take care to avoid slang or offensive language.
4 F Choose words, including less common words, that are most appropriate for the context. Very unusual words could be inappropriate or distracting.
5 F Assessment of grammatical accuracy is based not just on the frequency of mistakes but also their impact on intelligibility.
6 T But make sure you do not reduce clarity by using inappropriately complex structures.
7 F Stressed words should be pronounced more slowly, carefully and clearly; unstressed words should be said quickly and more quietly with short vowel sounds including the schwa.
8 F A foreign accent is acceptable as long as your speech is easily comprehensible to the examiner.

Exercise 2
The student should produce a more extended response with signposting and linking words.

Exercise 3
1 name the film and say something about the character's role in it
2 briefly summarize the plot

3 explain how the character's story represents this transition
4 explain why the character is interesting and give an example
5 explain what people of different ages would like about the film

Exercise 4

1 c <u>which</u> is an animated …
2 d <u>and</u> enter a spirit world … <u>and</u> Chihiro has to try …
<u>In the spirit world</u> … <u>like</u> the witch …
3 e <u>that</u> she has to overcome … <u>that</u> you need to acquire
4 a <u>At the beginning</u> she's kind of … <u>But in the spirit world,</u>
Chihiro … <u>also</u> develops … <u>At one point in the film,</u> <u>for</u>
<u>example,</u> she manages … <u>who</u> terrorizes …
5 b <u>whereas</u> adults might …

Exercise 5

1 famous (not *infamous* because it has a negative connotation) 2 get upset (not *freak out*, which is informal) 3 heavily (collocates with *criticized*) 4 Critics (not *Hypocrites* because it has a very negative connotation) 5 inappropriate (*rubbish* is informal) 6 glamourized (has a negative connotation appropriate for the sentence) 7 the rich (*posh* is informal) 8 perfectly (collocates with *reasonable*) 9 modernize (collocates with *a classic*; *renovate* collocates with physical structures, e.g. *house, building*) 10 valid (collocates with *reason*)

Exercise 6

I think they have changed a lot, **especially** since I bought a tablet. It's so **convenient**, so I spend more time both reading and viewing than before, but I change from one thing to another more **frequently**. Before I would maybe read several chapters of a novel **at a time**. Now I read maybe one chapter, then I get **distracted** by some notification on my phone, so I watch a vlog or something like that. Nowadays, I read more **non-fiction** and I watch more rubbish online. I've become more **impatient**.

Exercise 7

1 About two years ago my sister ~~taken~~ **took** me to an exhibition in London.
2 The exhibition was about **the** Mexican painter Frida Kahlo.
3 It was such **a** surprising experience.
4 I expected see~~ing~~ her paintings,
5 but the exhibition was mainly of her possessions, including her clothings, ~~jewelleries~~ **jewellery** and make-up.
6 I**'d** seen some of these things in her paintings
7 but I really enjoyed ~~to~~ see**ing** the actual objects.
8 Everything in the cases ~~were~~ **was** so colourful and unique.
9 I think the most interesting objects for me ~~was~~ **were** her dresses.

Exercise 8

About <u>two</u> <u>years</u> a<u>go</u> my <u>sister</u> <u>took</u> me to an <u>exhibition</u> in <u>London</u>. The <u>exhibition</u> was about the <u>Mexican</u> <u>painter</u> <u>Frida</u> <u>Kahlo</u>. It was <u>such</u> a <u>surprising</u> <u>experience</u>. I <u>expected</u> to <u>see</u> her <u>paintings</u>, but the <u>exhibition</u> was <u>mainly</u> of her <u>possessions, including</u> her <u>clothing</u>, <u>jewelry</u>, and <u>make-up</u>. I'd <u>seen</u> <u>some</u> of <u>these</u> <u>things</u> in her <u>paintings</u>, but I <u>really</u> <u>enjoyed</u> <u>seeing</u> the <u>actual</u> <u>objects</u>. <u>Everything</u> in the <u>cases</u> was <u>so</u> <u>colorful</u> and <u>unique</u>. I <u>think</u> the most <u>interesting</u> <u>objects</u> for me were her <u>dresses</u>.

Exercises 9–11

Students' own answers